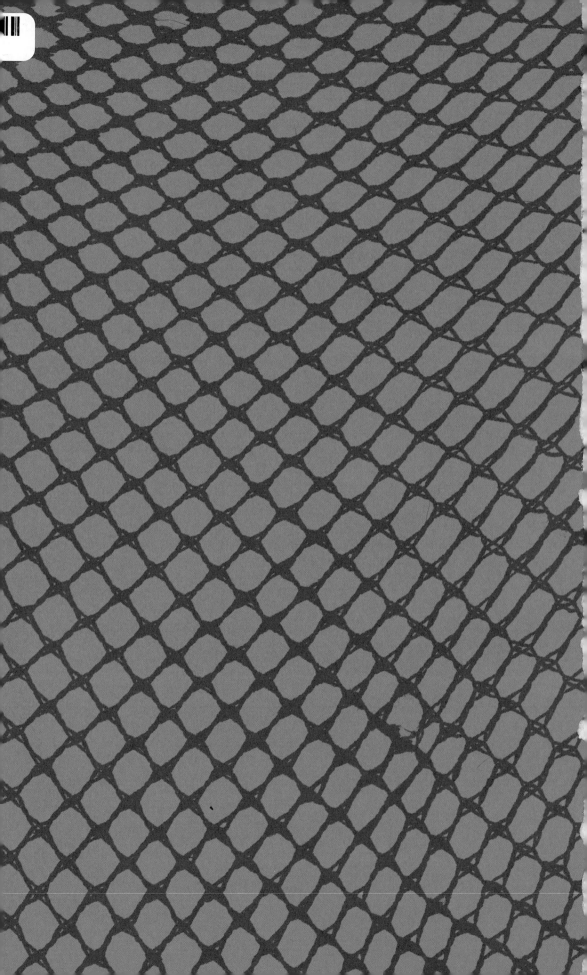

BLACK CANARY AND ZATANNA: BLOODSPELL

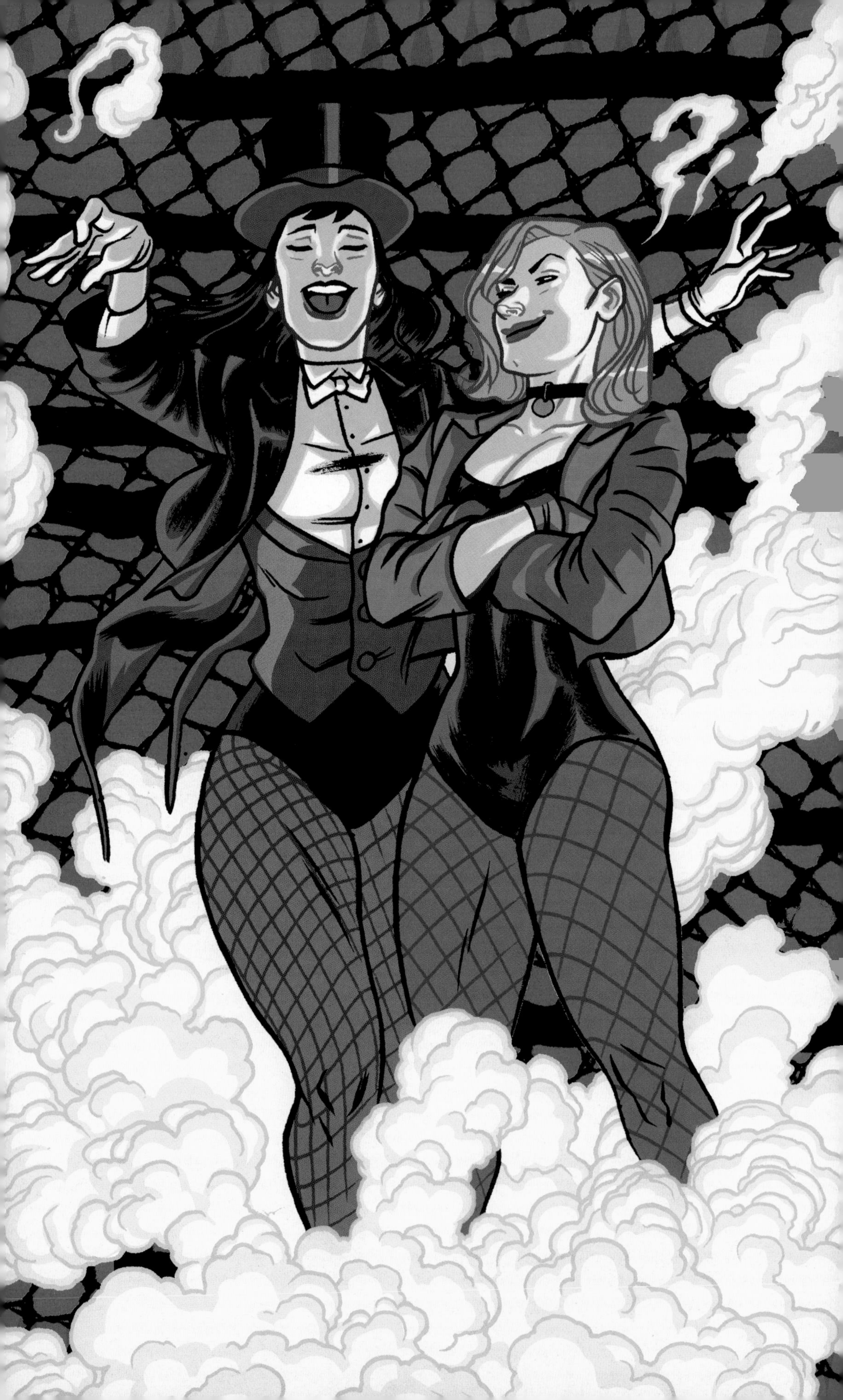

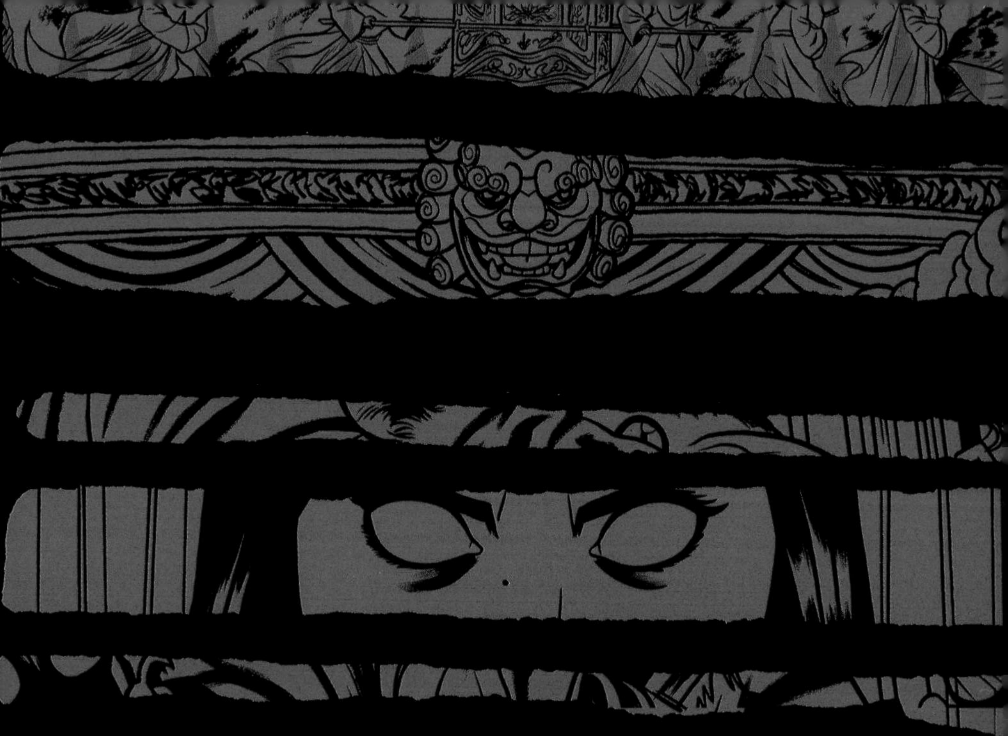

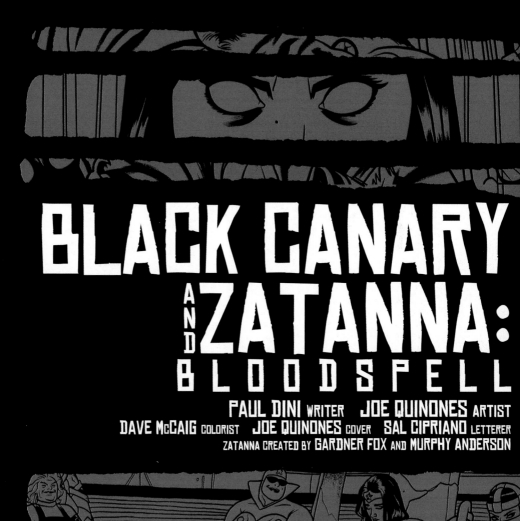

BLACK CANARY AND ZATANNA: BLOODSPELL

PAUL DINI WRITER JOE QUINONES ARTIST
DAVE McCAIG COLORIST JOE QUINONES COVER SAL CIPRIANO LETTERER

ZATANNA CREATED BY GARDNER FOX AND MURPHY ANDERSON

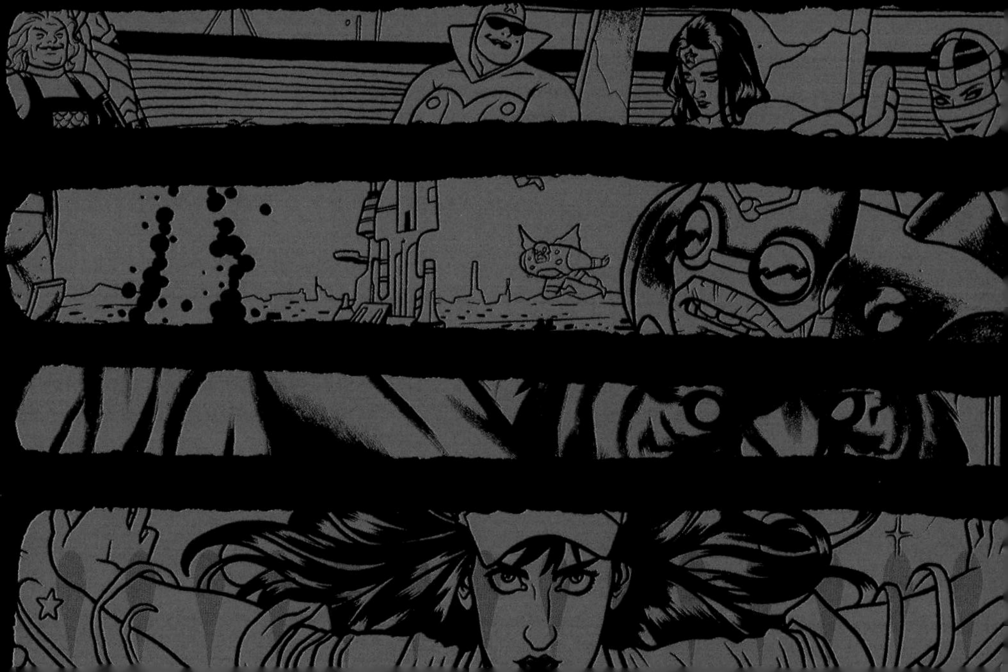

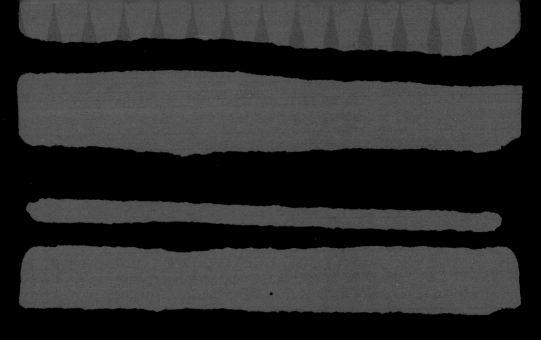

Matt Idelson Group Editor   Joey Cavalieri Editor   Chris Conroy Associate Editor   Kyle Andrukiewicz Assistant Editor   Robbin Brosterman Design Director – Books   Louis Prandi Publication Design

Bob Harras Senior VP – Editor-in-Chief, DC Comics

Diane Nelson President   Dan DiDio and Jim Lee Co-Publishers   Geoff Johns Chief Creative Officer   John Rood Executive VP – Sales, Marketing & Business Development   Amy Genkins Senior VP – Business & Legal Affairs

Nairi Gardiner Senior VP – Finance   Jeff Boison VP – Publishing Planning   Mark Chiarello VP – Art Direction & Design   John Cunningham VP – Marketing   Terri Cunningham VP – Editorial Administration

Alison Gill Senior VP – Manufacturing & Operations   Hank Kanalz Senior VP – Vertigo & Integrated Publishing   Jay Kogan VP – Business & Legal Affairs, Publishing   Jack Mahan VP – Business Affairs, Talent

Nick Napolitano VP – Manufacturing Administration   Sue Pohja VP – Book Sales   Courtney Simmons Senior VP – Publicity   Bob Wayne Senior VP – Sales

BLACK CANARY AND ZATANNA: BLOODSPELL

DC Comics, 1700 Broadway, New York, NY 10019. A Warner Bros. Entertainment Company. Printed by Transcontinental Interglobe, Beauceville, QC, Canada. 4/18/14.
First Printing. ISBN: 978-1-4012-1054-0

Library of Congress Cataloging-in-Publication Data

Dini, Paul, author.
Black Canary and Zatanna : Bloodspell / Paul Dini, Joe Quinones, Dave McCaig.
pages cm
ISBN 978-1-4012-1054-0 (hardback)
1. Graphic novels. I. Quinones, Joe, illustrator. II. McCaig, Dave, illustrator. III. Title. IV. Title: Bloodspell.
PN6727.D57B57 2014
741.5'973—dc23

2014001615

SUSTAINABLE FORESTRY INITIATIVE
Certified Chain of Custody
Promoting Sustainable Forestry
www.sfiprogram.org
SFI-00507
This label only applies to the text section.

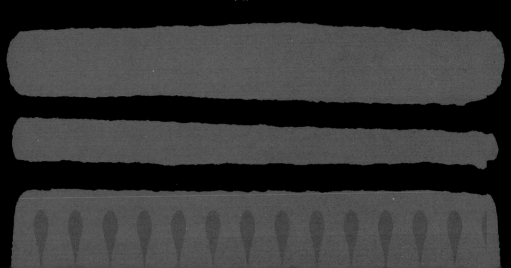

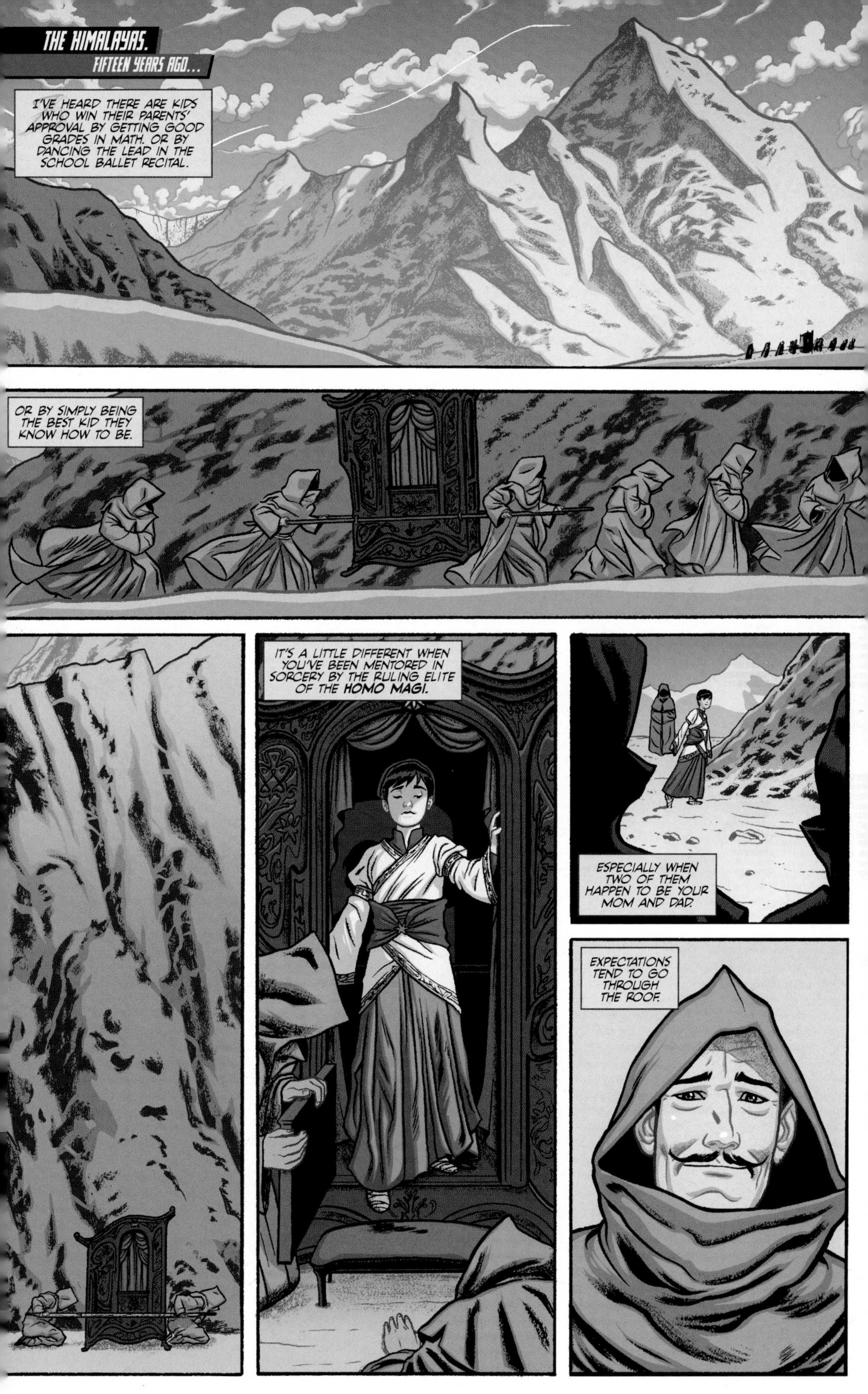
THE HIMALAYAS.
FIFTEEN YEARS AGO...
I'VE HEARD THERE ARE KIDS WHO WIN THEIR PARENTS' APPROVAL BY GETTING GOOD GRADES IN MATH. OR BY DANCING THE LEAD IN THE SCHOOL BALLET RECITAL.
OR BY SIMPLY BEING THE BEST KID THEY KNOW HOW TO BE.
IT'S A LITTLE DIFFERENT WHEN YOU'VE BEEN MENTORED IN SORCERY BY THE RULING ELITE OF THE HOMO MAGI.
ESPECIALLY WHEN TWO OF THEM HAPPEN TO BE YOUR MOM AND DAD.
EXPECTATIONS TEND TO GO THROUGH THE ROOF.

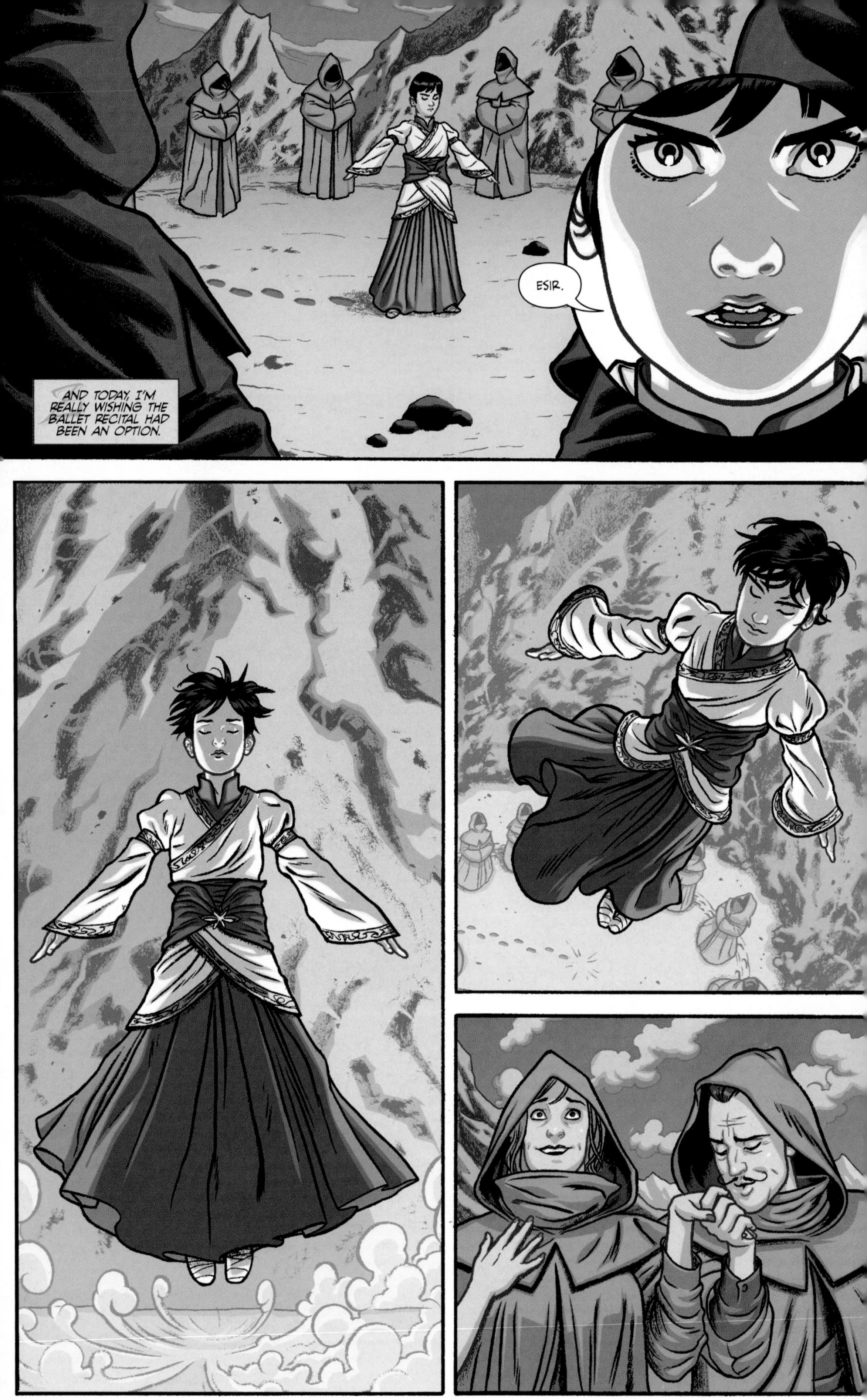
AND TODAY, I'M REALLY WISHING THE BALLET RECITAL HAD BEEN AN OPTION.
ESIR.

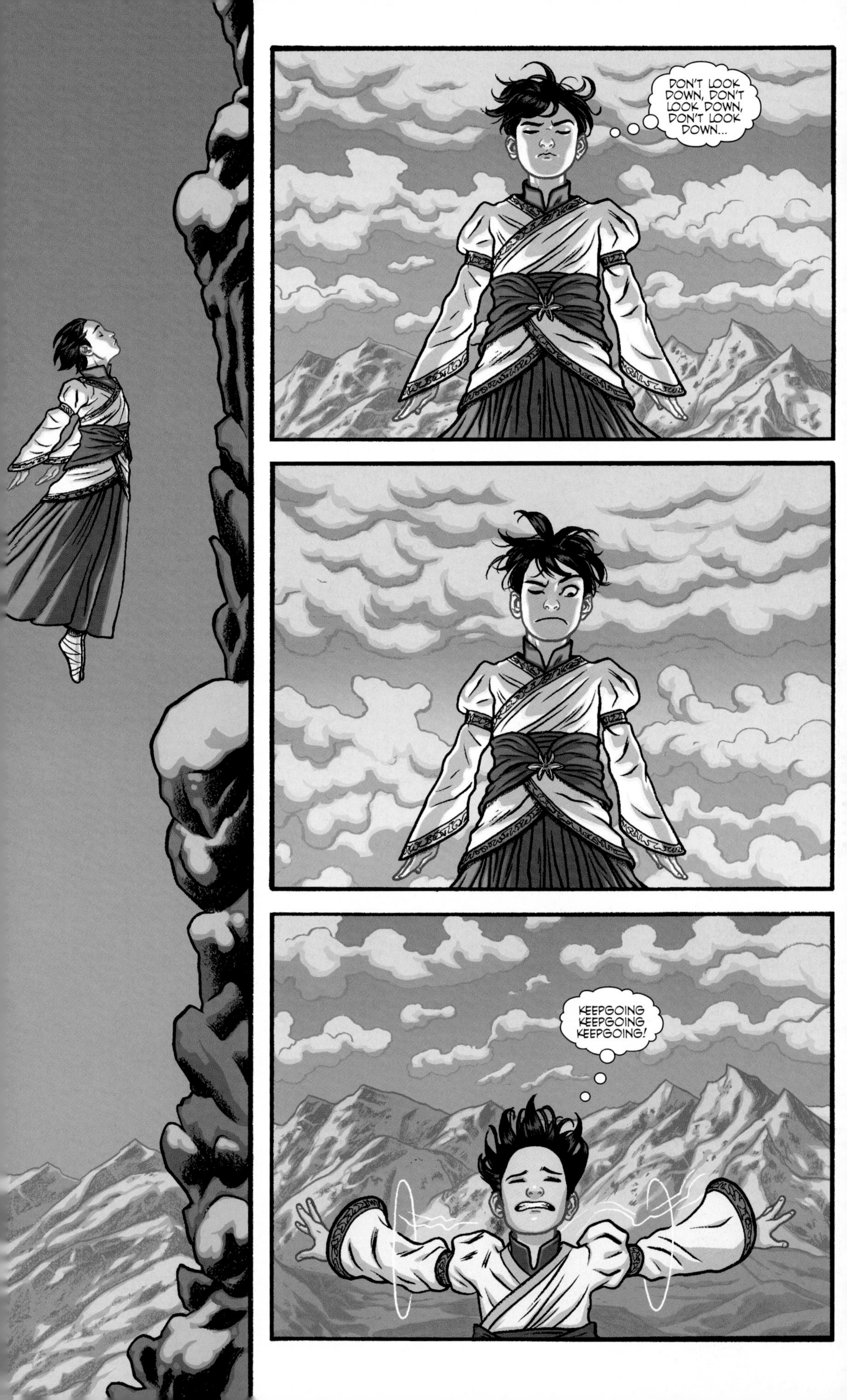
DON'T LOOK DOWN, DON'T LOOK DOWN, DON'T LOOK DOWN...
KEEPGOING KEEPGOING KEEPGOING!

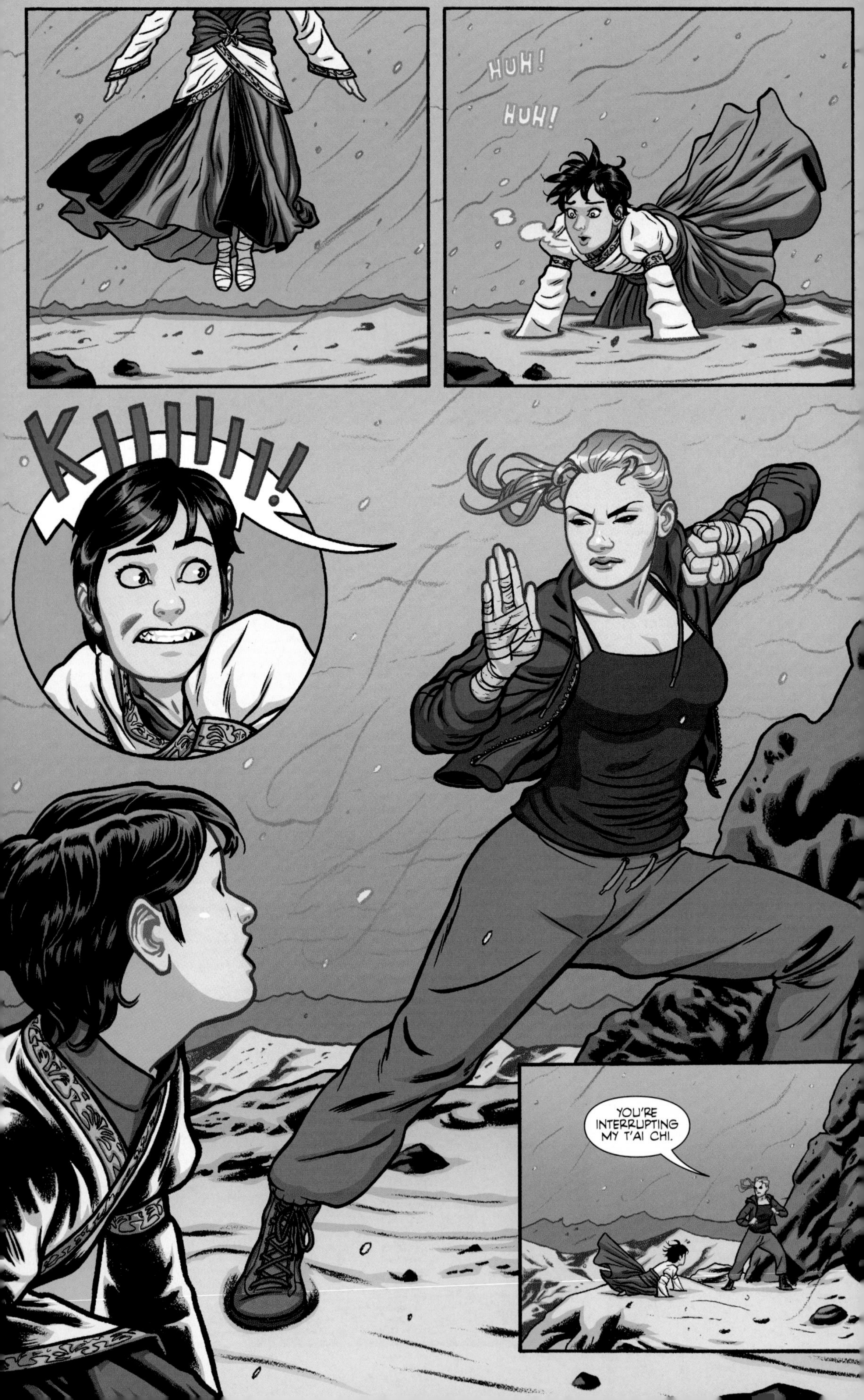
HUH!
HUH!
KIIIIII!
YOU'RE INTERRUPTING MY T'AI CHI.

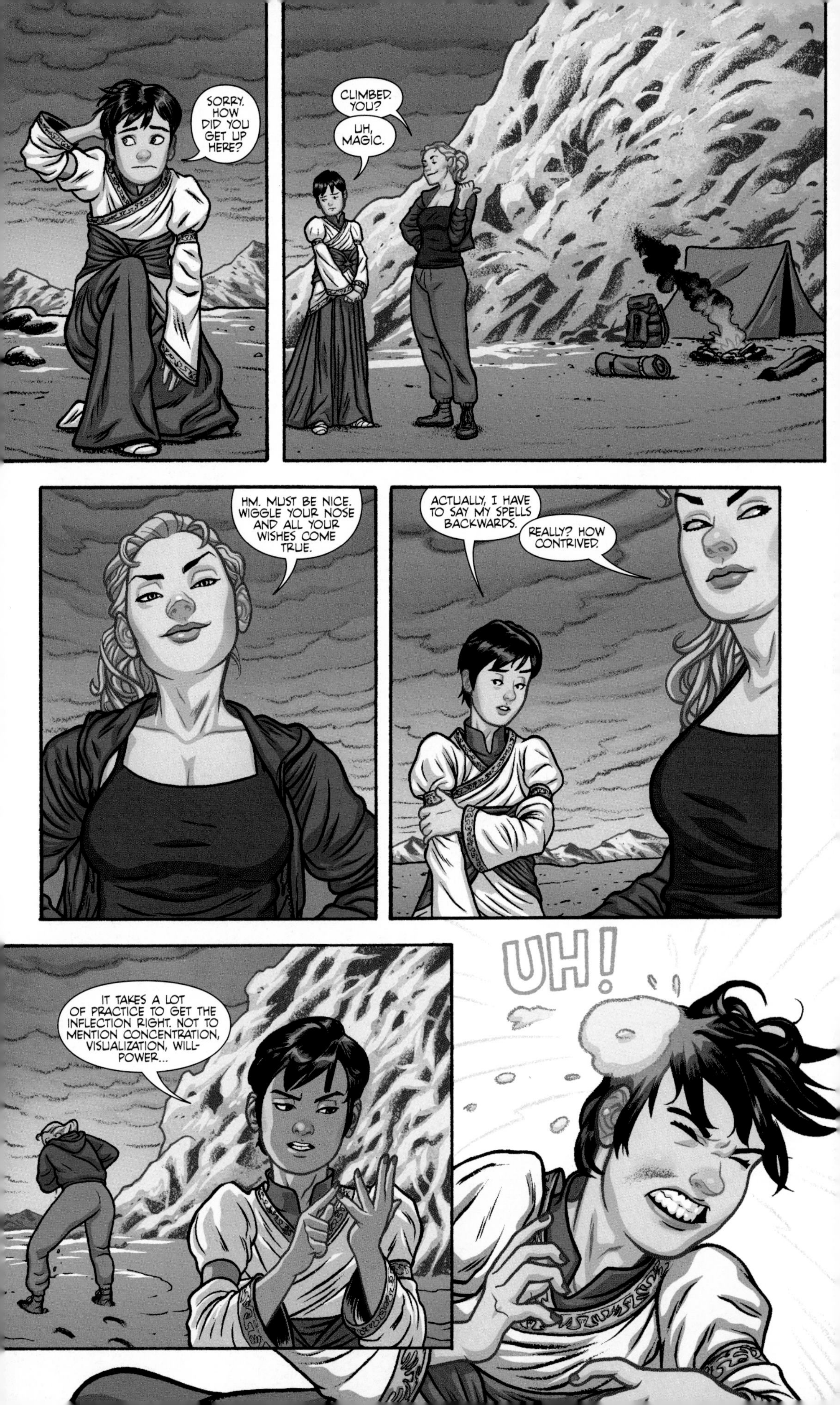

SORRY. HOW DID YOU GET UP HERE?
CLIMBED. YOU?
UH, MAGIC.
HM. MUST BE NICE. WIGGLE YOUR NOSE AND ALL YOUR WISHES COME TRUE.
ACTUALLY, I HAVE TO SAY MY SPELLS BACKWARDS.
REALLY? HOW CONTRIVED.
IT TAKES A LOT OF PRACTICE TO GET THE INFLECTION RIGHT. NOT TO MENTION CONCENTRATION, VISUALIZATION, WILL-POWER...
UH!

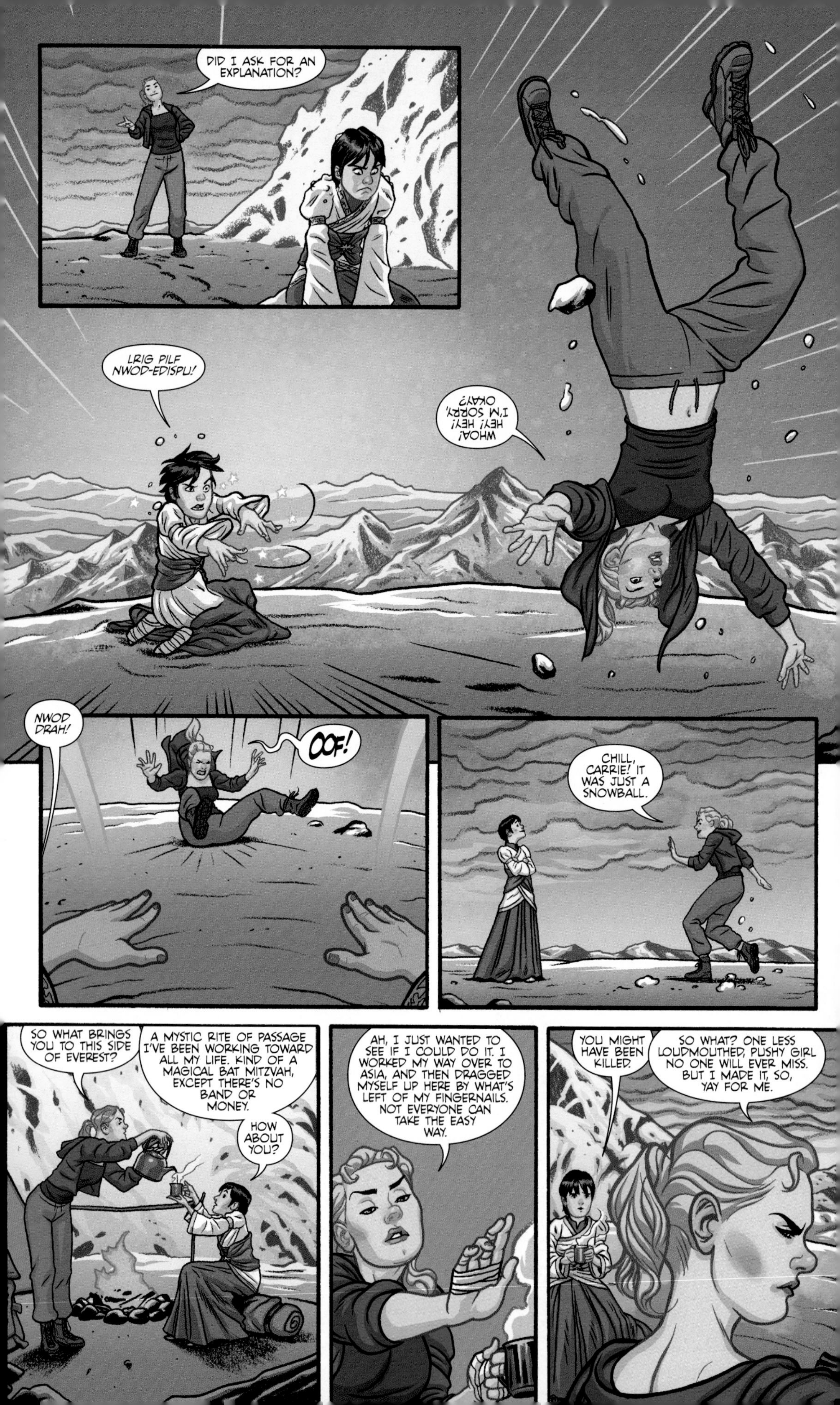
DID I ASK FOR AN EXPLANATION?
LRIG PILF NWOD-EDISPU!
WHOA! HEY! HEY! I'M SORRY, OKAY?
NWOD DRAH!
OOF!
CHILL, CARRIE! IT WAS JUST A SNOWBALL.
SO WHAT BRINGS YOU TO THIS SIDE OF EVEREST?
A MYSTIC RITE OF PASSAGE I'VE BEEN WORKING TOWARD ALL MY LIFE. KIND OF A MAGICAL BAT MITZVAH, EXCEPT THERE'S NO BAND OR MONEY.
HOW ABOUT YOU?
AH, I JUST WANTED TO SEE IF I COULD DO IT. I WORKED MY WAY OVER TO ASIA, AND THEN DRAGGED MYSELF UP HERE BY WHAT'S LEFT OF MY FINGERNAILS. NOT EVERYONE CAN TAKE THE EASY WAY.
YOU MIGHT HAVE BEEN KILLED.
SO WHAT? ONE LESS LOUDMOUTHED, PUSHY GIRL NO ONE WILL EVER MISS. BUT I MADE IT, SO, YAY FOR ME.

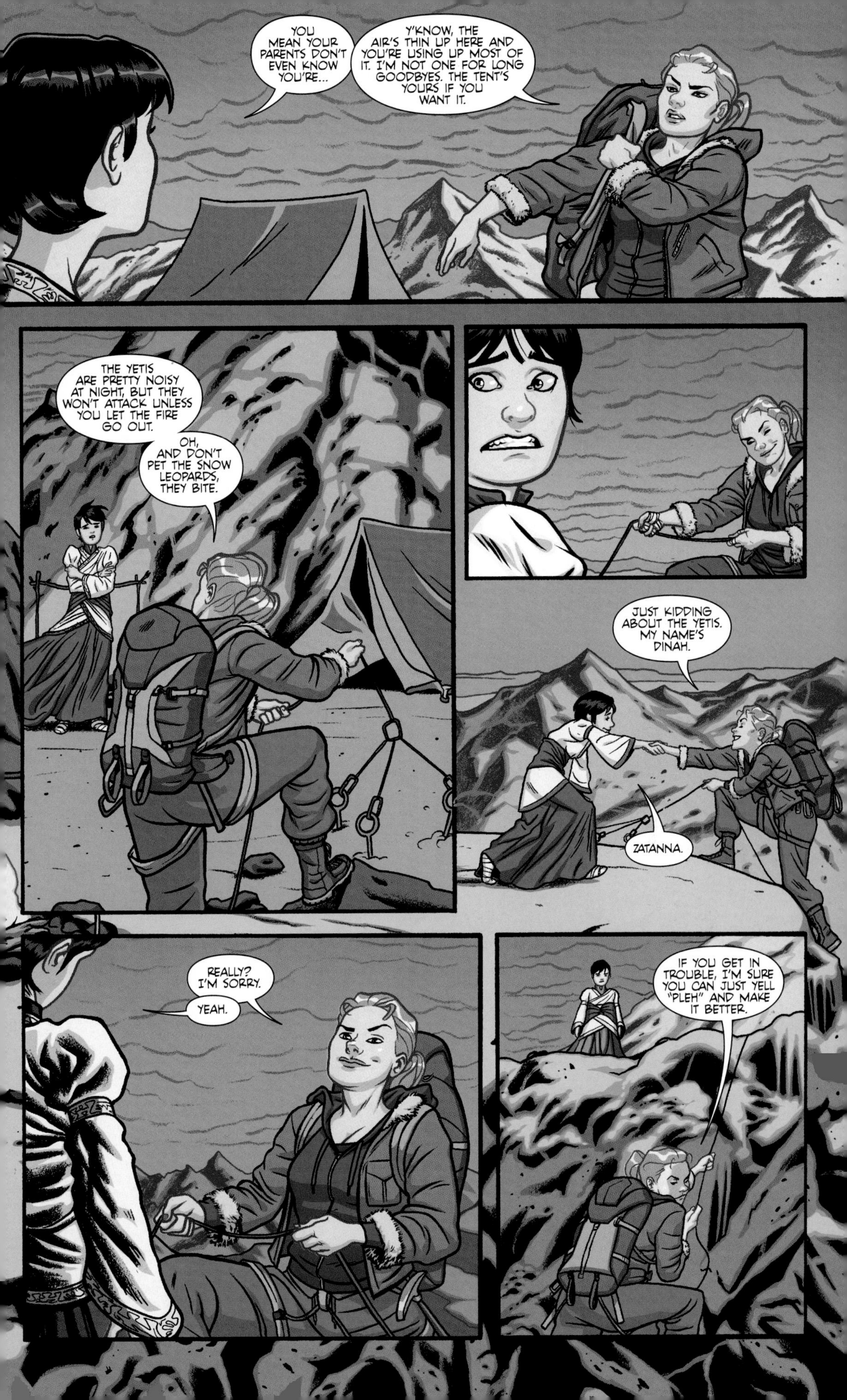
YOU MEAN YOUR PARENTS DON'T EVEN KNOW YOU'RE...
Y'KNOW, THE AIR'S THIN UP HERE AND YOU'RE USING UP MOST OF IT. I'M NOT ONE FOR LONG GOODBYES. THE TENT'S YOURS IF YOU WANT IT.
THE YETIS ARE PRETTY NOISY AT NIGHT, BUT THEY WON'T ATTACK UNLESS YOU LET THE FIRE GO OUT.
OH, AND DON'T PET THE SNOW LEOPARDS, THEY BITE.
JUST KIDDING ABOUT THE YETIS. MY NAME'S DINAH.
ZATANNA.
REALLY? I'M SORRY.
YEAH.
IF YOU GET IN TROUBLE, I'M SURE YOU CAN JUST YELL "PLEH" AND MAKE IT BETTER.

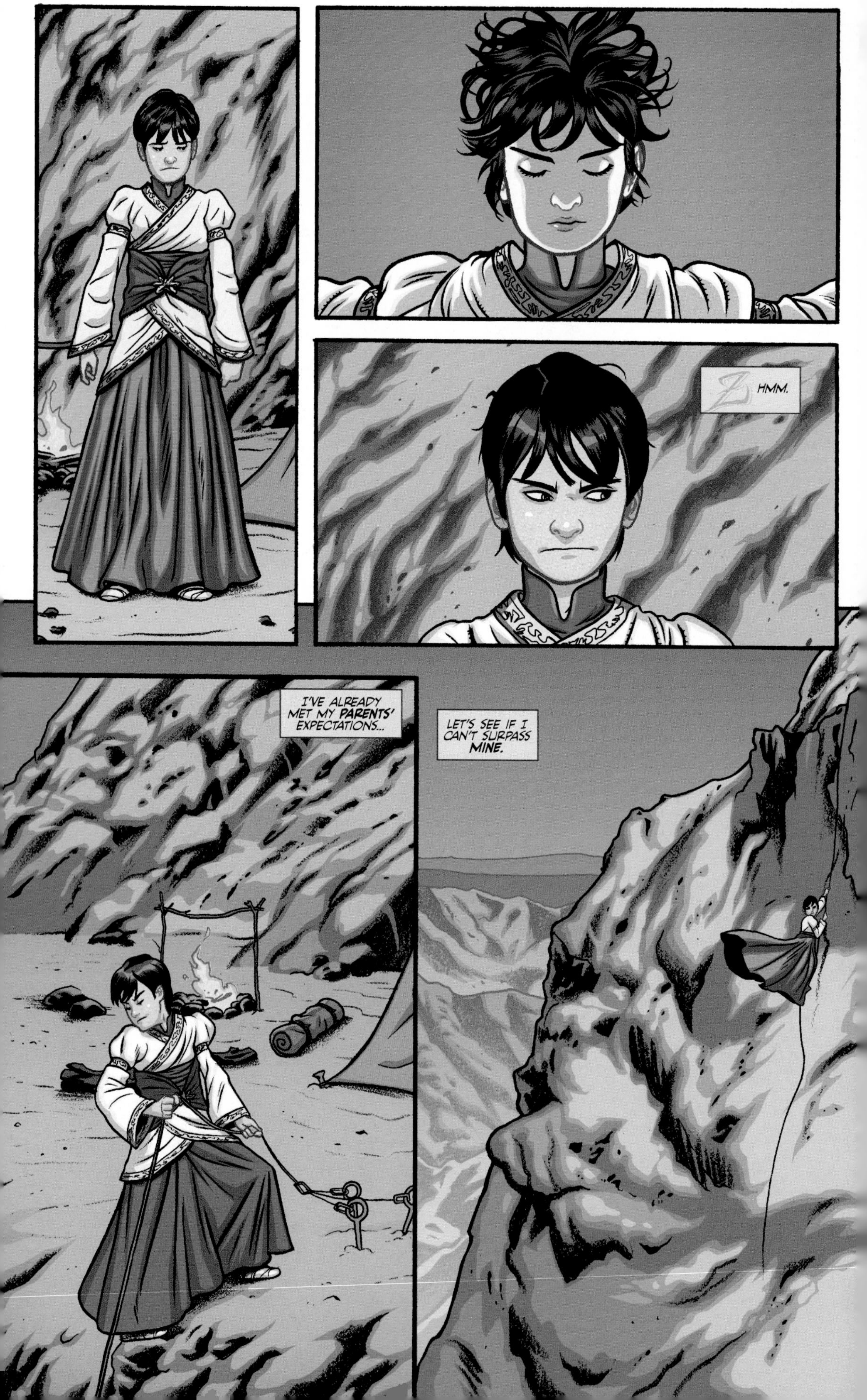
HMM.
I'VE ALREADY MET MY PARENTS' EXPECTATIONS...
LET'S SEE IF I CAN'T SURPASS MINE.

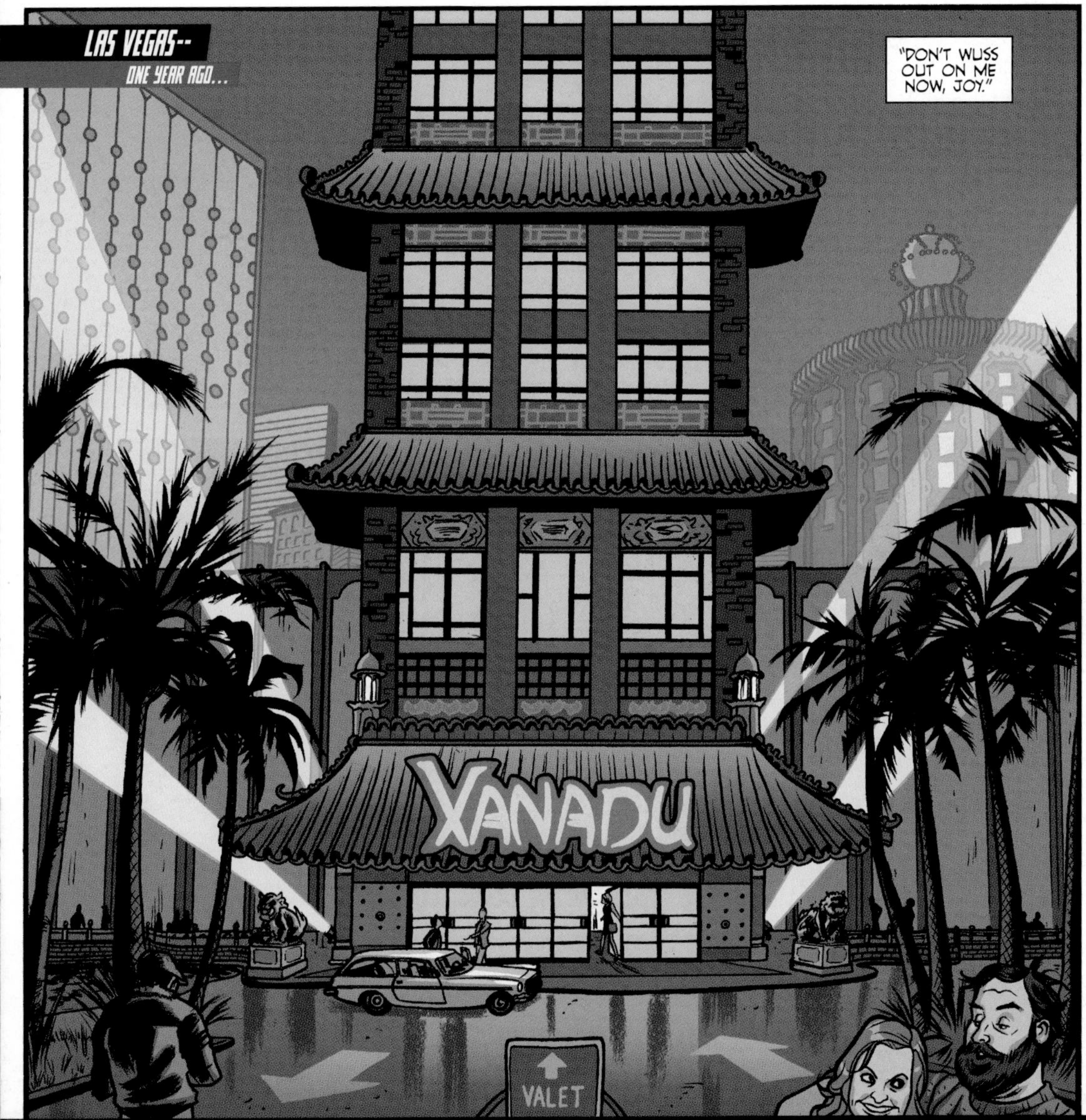
LAS VEGAS--
ONE YEAR AGO...
"DON'T WUSS OUT ON ME NOW, JOY."
XANADU
VALET

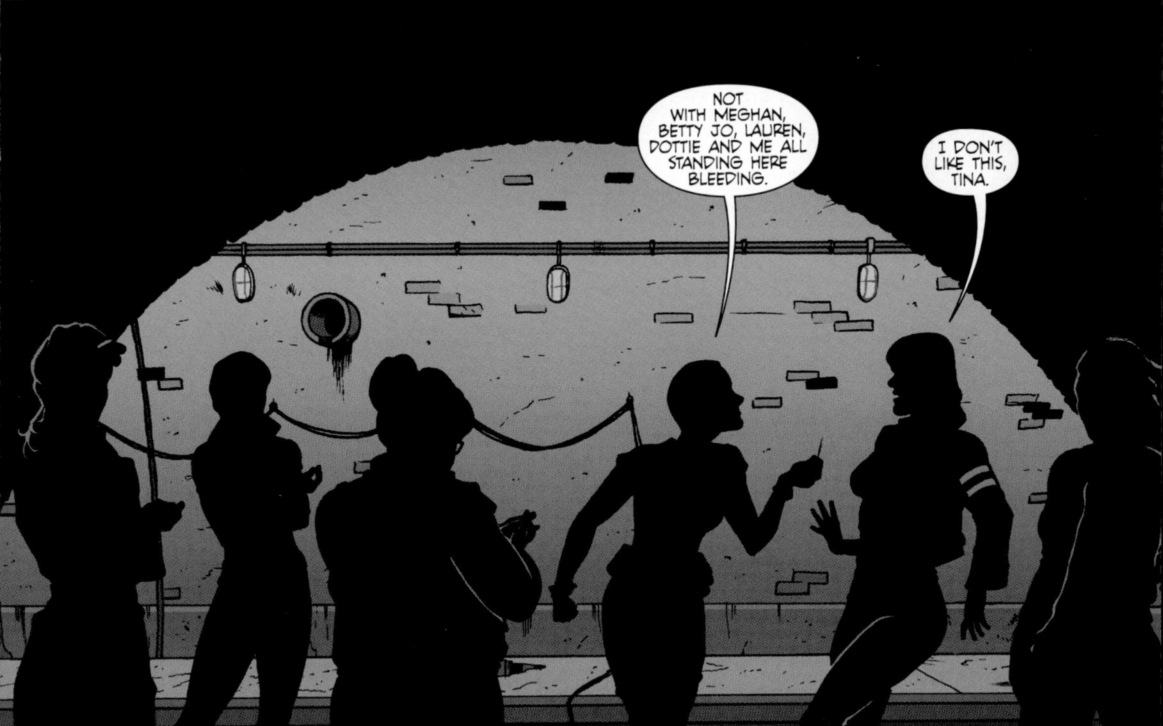
NOT WITH MEGHAN, BETTY JO, LAUREN, DOTTIE AND ME ALL STANDING HERE BLEEDING.
I DON'T LIKE THIS, TINA.

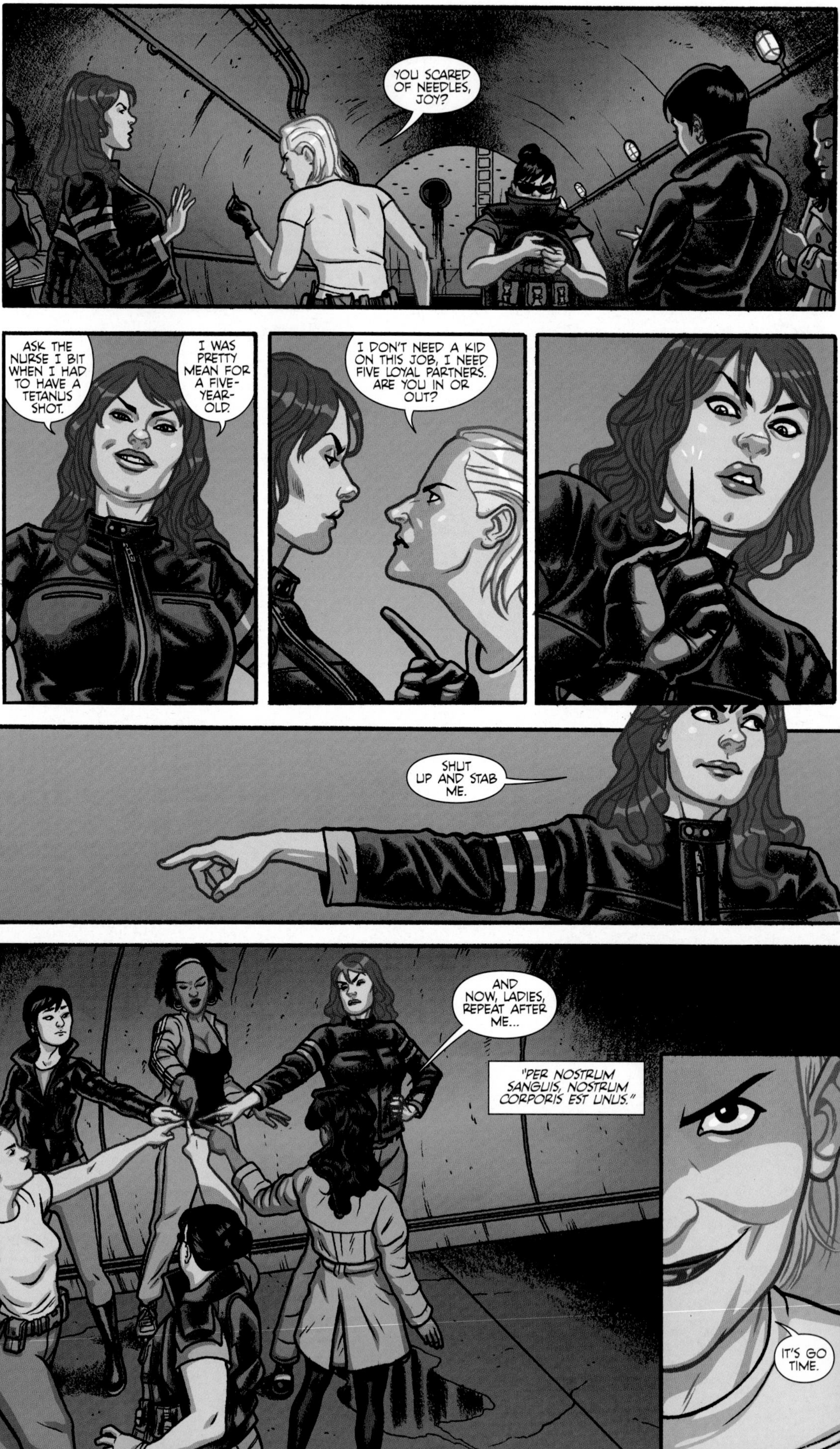
YOU SCARED OF NEEDLES, JOY?
ASK THE NURSE I BIT WHEN I HAD TO HAVE A TETANUS SHOT.
I WAS PRETTY MEAN FOR A FIVE-YEAR-OLD.
I DON'T NEED A KID ON THIS JOB, I NEED FIVE LOYAL PARTNERS. ARE YOU IN OR OUT?
SHUT UP AND STAB ME.
AND NOW, LADIES, REPEAT AFTER ME...
"PER NOSTRUM SANGUIS, NOSTRUM CORPORIS EST UNUS."
IT'S GO TIME.

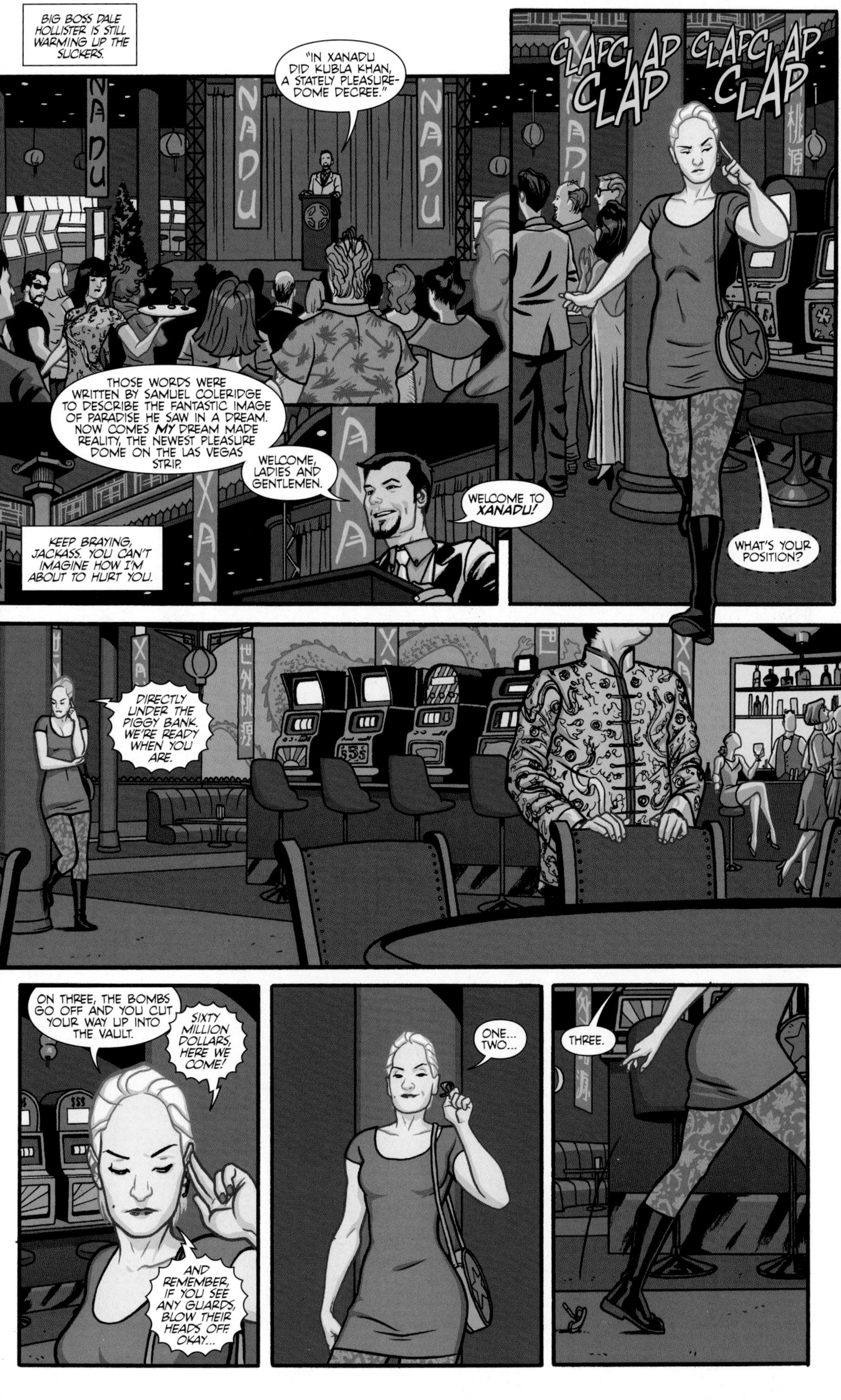
BIG BOSS DALE HOLLISTER IS STILL WARMING UP THE SUCKERS.
"IN XANADU DID KUBLA KHAN, A STATELY PLEASURE-DOME DECREE."
CLAP CLAP CLAP CLAP CLAP CLAP
THOSE WORDS WERE WRITTEN BY SAMUEL COLERIDGE TO DESCRIBE THE FANTASTIC IMAGE OF PARADISE HE SAW IN A DREAM. NOW COMES MY DREAM MADE REALITY, THE NEWEST PLEASURE DOME ON THE LAS VEGAS STRIP.
WELCOME, LADIES AND GENTLEMEN.
WELCOME TO XANADU!
KEEP BRAYING, JACKASS. YOU CAN'T IMAGINE HOW I'M ABOUT TO HURT YOU.
WHAT'S YOUR POSITION?
DIRECTLY UNDER THE PIGGY BANK. WE'RE READY WHEN YOU ARE.
ON THREE, THE BOMBS GO OFF AND YOU CUT YOUR WAY UP INTO THE VAULT.
SIXTY MILLION DOLLARS, HERE WE COME!
AND REMEMBER, IF YOU SEE ANY GUARDS, BLOW THEIR HEADS OFF. OKAY...
ONE... TWO...
THREE.

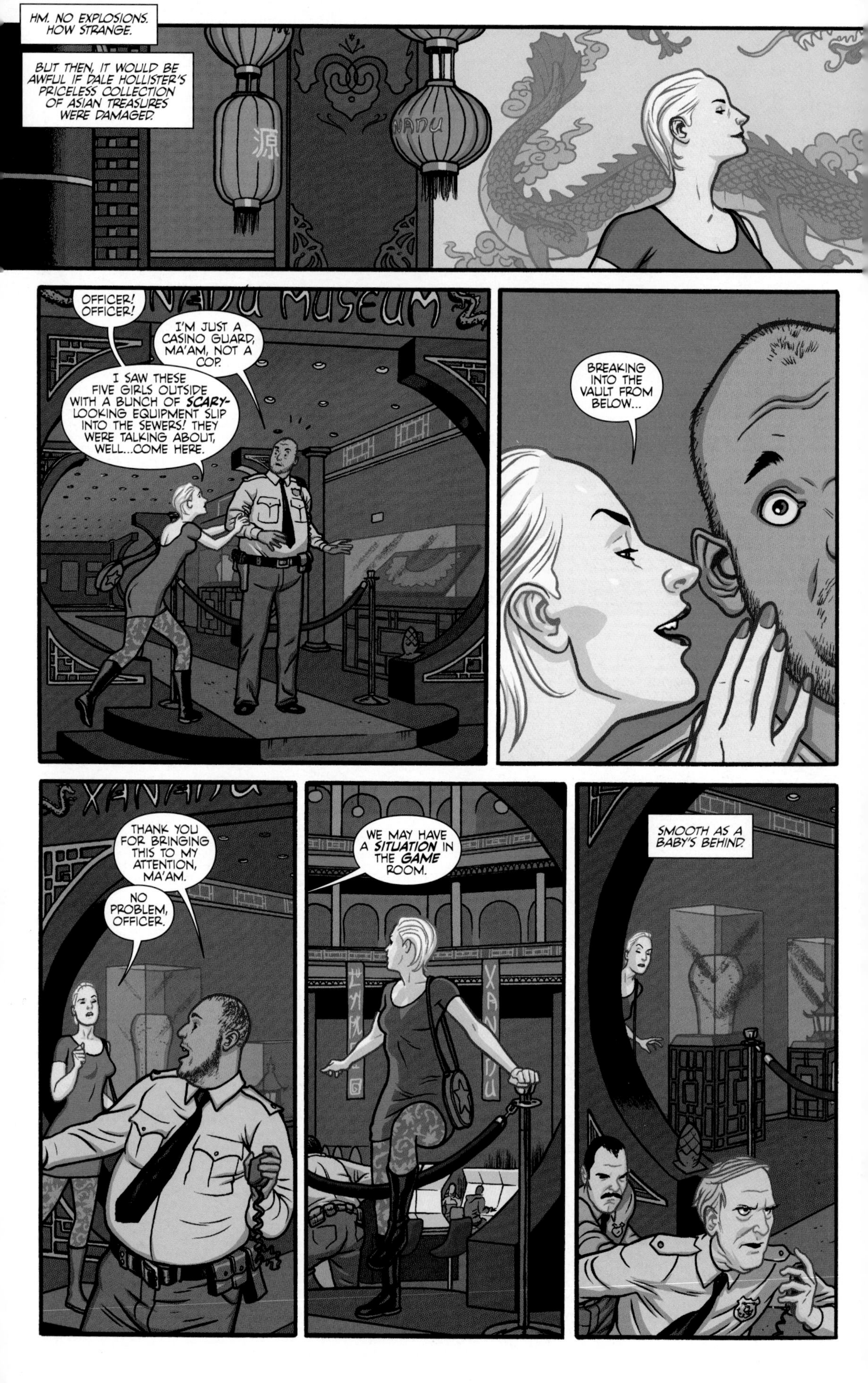
HM. NO EXPLOSIONS. HOW STRANGE.
BUT THEN, IT WOULD BE AWFUL IF DALE HOLLISTER'S PRICELESS COLLECTION OF ASIAN TREASURES WERE DAMAGED.
OFFICER! OFFICER!
I'M JUST A CASINO GUARD, MA'AM, NOT A COP.
I SAW THESE FIVE GIRLS OUTSIDE WITH A BUNCH OF SCARY-LOOKING EQUIPMENT SLIP INTO THE SEWERS! THEY WERE TALKING ABOUT, WELL...COME HERE.
BREAKING INTO THE VAULT FROM BELOW...
THANK YOU FOR BRINGING THIS TO MY ATTENTION, MA'AM.
NO PROBLEM, OFFICER.
WE MAY HAVE A SITUATION IN THE GAME ROOM.
SMOOTH AS A BABY'S BEHIND.

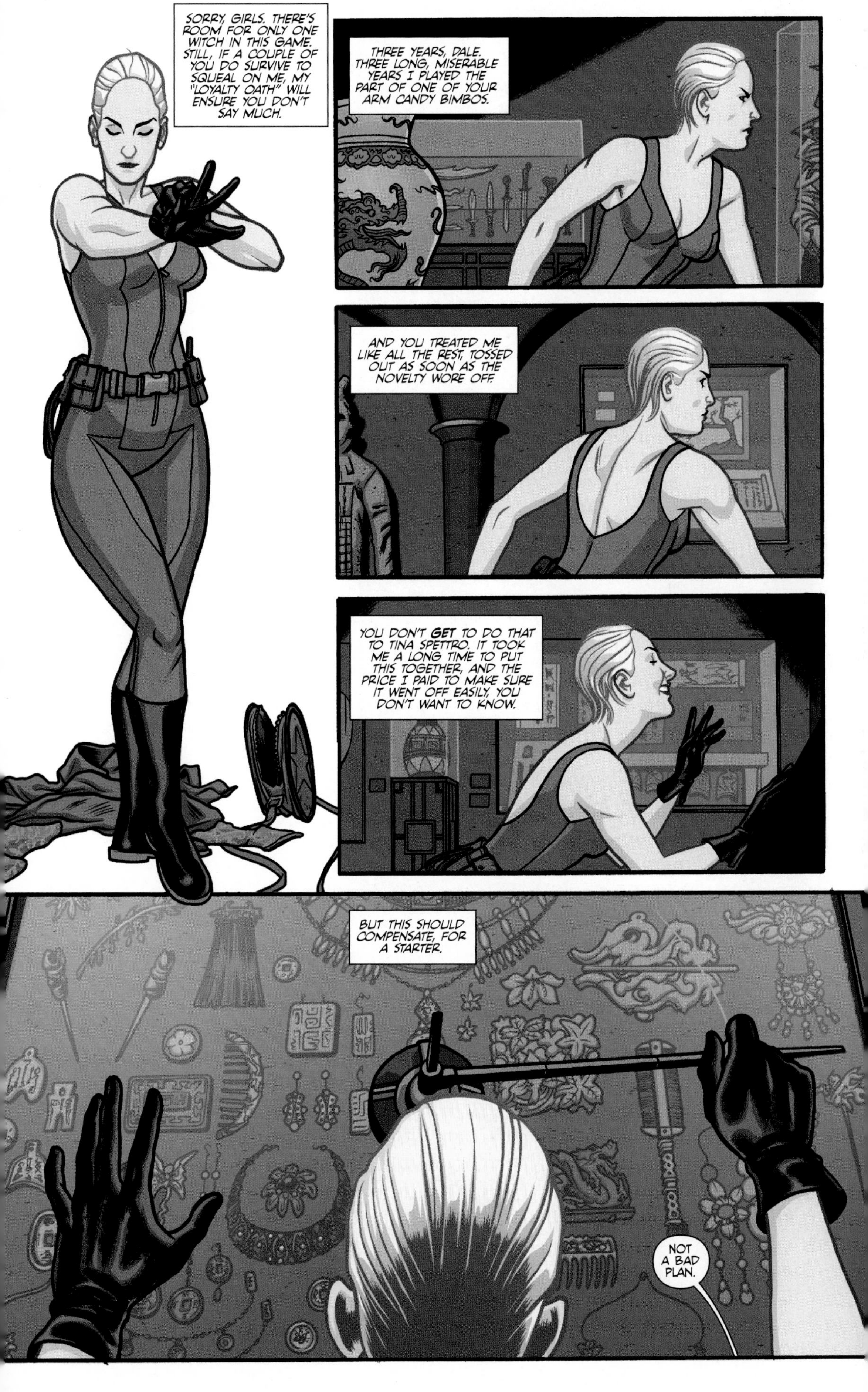
SORRY, GIRLS. THERE'S ROOM FOR ONLY ONE WITCH IN THIS GAME. STILL, IF A COUPLE OF YOU DO SURVIVE TO SQUEAL ON ME, MY "LOYALTY OATH" WILL ENSURE YOU DON'T SAY MUCH.
THREE YEARS, DALE. THREE LONG, MISERABLE YEARS I PLAYED THE PART OF ONE OF YOUR ARM CANDY BIMBOS.
AND YOU TREATED ME LIKE ALL THE REST, TOSSED OUT AS SOON AS THE NOVELTY WORE OFF.
YOU DON'T GET TO DO THAT TO TINA SPETTRO. IT TOOK ME A LONG TIME TO PUT THIS TOGETHER, AND THE PRICE I PAID TO MAKE SURE IT WENT OFF EASILY, YOU DON'T WANT TO KNOW.
BUT THIS SHOULD COMPENSATE, FOR A STARTER.
NOT A BAD PLAN.

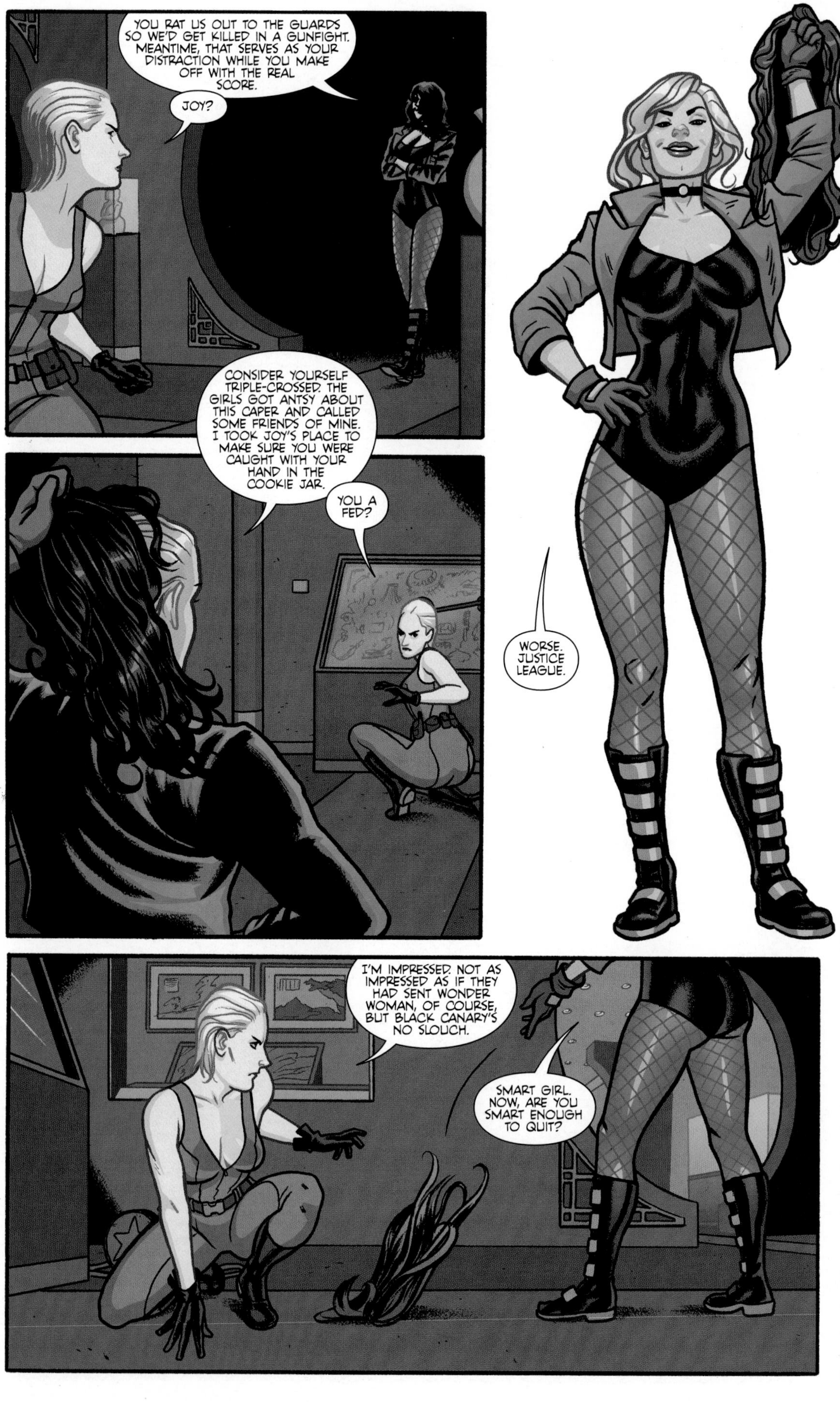
YOU RAT US OUT TO THE GUARDS SO WE'D GET KILLED IN A GUNFIGHT. MEANTIME, THAT SERVES AS YOUR DISTRACTION WHILE YOU MAKE OFF WITH THE REAL SCORE.
JOY?
CONSIDER YOURSELF TRIPLE-CROSSED. THE GIRLS GOT ANTSY ABOUT THIS CAPER AND CALLED SOME FRIENDS OF MINE. I TOOK JOY'S PLACE TO MAKE SURE YOU WERE CAUGHT WITH YOUR HAND IN THE COOKIE JAR.
YOU A FED?
WORSE. JUSTICE LEAGUE.
I'M IMPRESSED. NOT AS IMPRESSED AS IF THEY HAD SENT WONDER WOMAN, OF COURSE, BUT BLACK CANARY'S NO SLOUCH.
SMART GIRL. NOW, ARE YOU SMART ENOUGH TO QUIT?

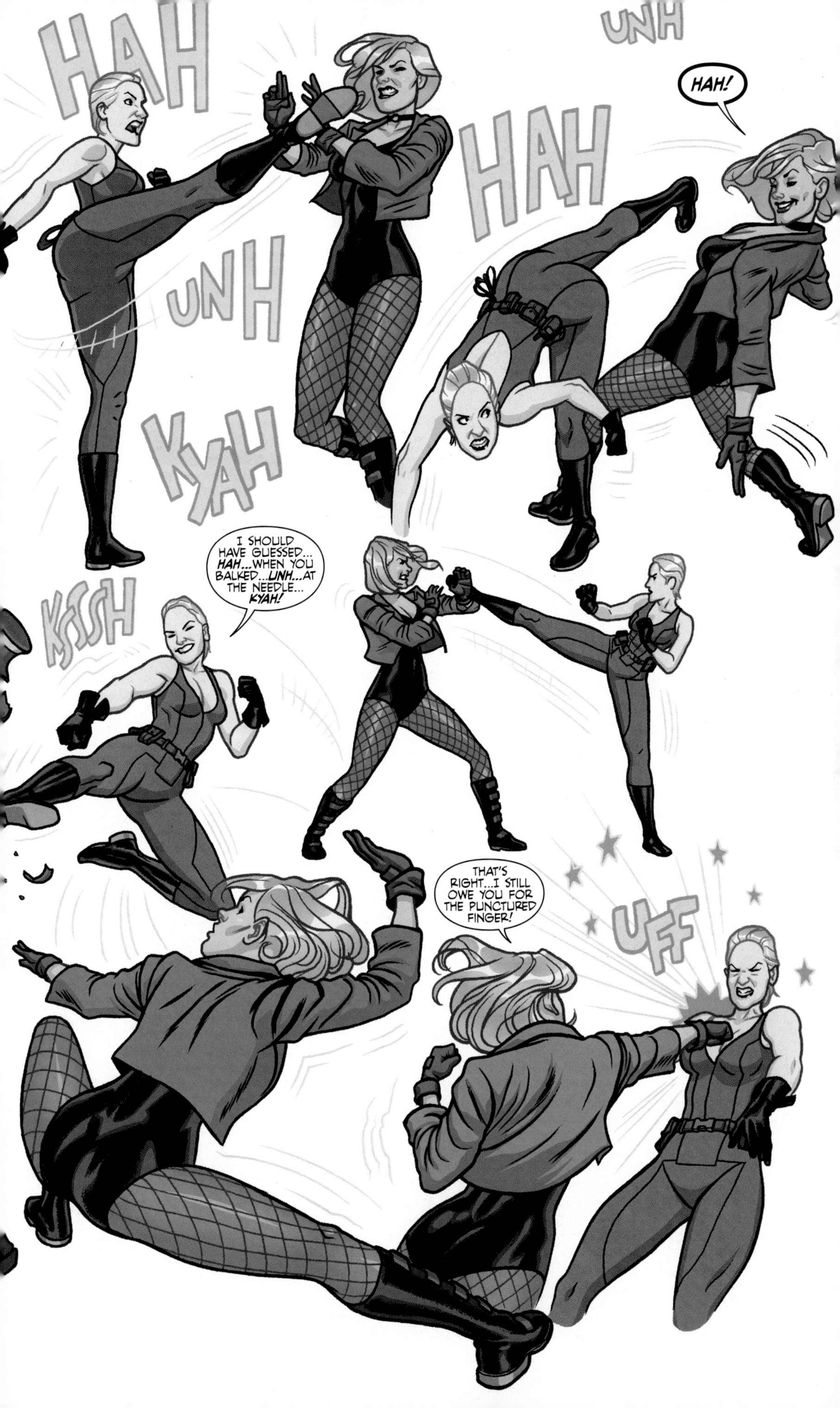

HAH
UNH
HAH!
HAH
UNH
KYAH
KSSH
I SHOULD HAVE GUESSED... HAH...WHEN YOU BALKED...UNH...AT THE NEEDLE... KYAH!
THAT'S RIGHT...I STILL OWE YOU FOR THE PUNCTURED FINGER!
UFF

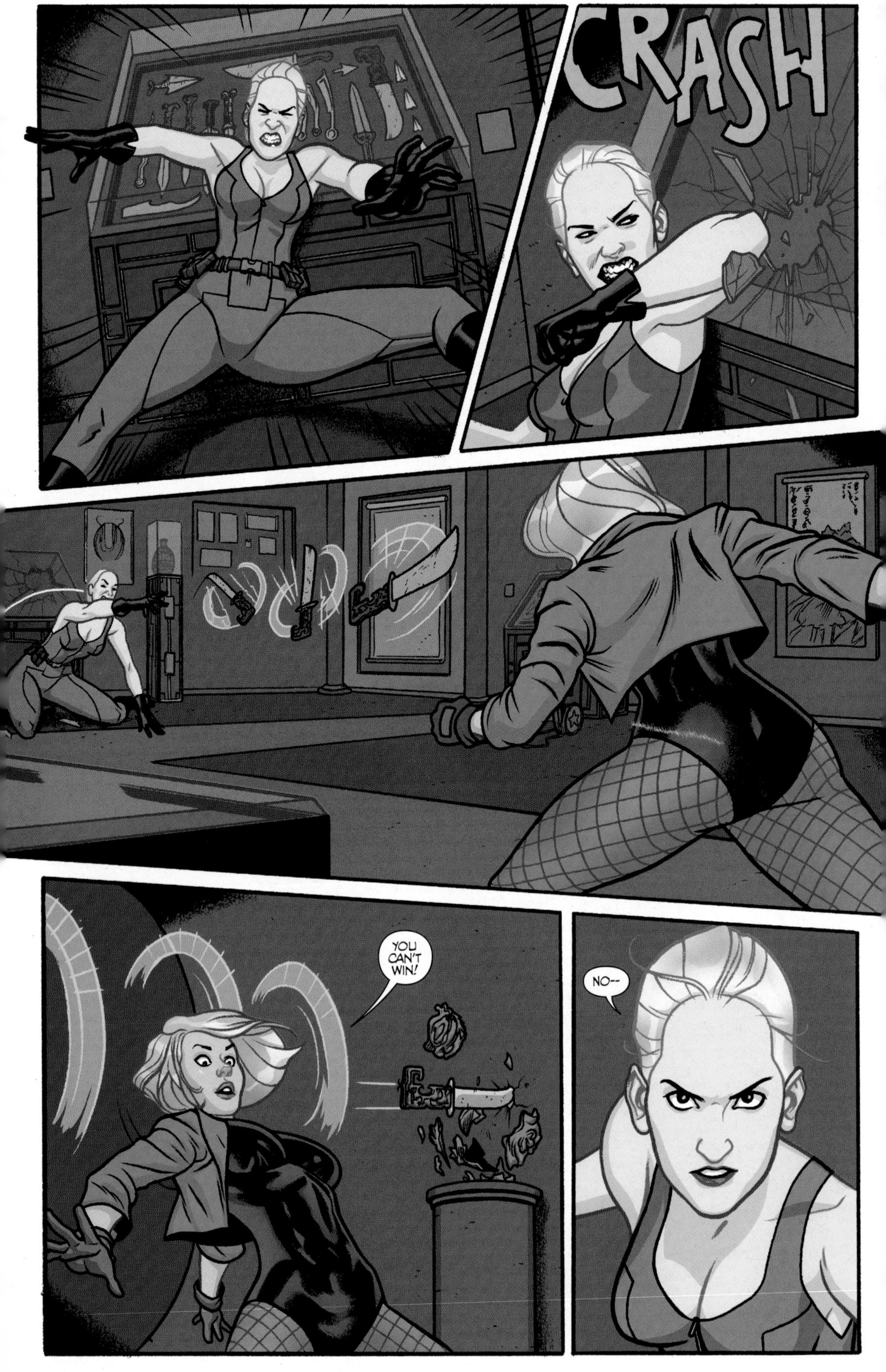
CRASH
YOU CAN'T WIN!
NO--

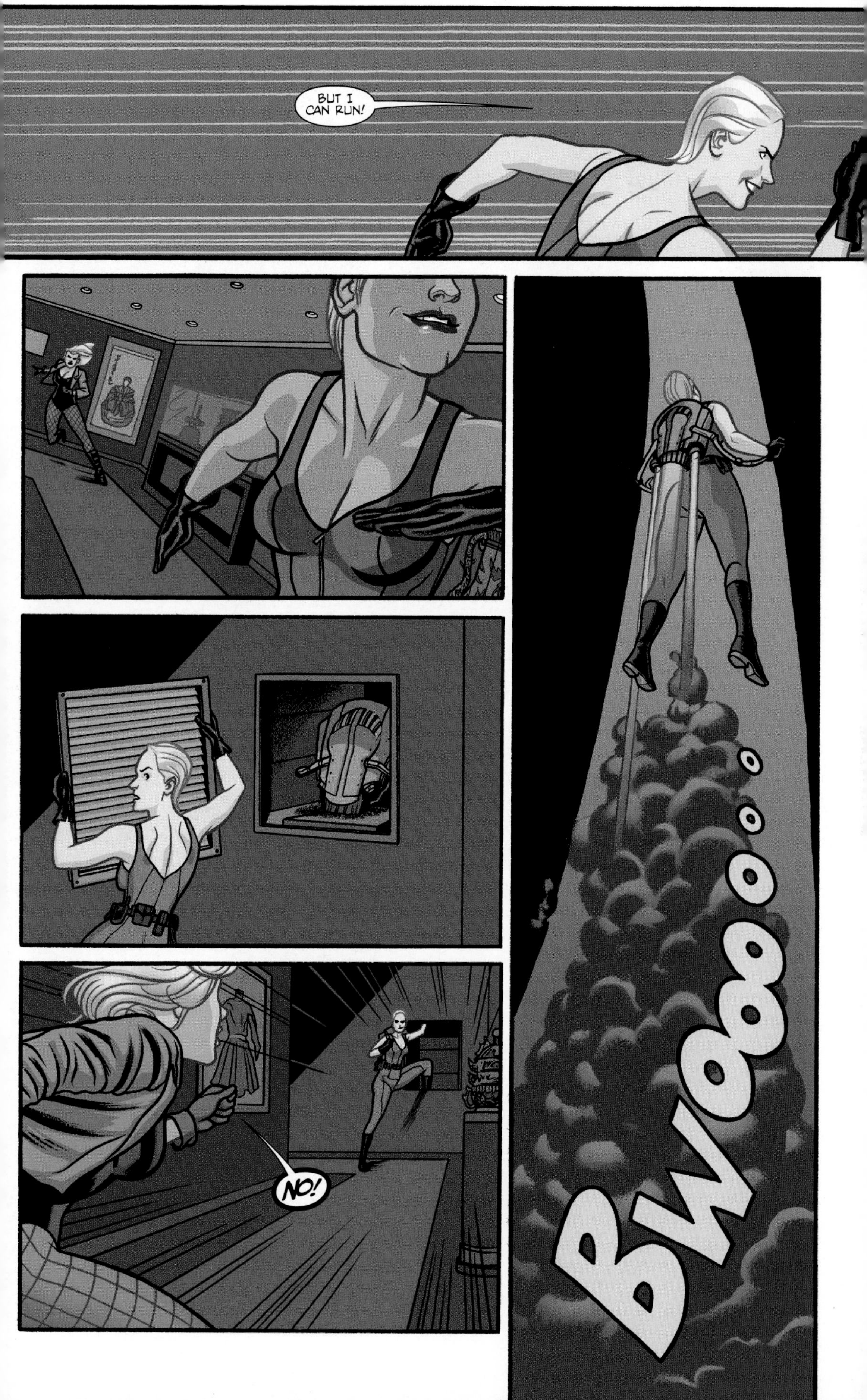
BUT I CAN RUN!
NO!
BWOOOOOOOO

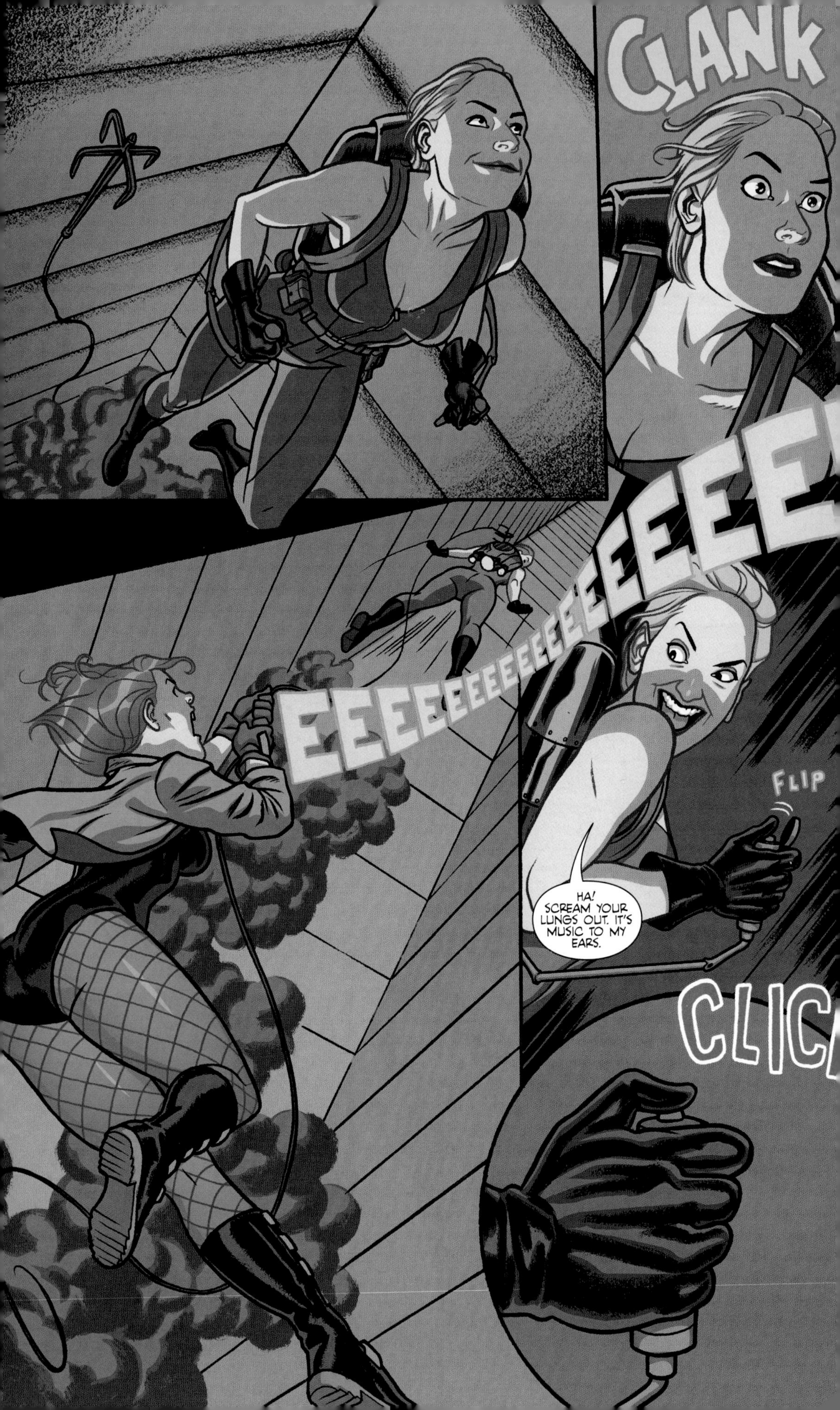
CLANK
EEEEEEEEEEEEEEEEEEE
FLIP
HA! SCREAM YOUR LUNGS OUT. IT'S MUSIC TO MY EARS.
CLIC

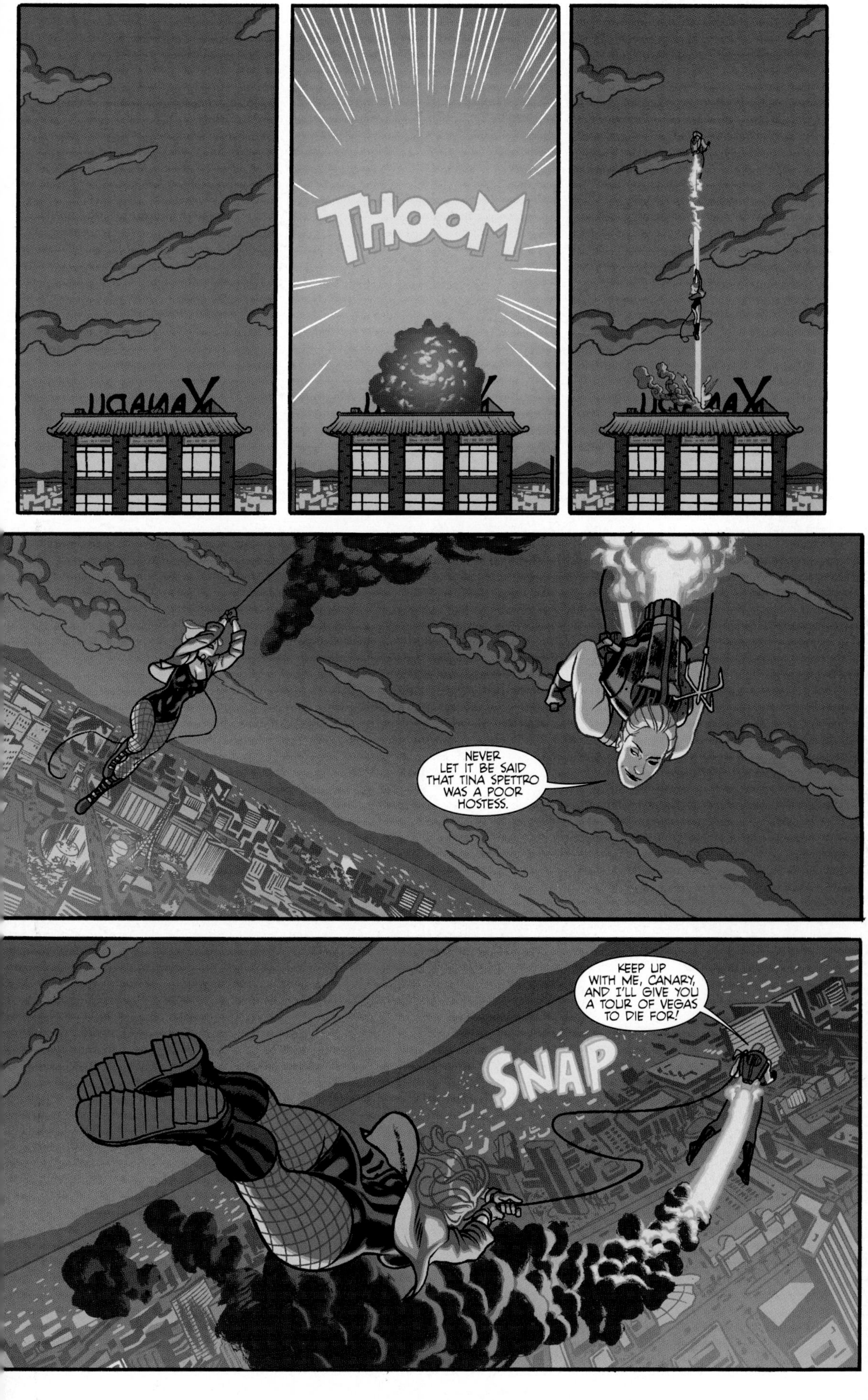

THOOM
NEVER LET IT BE SAID THAT TINA SPETTRO WAS A POOR HOSTESS.
KEEP UP WITH ME, CANARY, AND I'LL GIVE YOU A TOUR OF VEGAS TO DIE FOR!
SNAP

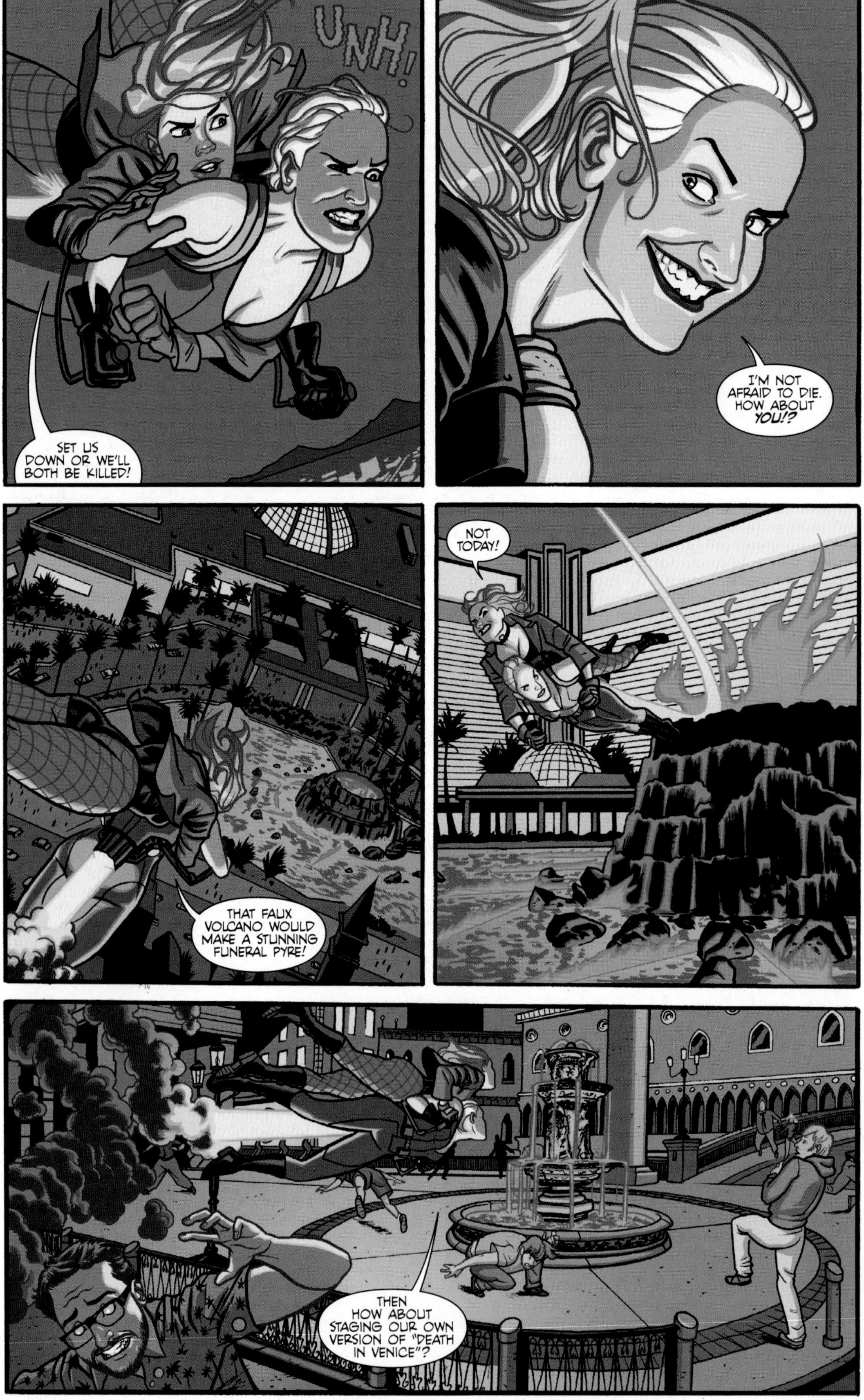
UNH!
SET US DOWN OR WE'LL BOTH BE KILLED!
I'M NOT AFRAID TO DIE. HOW ABOUT YOU!?
THAT FAUX VOLCANO WOULD MAKE A STUNNING FUNERAL PYRE!
NOT TODAY!
THEN HOW ABOUT STAGING OUR OWN VERSION OF "DEATH IN VENICE"?

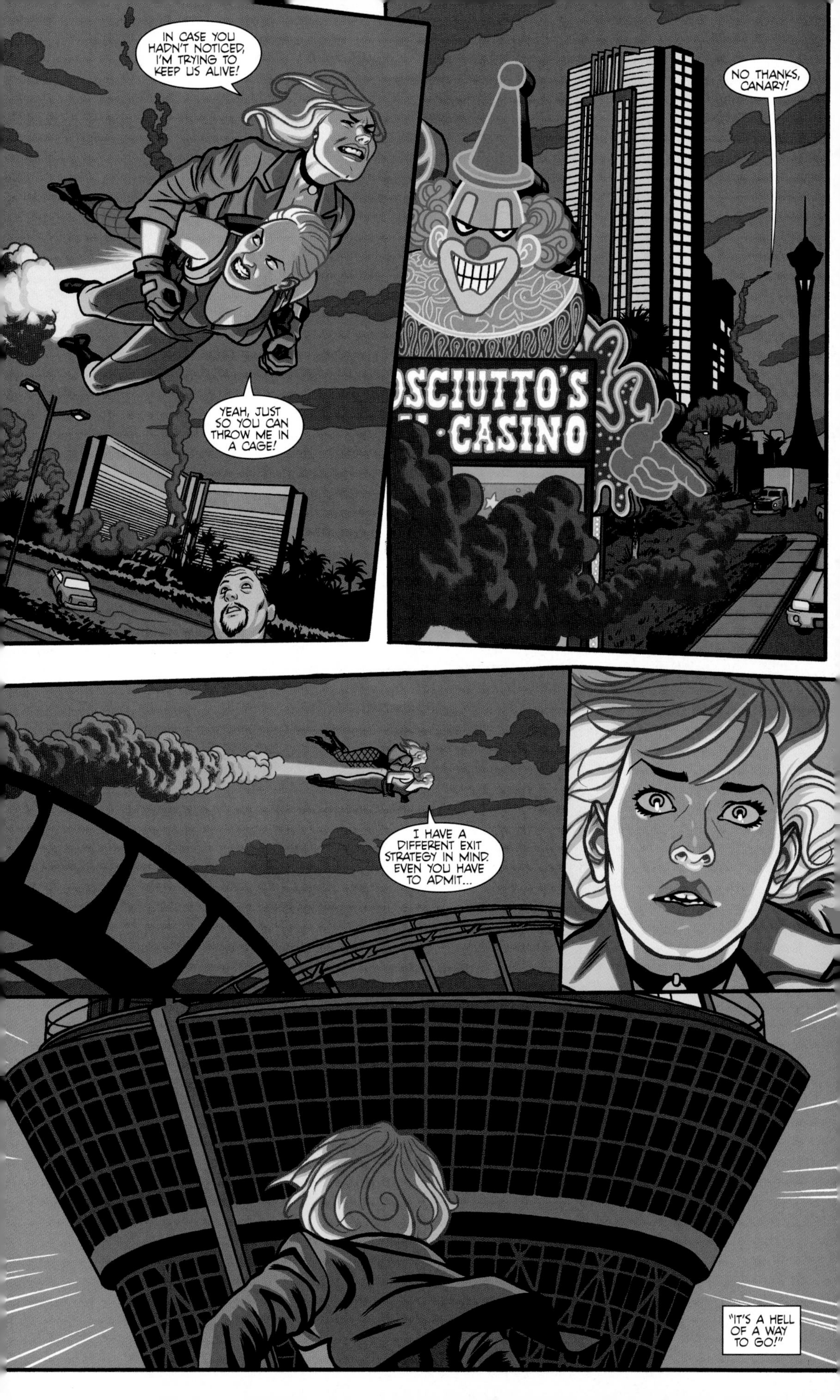
IN CASE YOU HADN'T NOTICED, I'M TRYING TO KEEP US ALIVE!
YEAH, JUST SO YOU CAN THROW ME IN A CAGE!
OSCIUTTO'S
CASINO
NO THANKS, CANARY!
I HAVE A DIFFERENT EXIT STRATEGY IN MIND. EVEN YOU HAVE TO ADMIT...
"IT'S A HELL OF A WAY TO GO!"

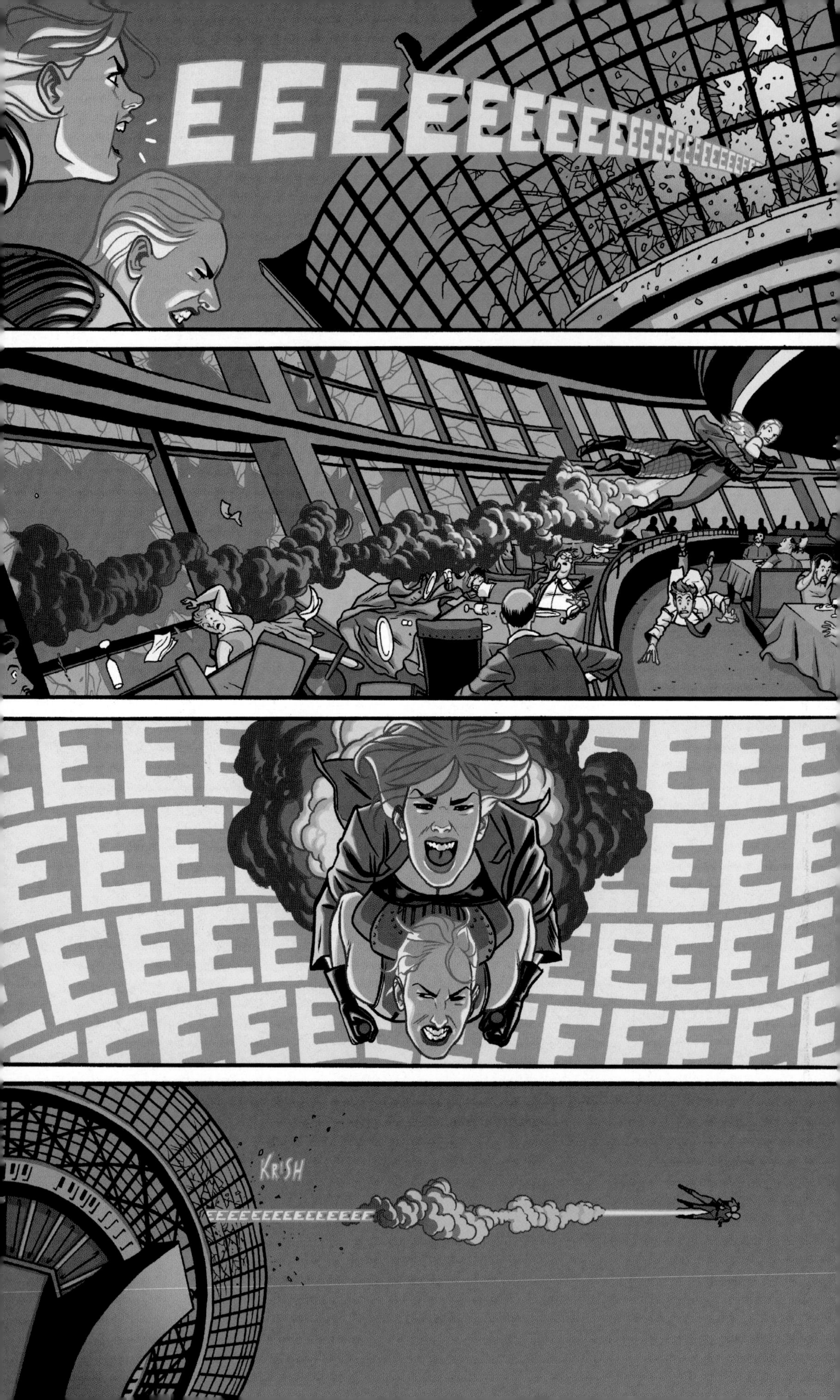

EEEEEEEEEEEEEEEEEEEEEEEEE
EEEEEEEEEEEEEEEEEEEEEEEEEEEEEE
KRISH
EEEEEEEEEEEEEEEE

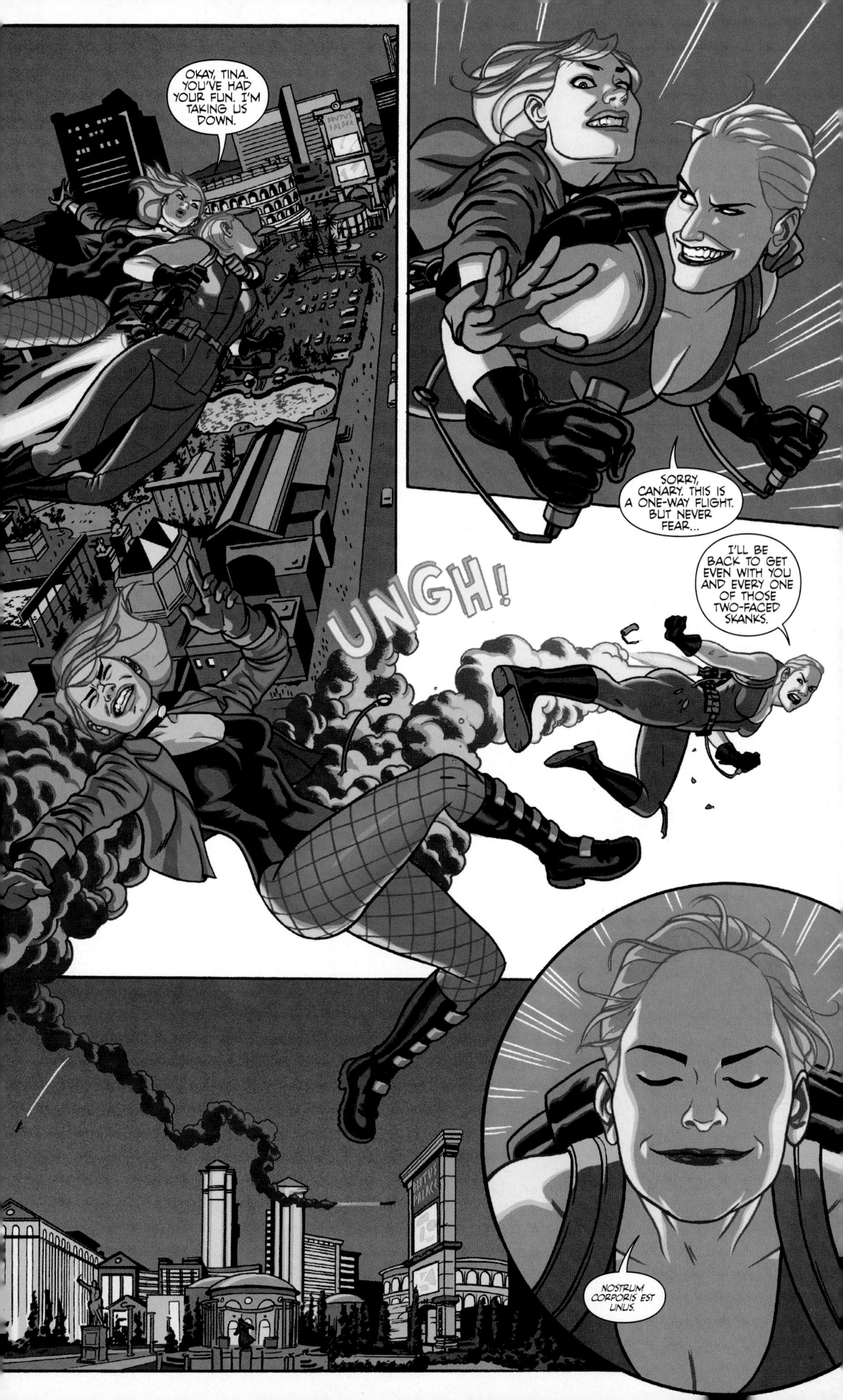
OKAY, TINA. YOU'VE HAD YOUR FUN. I'M TAKING US DOWN.
BRUTUS PALACE
SORRY, CANARY. THIS IS A ONE-WAY FLIGHT. BUT NEVER FEAR...
I'LL BE BACK TO GET EVEN WITH YOU AND EVERY ONE OF THOSE TWO-FACED SKANKS.
UNGH!
BRUTUS PALACE
NOSTRUM CORPORIS EST UNUS.

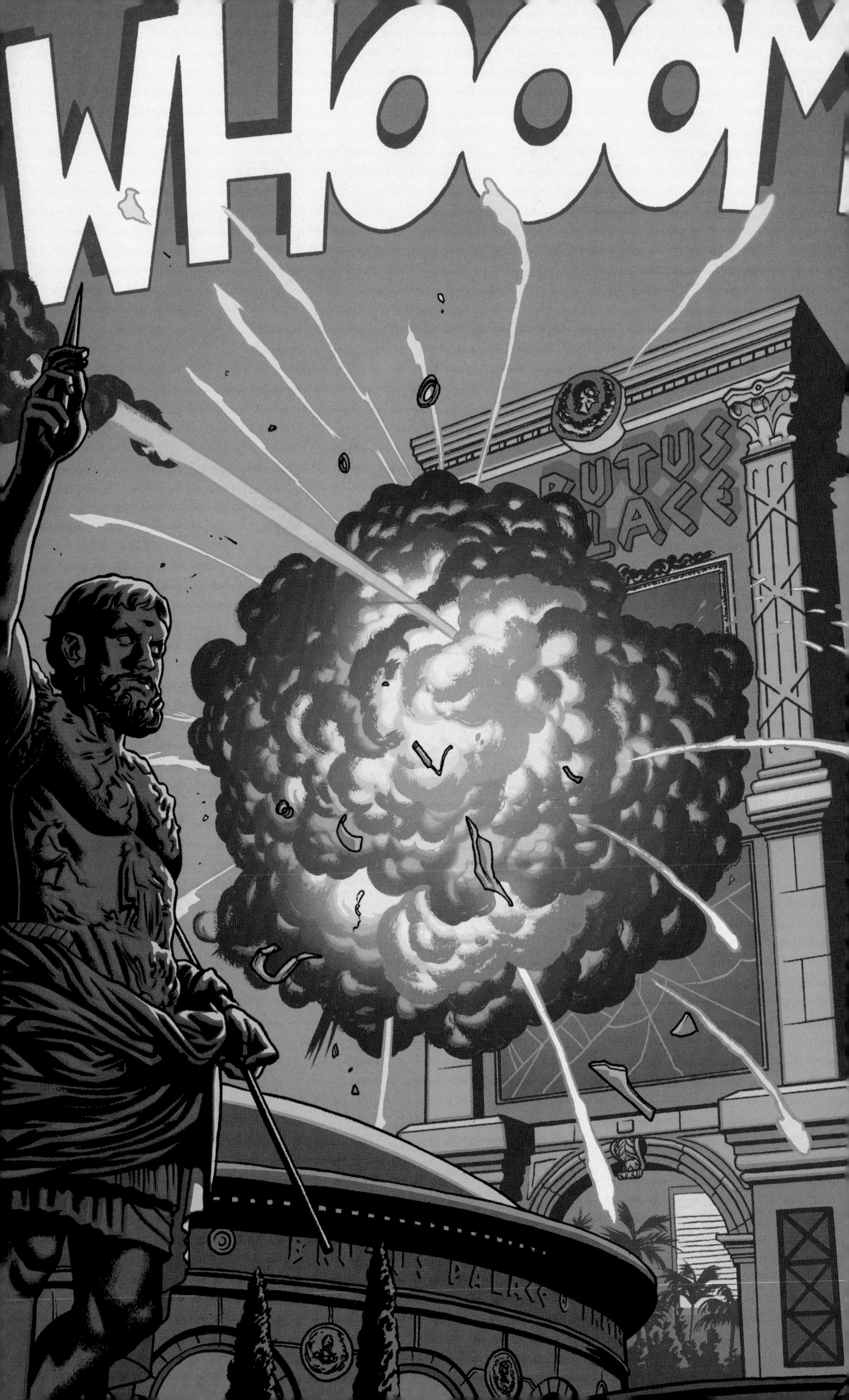
WHOOOM

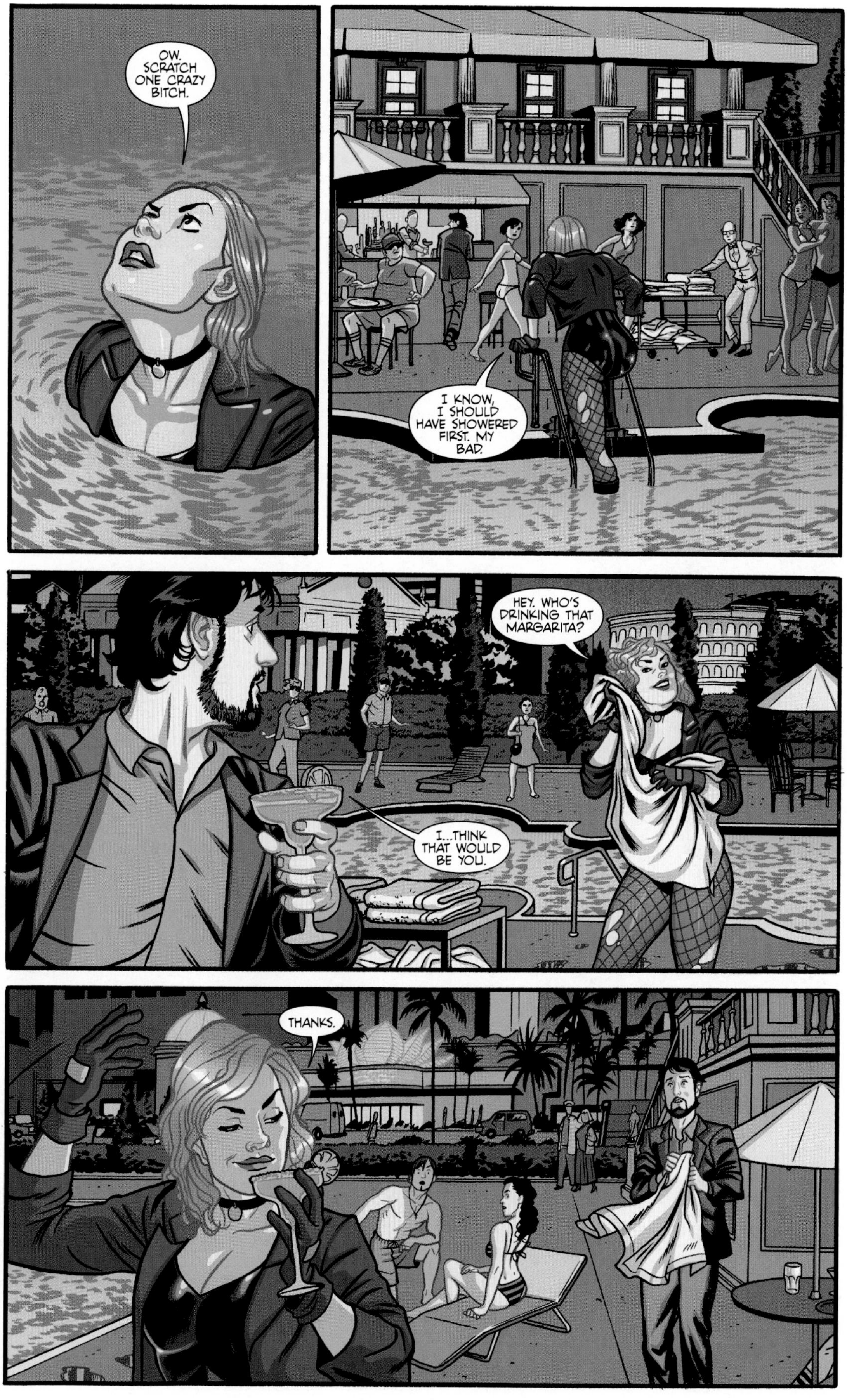

OW. SCRATCH ONE CRAZY BITCH.
I KNOW, I SHOULD HAVE SHOWERED FIRST. MY BAD.
HEY. WHO'S DRINKING THAT MARGARITA?
I...THINK THAT WOULD BE YOU.
THANKS.

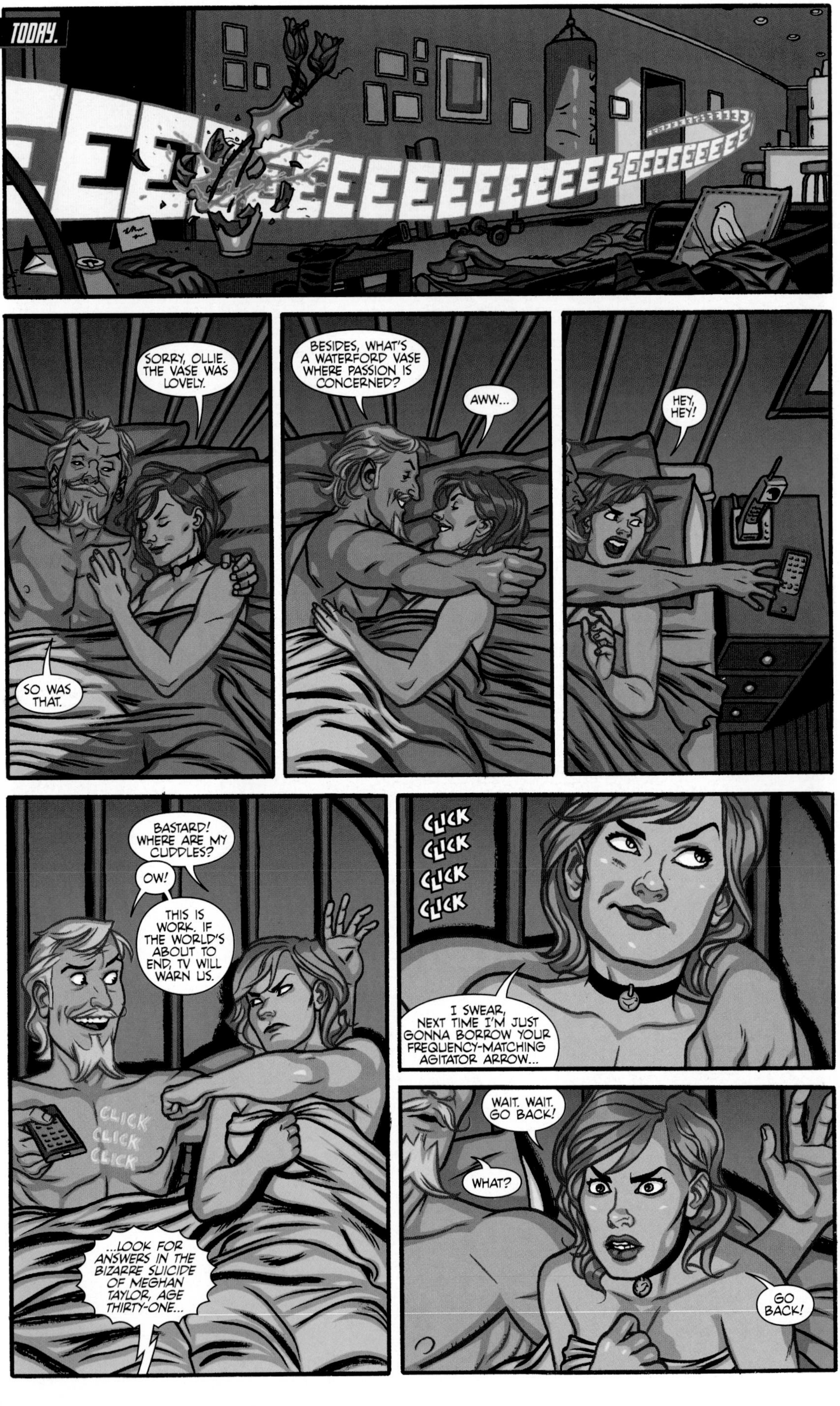

TODAY.
EEEEEEEEEEEEEEEEEEEEEEEEEEEEEEE
SORRY, OLLIE. THE VASE WAS LOVELY.
SO WAS THAT.
BESIDES, WHAT'S A WATERFORD VASE WHERE PASSION IS CONCERNED?
AWW...
HEY, HEY!
BASTARD! WHERE ARE MY CUDDLES?
OW!
THIS IS WORK. IF THE WORLD'S ABOUT TO END, TV WILL WARN US.
CLICK CLICK CLICK
...LOOK FOR ANSWERS IN THE BIZARRE SUICIDE OF MEGHAN TAYLOR, AGE THIRTY-ONE...
CLICK
CLICK
CLICK
CLICK
I SWEAR, NEXT TIME I'M JUST GONNA BORROW YOUR FREQUENCY-MATCHING AGITATOR ARROW...
WAIT. WAIT. GO BACK!
WHAT?
GO BACK!

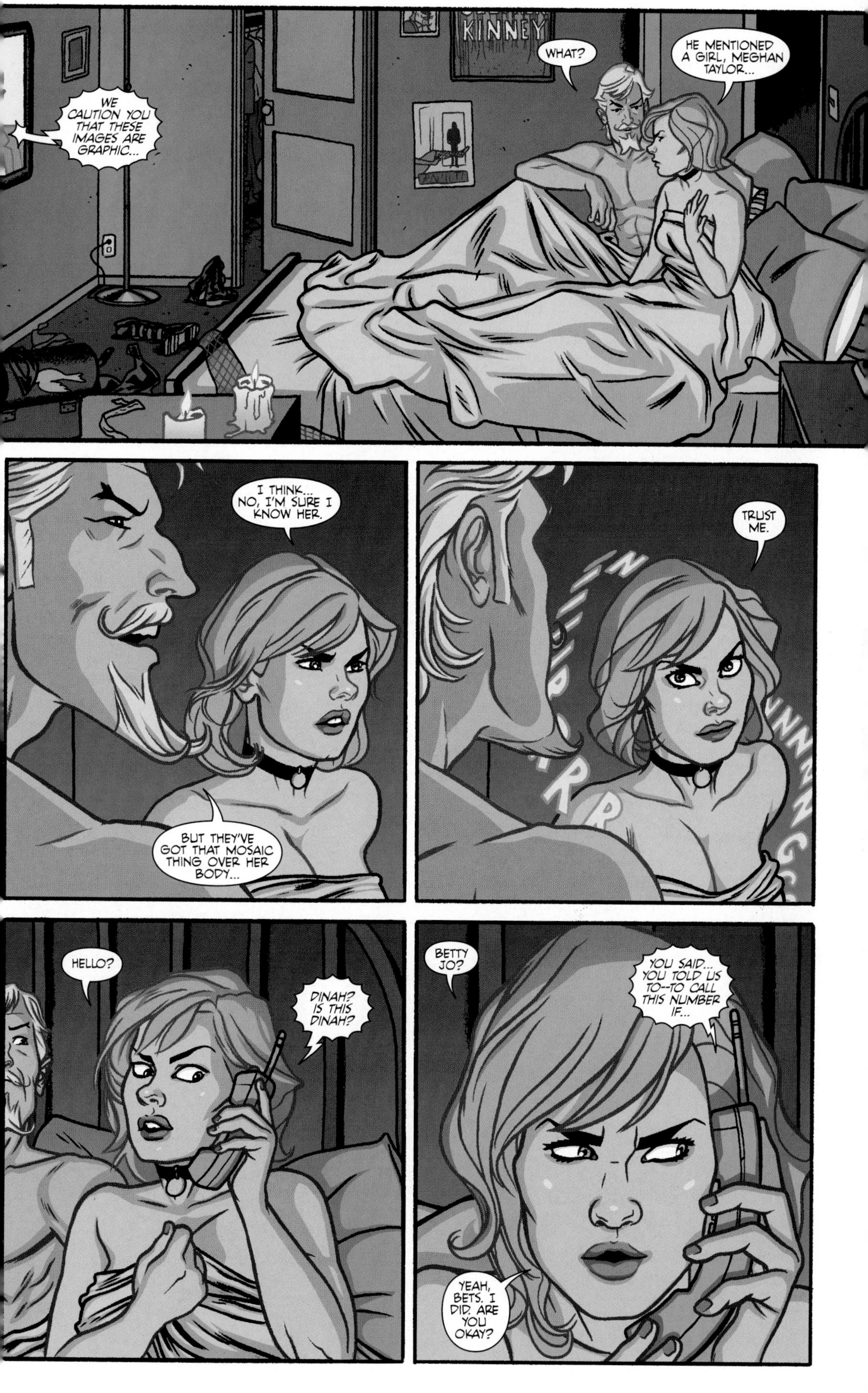
WE CAUTION YOU THAT THESE IMAGES ARE GRAPHIC...
KINNEY
WHAT?
HE MENTIONED A GIRL, MEGHAN TAYLOR...
I THINK... NO, I'M SURE I KNOW HER.
BUT THEY'VE GOT THAT MOSAIC THING OVER HER BODY...
TRUST ME.
HELLO?
DINAH? IS THIS DINAH?
BETTY JO?
YOU SAID... YOU TOLD US TO--TO CALL THIS NUMBER IF...
YEAH, BETS. I DID. ARE YOU OKAY?

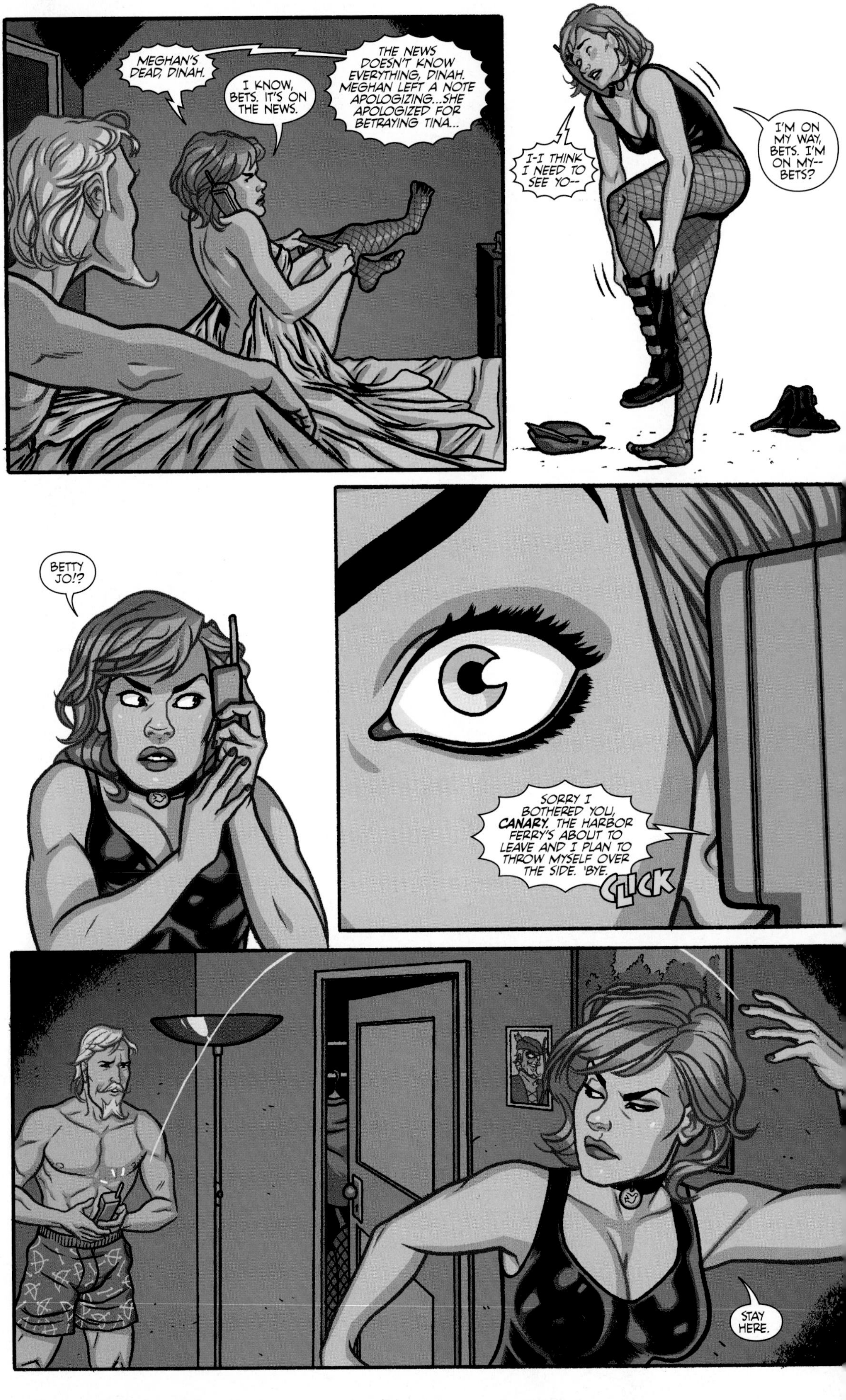
MEGHAN'S DEAD, DINAH.
I KNOW, BETS. IT'S ON THE NEWS.
THE NEWS DOESN'T KNOW EVERYTHING, DINAH. MEGHAN LEFT A NOTE APOLOGIZING...SHE APOLOGIZED FOR BETRAYING TINA...
I-I THINK I NEED TO SEE YO--
I'M ON MY WAY, BETS. I'M ON MY-- BETS?
BETTY JO!?
SORRY I BOTHERED YOU, **CANARY.** THE HARBOR FERRY'S ABOUT TO LEAVE AND I PLAN TO THROW MYSELF OVER THE SIDE. 'BYE.
CLICK
STAY HERE.

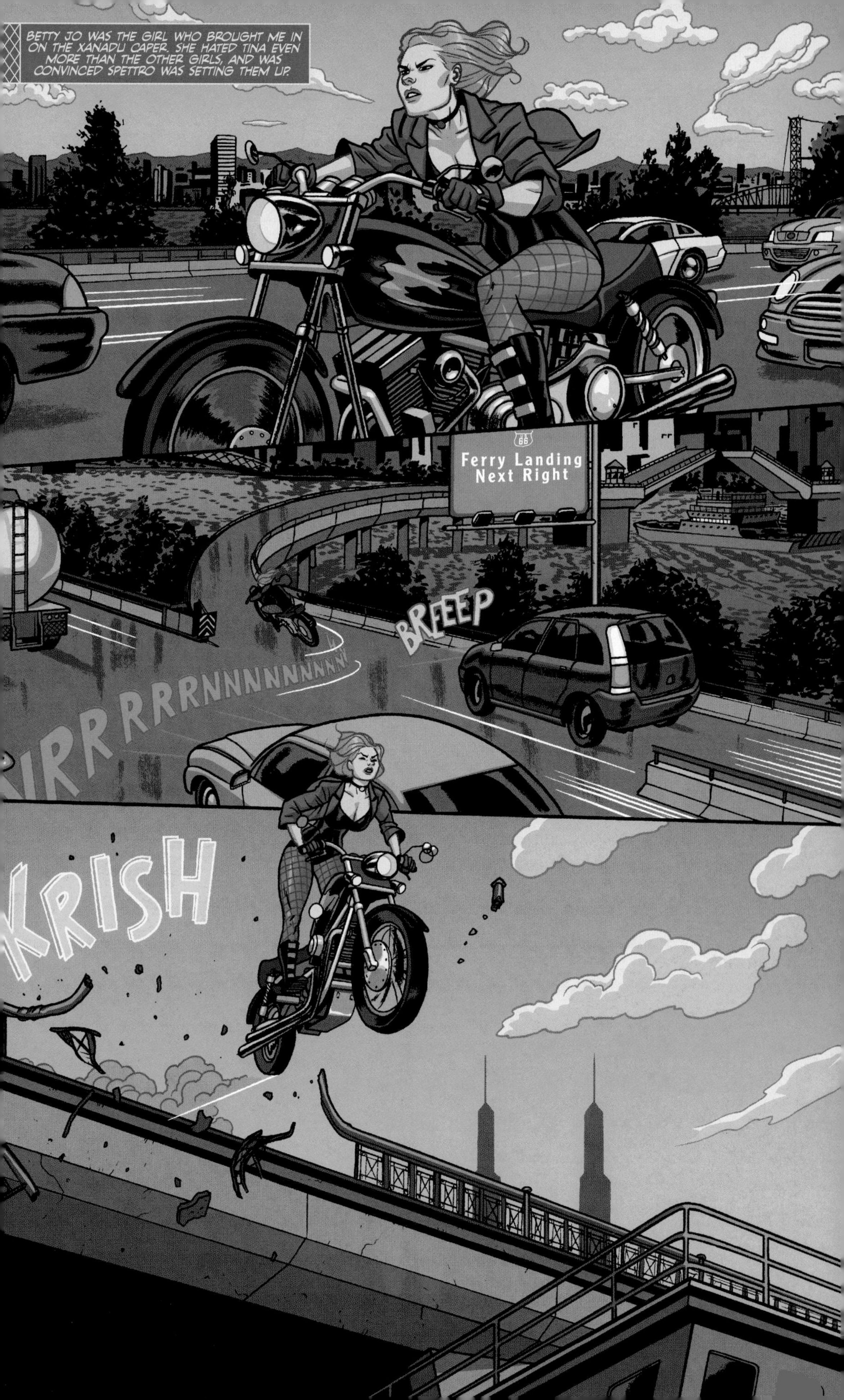
BETTY JO WAS THE GIRL WHO BROUGHT ME IN ON THE XANADU CAPER. SHE HATED TINA EVEN MORE THAN THE OTHER GIRLS, AND WAS CONVINCED SPETTRO WAS SETTING THEM UP.
Ferry Landing
Next Right
BREEEP
RRRRRRRNNNNNNNNNNN
KRISH

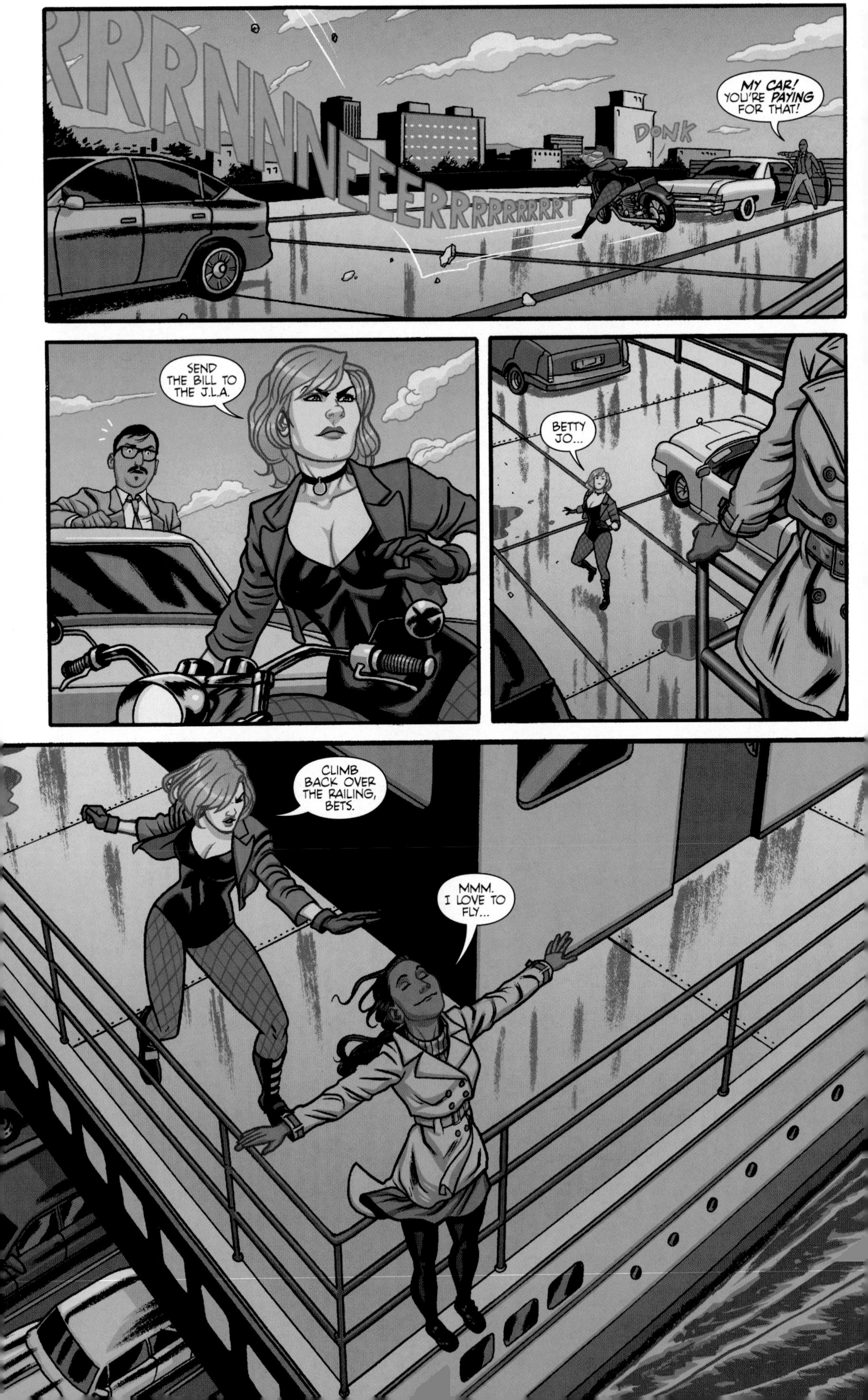
RRRNNNNEEERRRRRRRRRRT
DONK
MY CAR! YOU'RE PAYING FOR THAT!
SEND THE BILL TO THE J.L.A.
BETTY JO...
CLIMB BACK OVER THE RAILING, BETS.
MMM. I LOVE TO FLY...

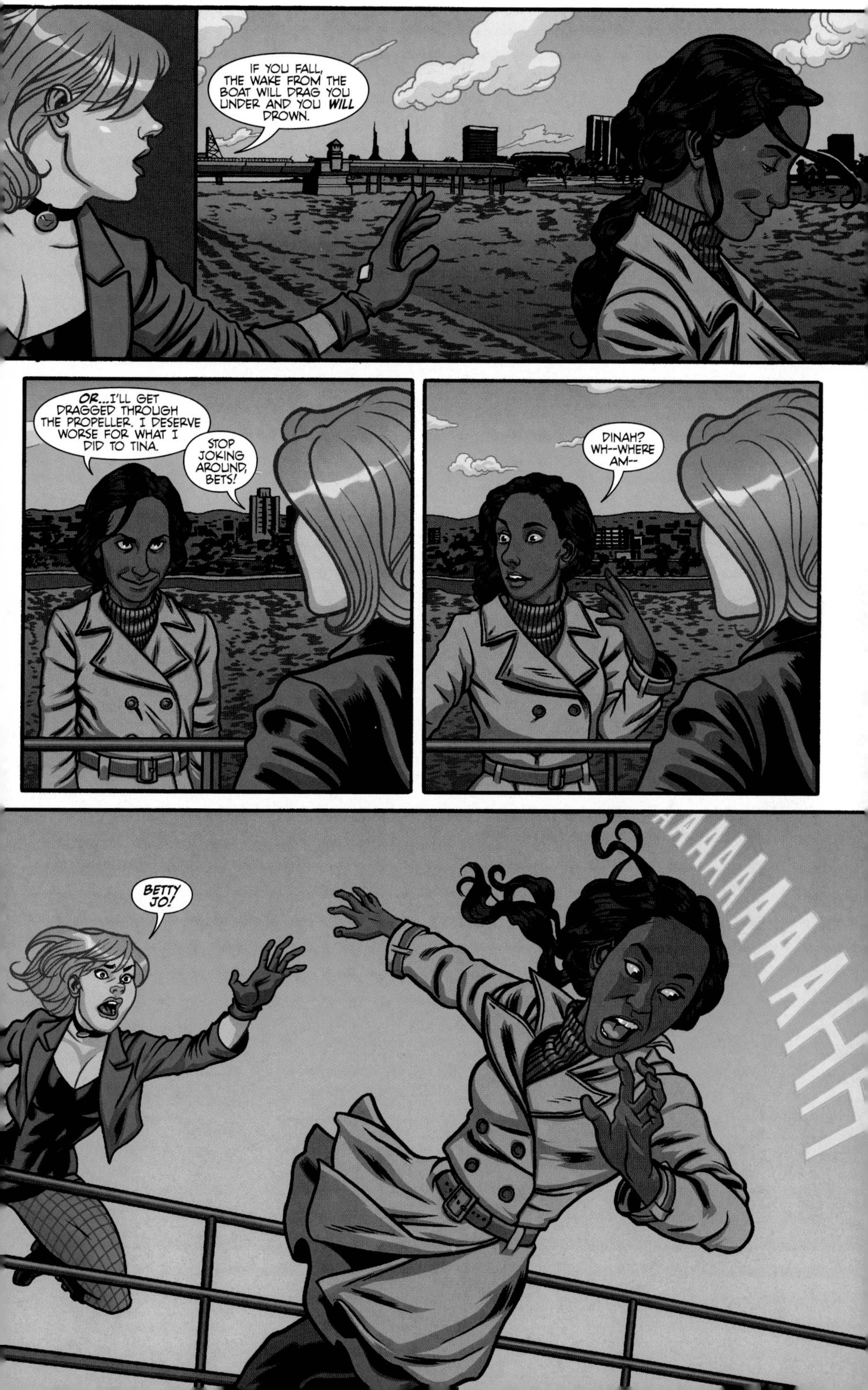
IF YOU FALL, THE WAKE FROM THE BOAT WILL DRAG YOU UNDER AND YOU WILL DROWN.
OR...I'LL GET DRAGGED THROUGH THE PROPELLER. I DESERVE WORSE FOR WHAT I DID TO TINA.
STOP JOKING AROUND, BETS!
DINAH? WH--WHERE AM--
BETTY JO!
AAAAAAAAAAAHH!

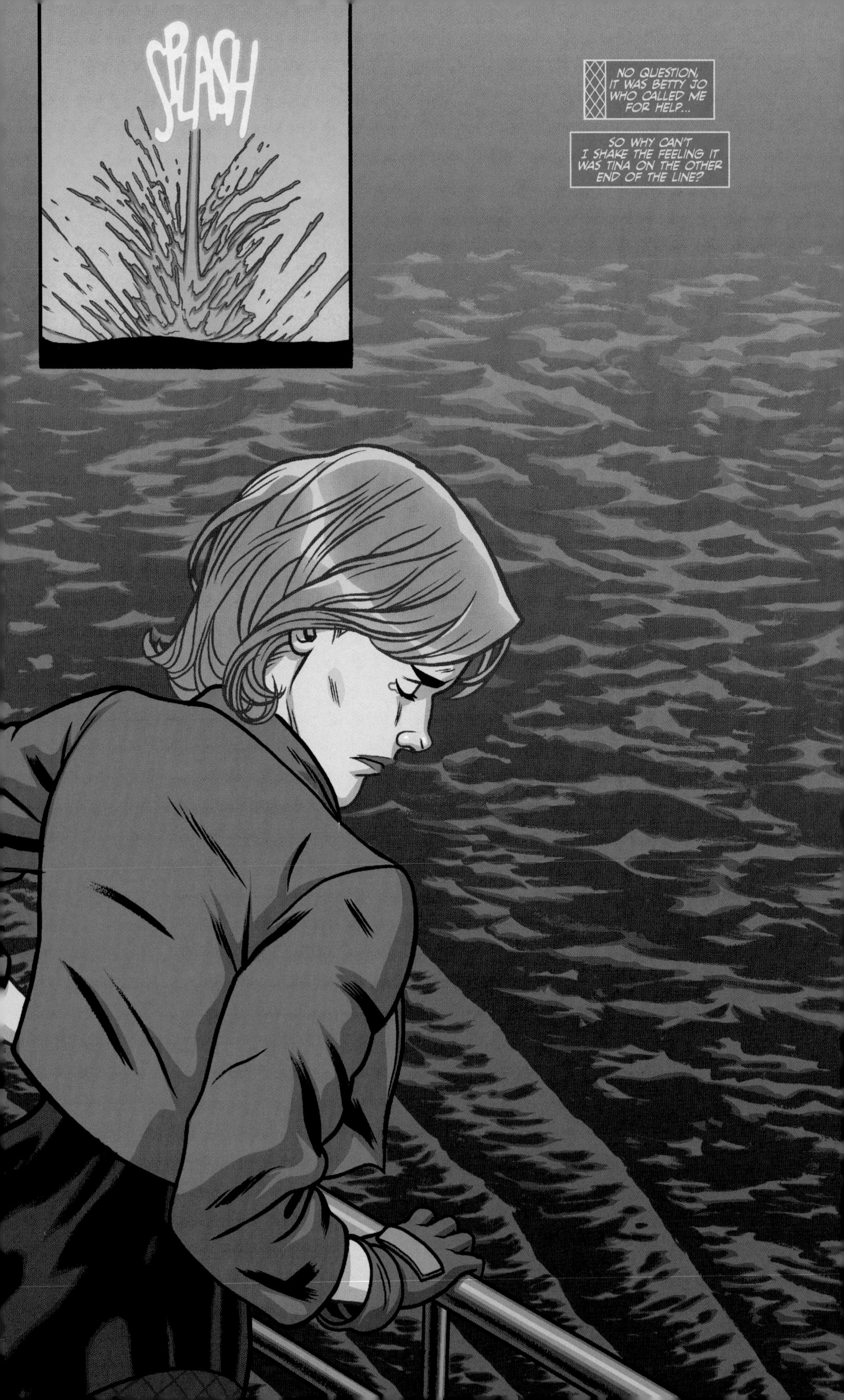
SPLASH
NO QUESTION, IT WAS BETTY JO WHO CALLED ME FOR HELP...
SO WHY CAN'T I SHAKE THE FEELING IT WAS TINA ON THE OTHER END OF THE LINE?

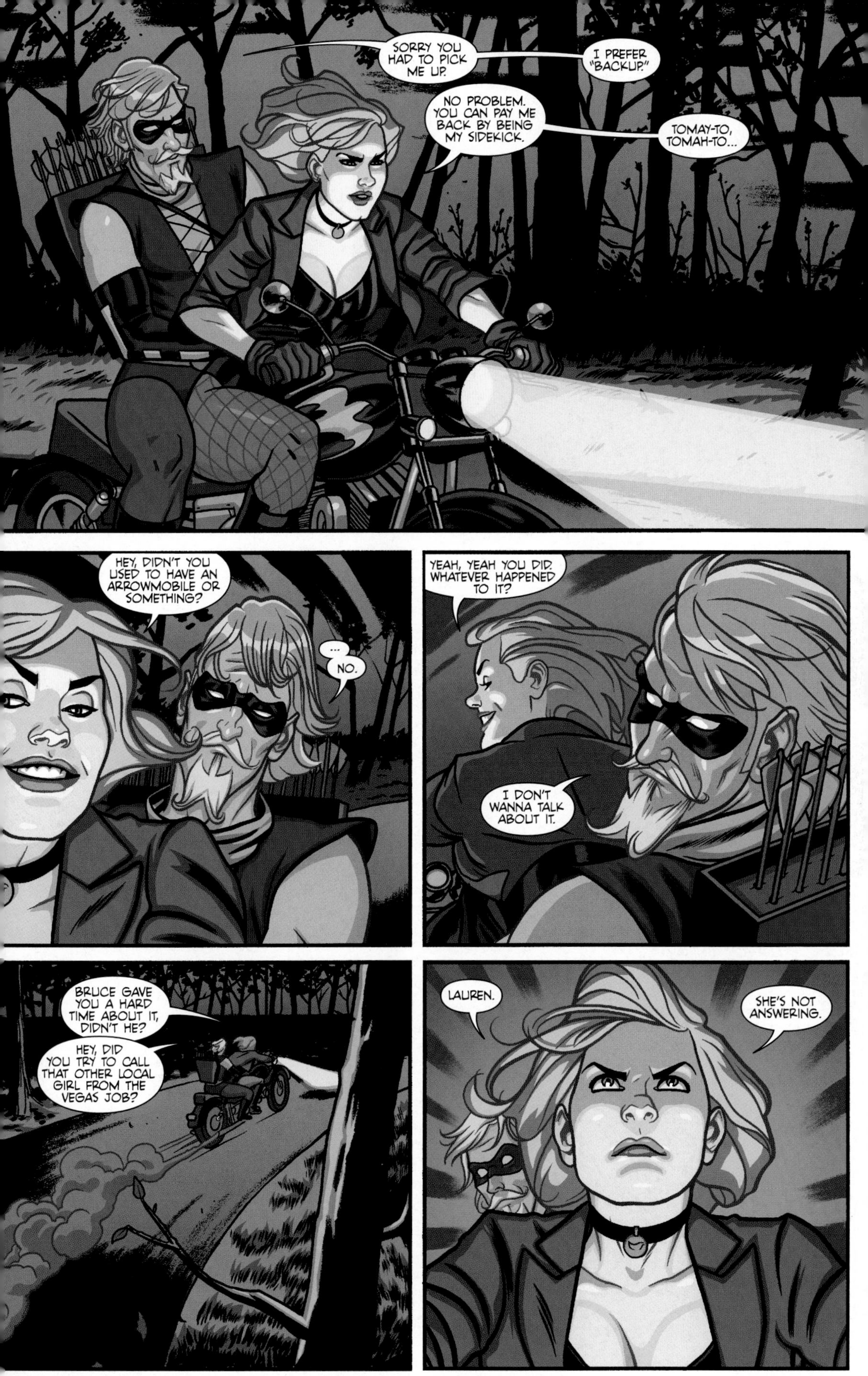
SORRY YOU HAD TO PICK ME UP.
I PREFER "BACKUP."
NO PROBLEM. YOU CAN PAY ME BACK BY BEING MY SIDEKICK.
TOMAY-TO, TOMAH-TO...
HEY, DIDN'T YOU USED TO HAVE AN ARROWMOBILE OR SOMETHING?
... NO.
YEAH, YEAH YOU DID. WHATEVER HAPPENED TO IT?
I DON'T WANNA TALK ABOUT IT.
BRUCE GAVE YOU A HARD TIME ABOUT IT, DIDN'T HE?
HEY, DID YOU TRY TO CALL THAT OTHER LOCAL GIRL FROM THE VEGAS JOB?
LAUREN.
SHE'S NOT ANSWERING.

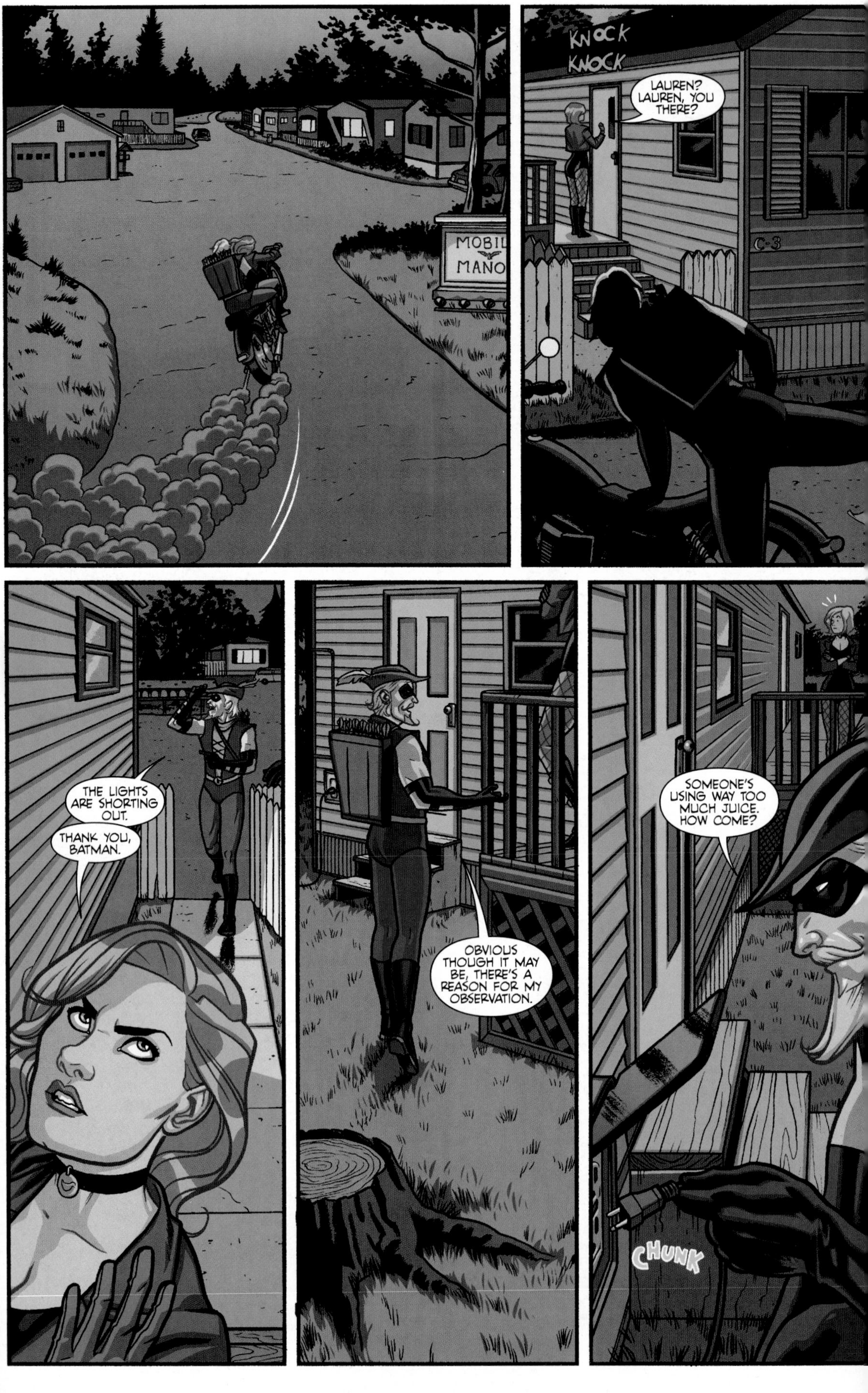

MOBIL
MANO
KNOCK
KNOCK
LAUREN? LAUREN, YOU THERE?
C-3
THE LIGHTS ARE SHORTING OUT.
THANK YOU, BATMAN.
OBVIOUS THOUGH IT MAY BE, THERE'S A REASON FOR MY OBSERVATION.
SOMEONE'S USING WAY TOO MUCH JUICE. HOW COME?
CHUNK

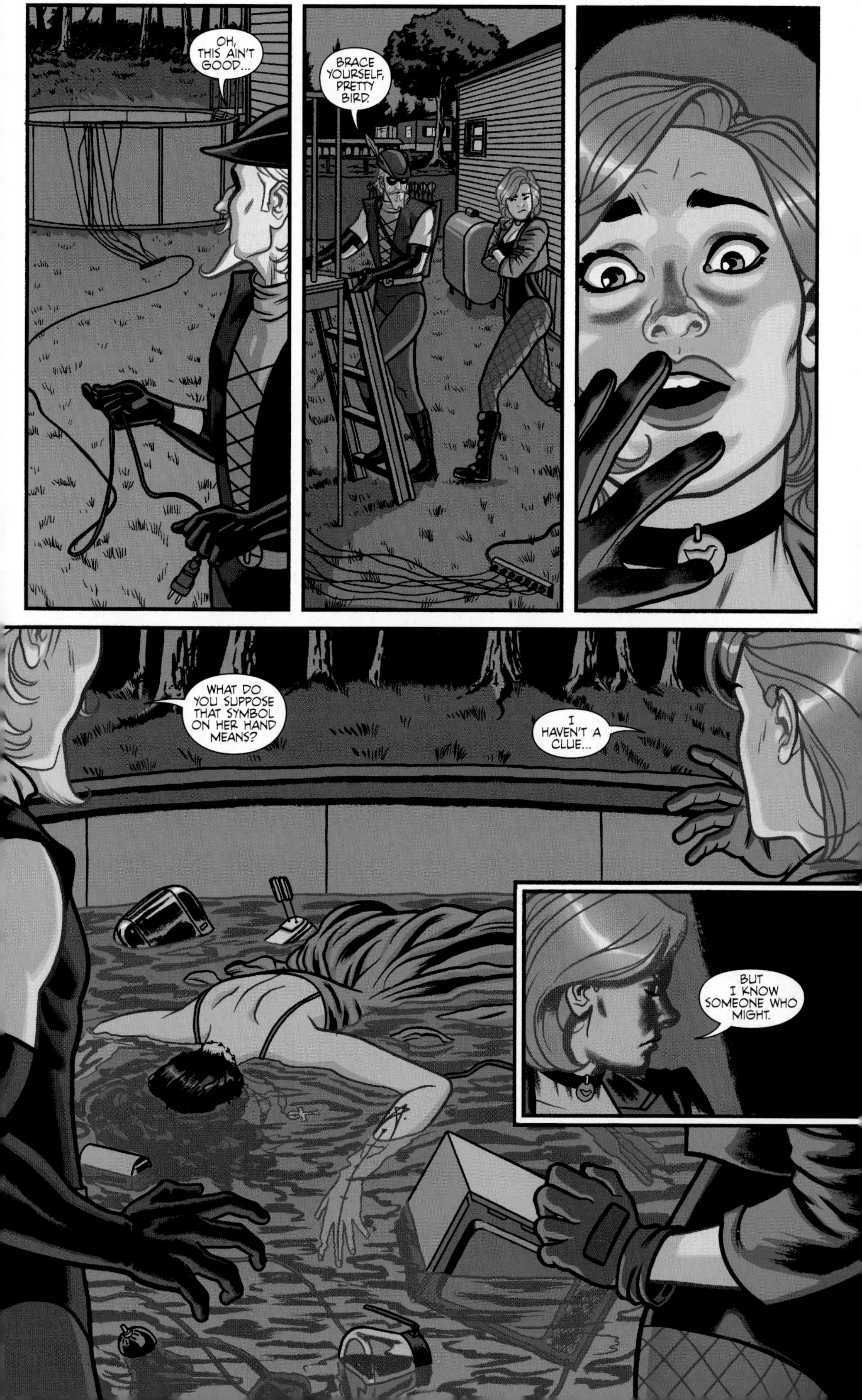
OH, THIS AIN'T GOOD...
BRACE YOURSELF, PRETTY BIRD.
WHAT DO YOU SUPPOSE THAT SYMBOL ON HER HAND MEANS?
I HAVEN'T A CLUE...
BUT I KNOW SOMEONE WHO MIGHT.

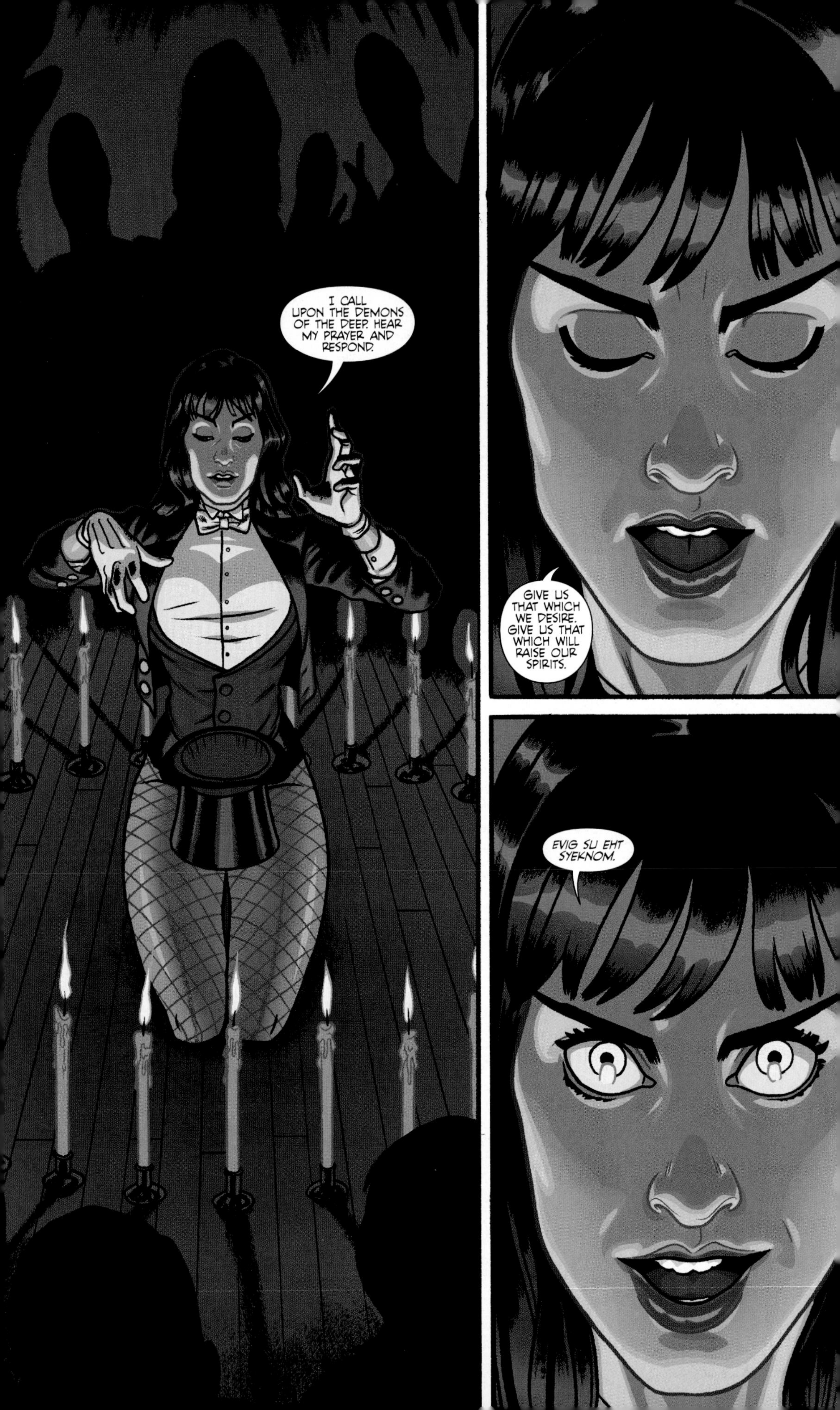
I CALL UPON THE DEMONS OF THE DEEP. HEAR MY PRAYER AND RESPOND.
GIVE US THAT WHICH WE DESIRE. GIVE US THAT WHICH WILL RAISE OUR SPIRITS.
EVIG SU EHT SYEKNOM.

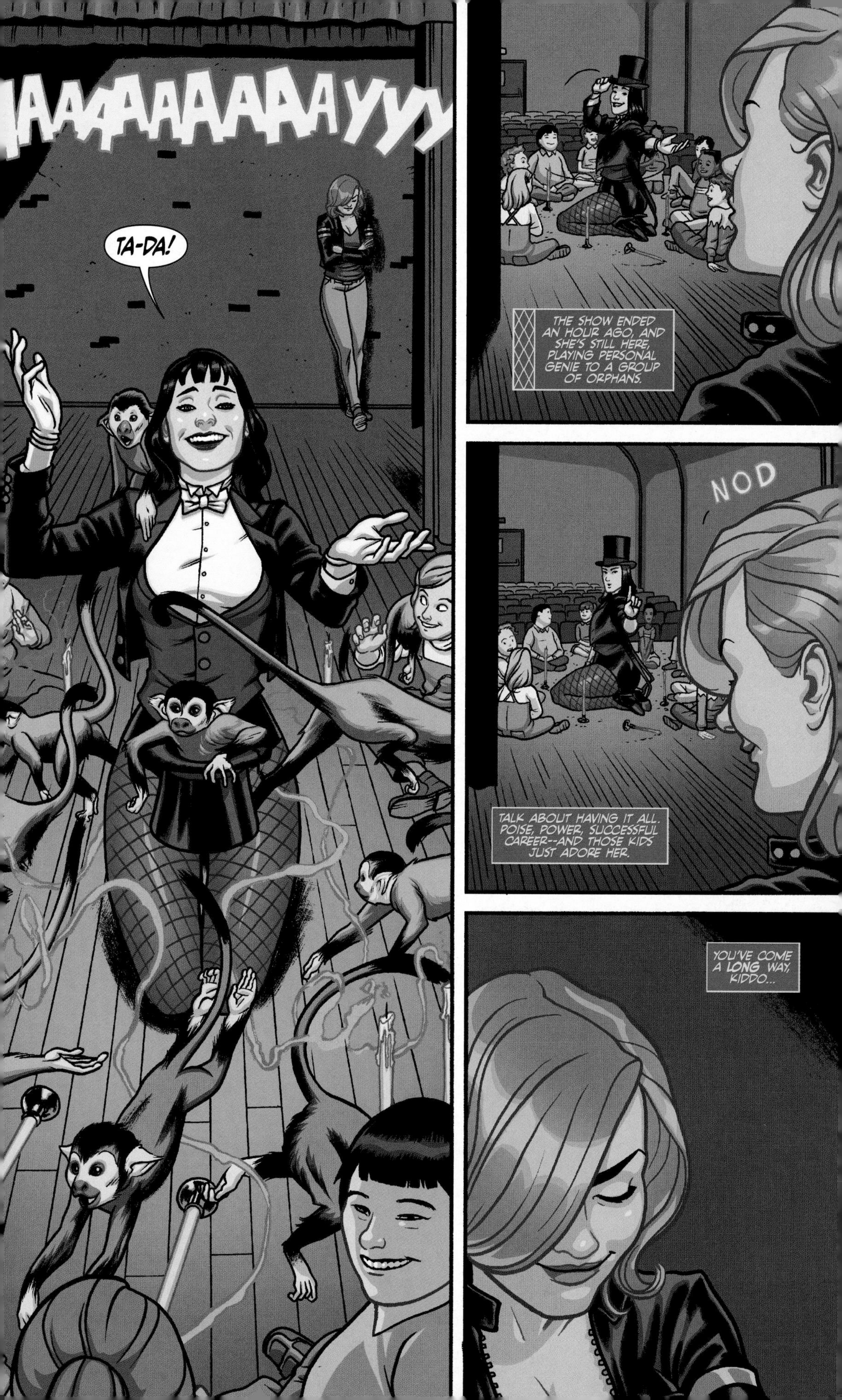
AAAAAAAAAAYYY
TA-DA!
THE SHOW ENDED AN HOUR AGO, AND SHE'S STILL HERE, PLAYING PERSONAL GENIE TO A GROUP OF ORPHANS.
NOD
TALK ABOUT HAVING IT ALL. POISE, POWER, SUCCESSFUL CAREER--AND THOSE KIDS JUST ADORE HER.
YOU'VE COME A LONG WAY, KIDDO...

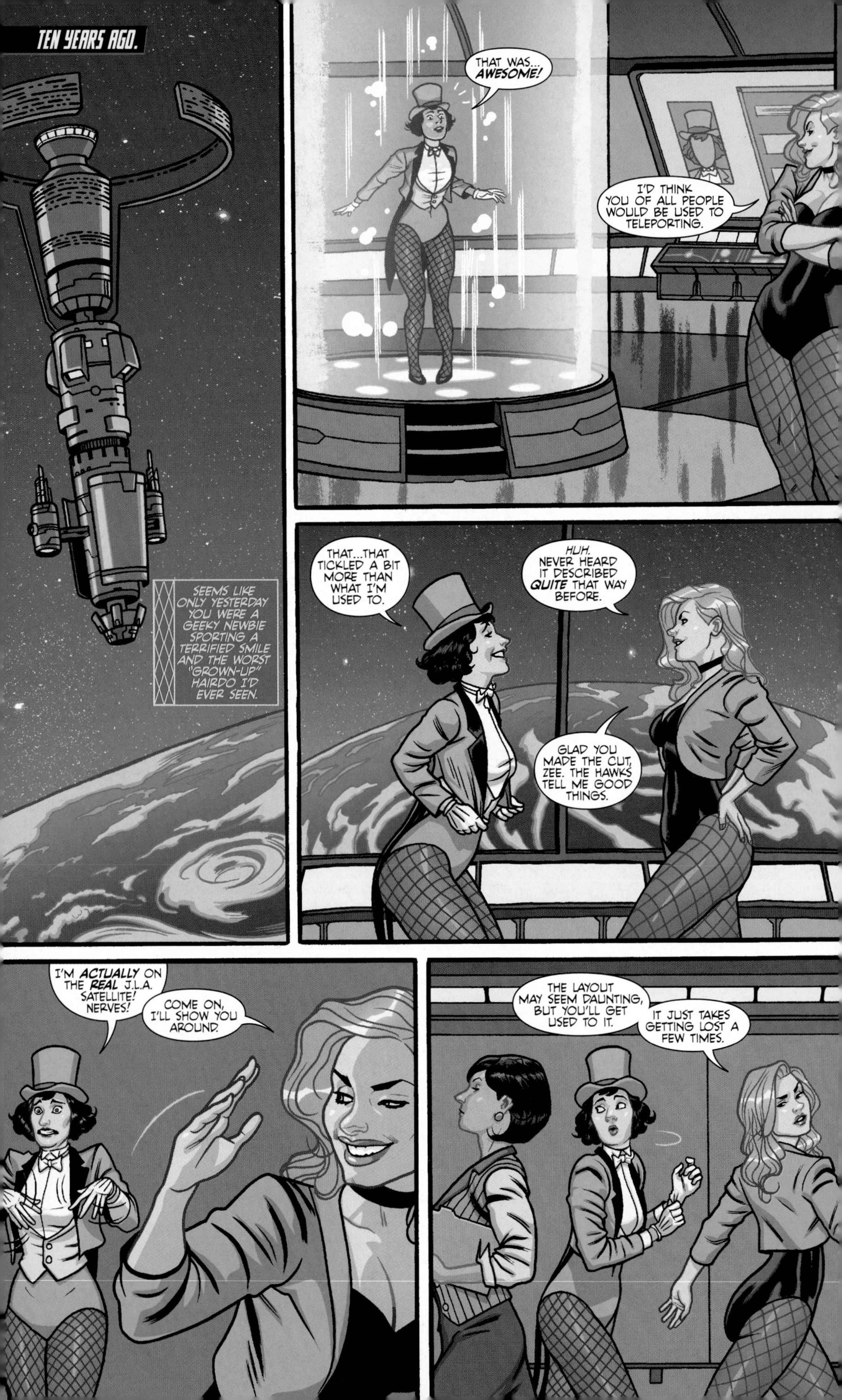
TEN YEARS AGO.
SEEMS LIKE ONLY YESTERDAY YOU WERE A GEEKY NEWBIE SPORTING A TERRIFIED SMILE AND THE WORST "GROWN-UP" HAIRDO I'D EVER SEEN.
THAT WAS... AWESOME!
I'D THINK YOU OF ALL PEOPLE WOULD BE USED TO TELEPORTING.
THAT...THAT TICKLED A BIT MORE THAN WHAT I'M USED TO.
HUH. NEVER HEARD IT DESCRIBED QUITE THAT WAY BEFORE.
GLAD YOU MADE THE CUT, ZEE. THE HAWKS TELL ME GOOD THINGS.
I'M ACTUALLY ON THE REAL J.L.A. SATELLITE! NERVES!
COME ON, I'LL SHOW YOU AROUND.
THE LAYOUT MAY SEEM DAUNTING, BUT YOU'LL GET USED TO IT.
IT JUST TAKES GETTING LOST A FEW TIMES.

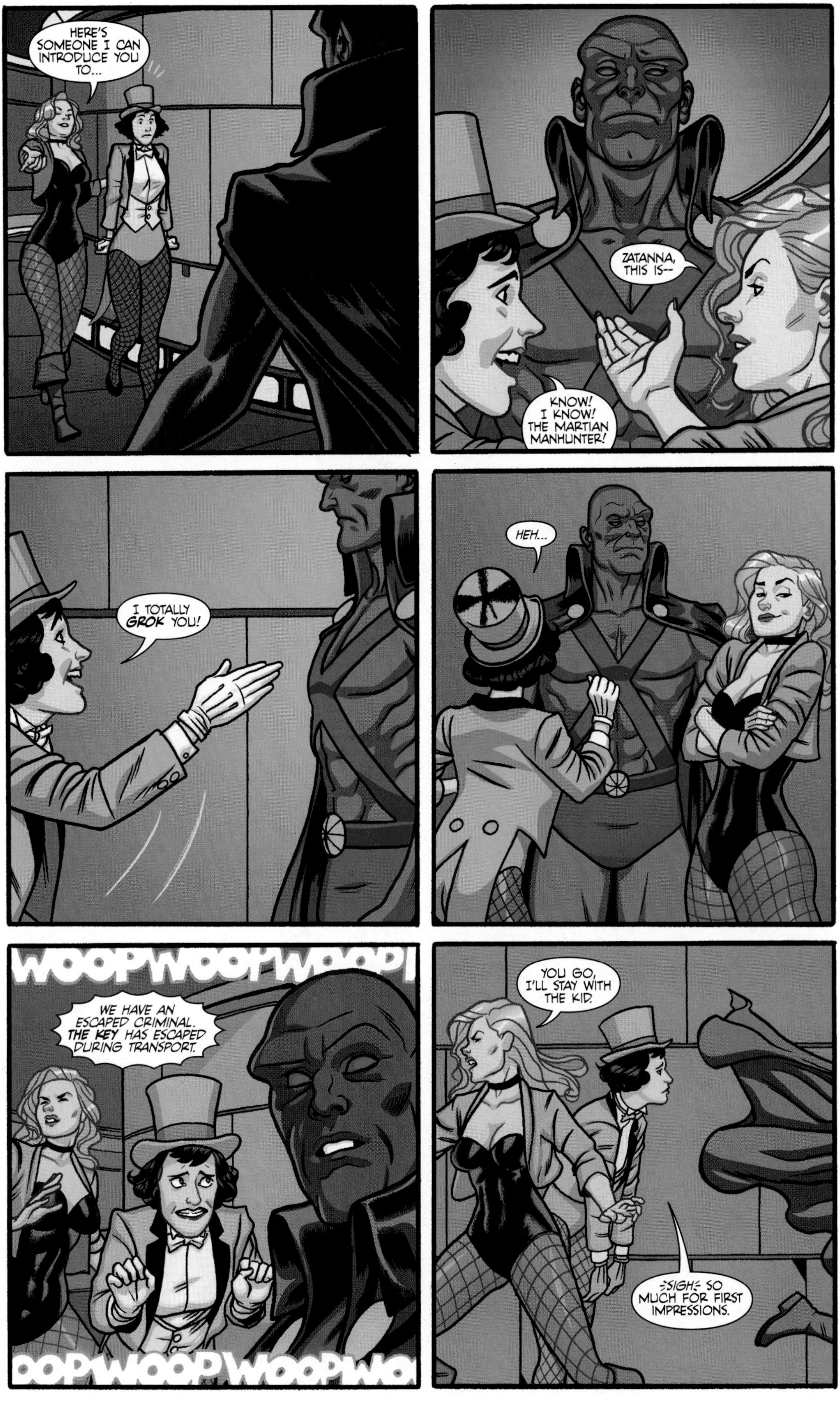
HERE'S SOMEONE I CAN INTRODUCE YOU TO...
ZATANNA, THIS IS--
KNOW! I KNOW! THE MARTIAN MANHUNTER!
I TOTALLY GROK YOU!
HEH...
WOOPWOOPWOOP
WE HAVE AN ESCAPED CRIMINAL. THE KEY HAS ESCAPED DURING TRANSPORT.
OOPWOOPWOOPWO
YOU GO, I'LL STAY WITH THE KID.
SIGH SO MUCH FOR FIRST IMPRESSIONS.

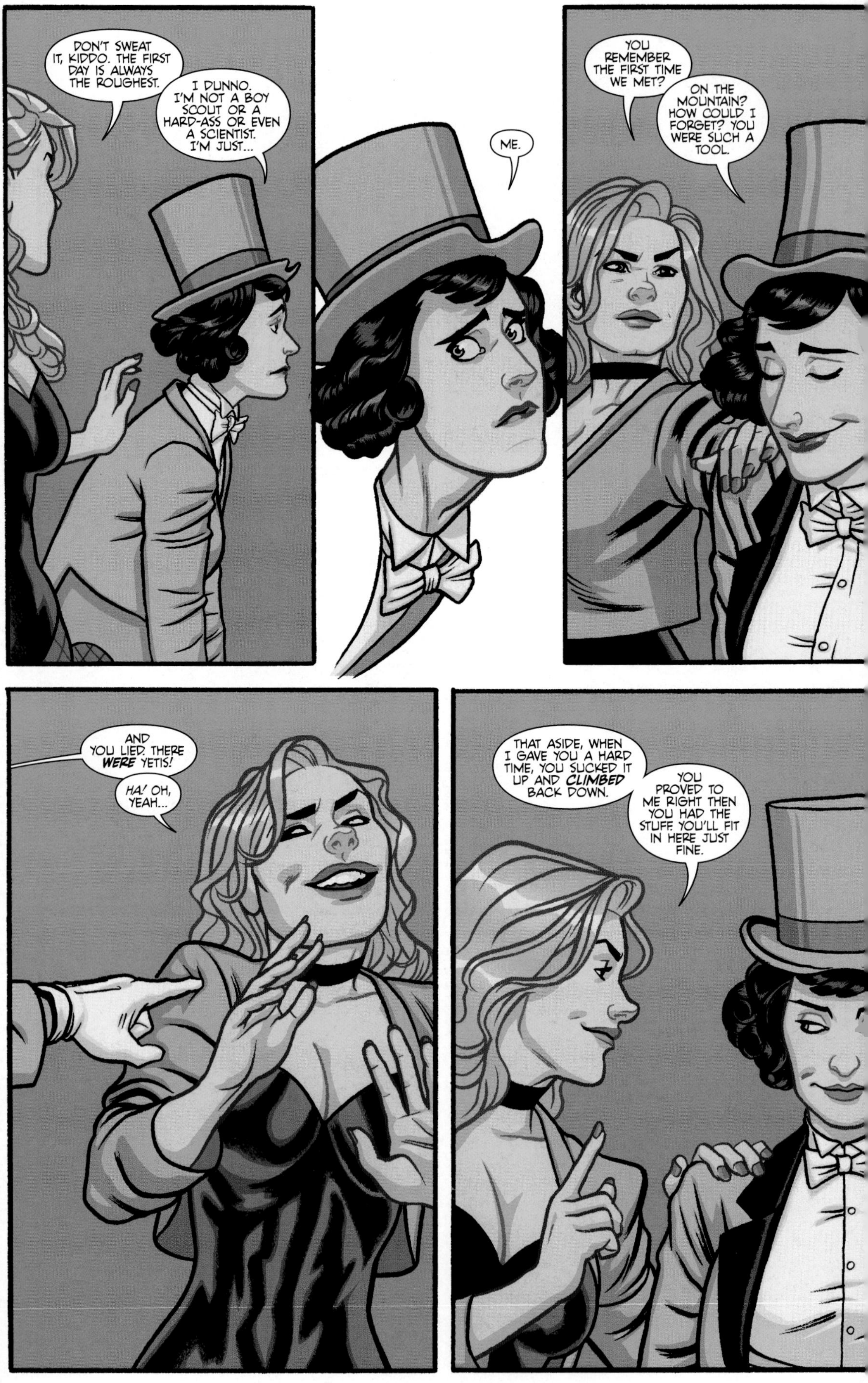
DON'T SWEAT IT, KIDDO. THE FIRST DAY IS ALWAYS THE ROUGHEST.
I DUNNO. I'M NOT A BOY SCOUT OR A HARD-ASS OR EVEN A SCIENTIST. I'M JUST...
ME.
YOU REMEMBER THE FIRST TIME WE MET?
ON THE MOUNTAIN? HOW COULD I FORGET? YOU WERE SUCH A TOOL.
AND YOU LIED. THERE *WERE* YETIS!
HA! OH, YEAH...
THAT ASIDE, WHEN I GAVE YOU A HARD TIME, YOU SUCKED IT UP AND ***CLIMBED*** BACK DOWN.
YOU PROVED TO ME RIGHT THEN YOU HAD THE STUFF. YOU'LL FIT IN HERE JUST FINE.

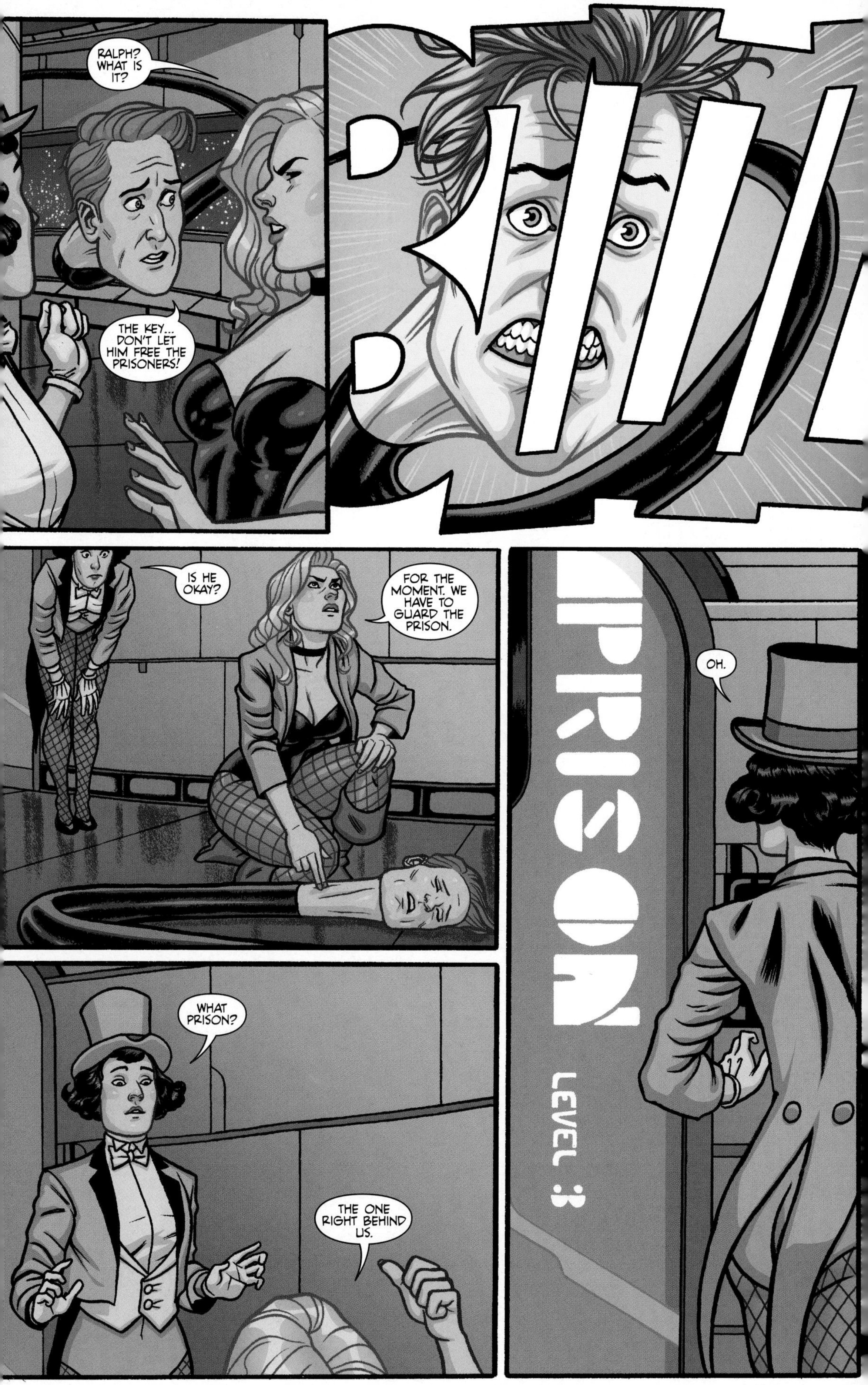
RALPH? WHAT IS IT?
THE KEY... DON'T LET HIM FREE THE PRISONERS!
IS HE OKAY?
FOR THE MOMENT. WE HAVE TO GUARD THE PRISON.
WHAT PRISON?
THE ONE RIGHT BEHIND US.
PRISON
LEVEL 3
OH.

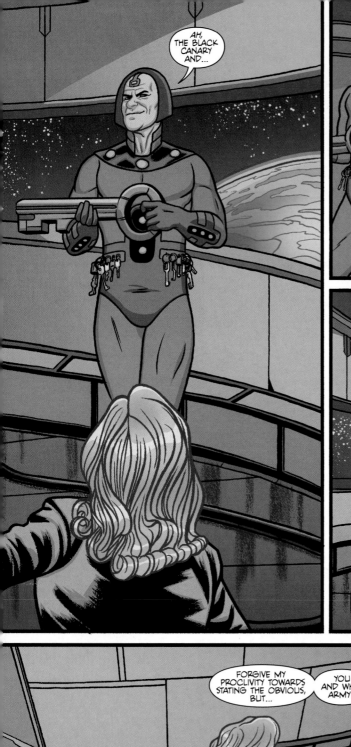

AH, THE BLACK CANARY AND...

...AND WHAT ARE YOU SUPPOSED TO BE? A COCKTAIL WAITRESS?

YOU'RE *NOT* FREEING THE PRISONERS. I *WILL* STOP YOU.

FORGIVE MY PROCLIVITY TOWARDS STATING THE OBVIOUS, BUT...

YOU AND WHAT ARMY?

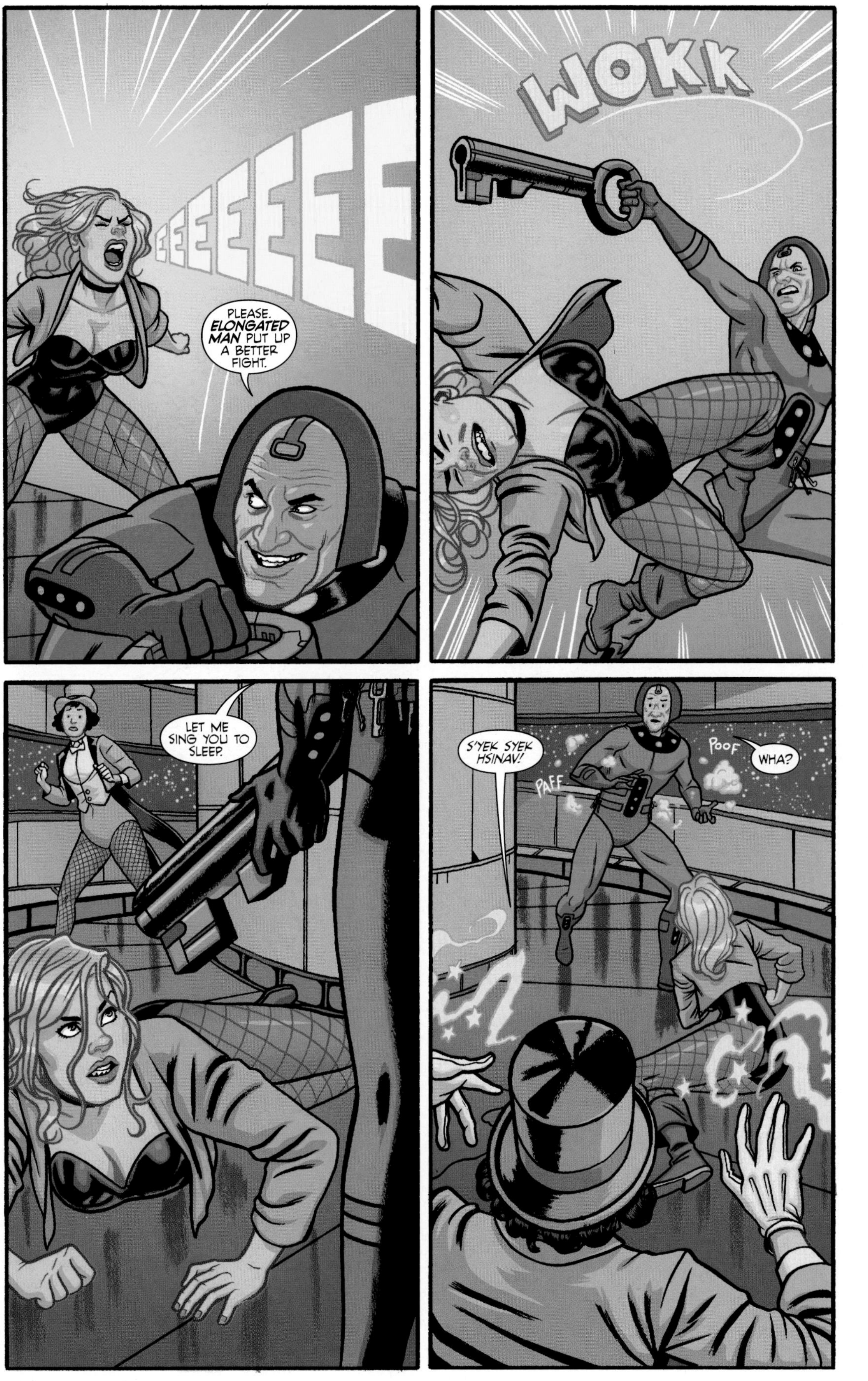
EEEEEEE
PLEASE. ELONGATED MAN PUT UP A BETTER FIGHT.
WOKK
LET ME SING YOU TO SLEEP.
S'YEK SYEK HSINAV!
PAFF
POOF
WHA?

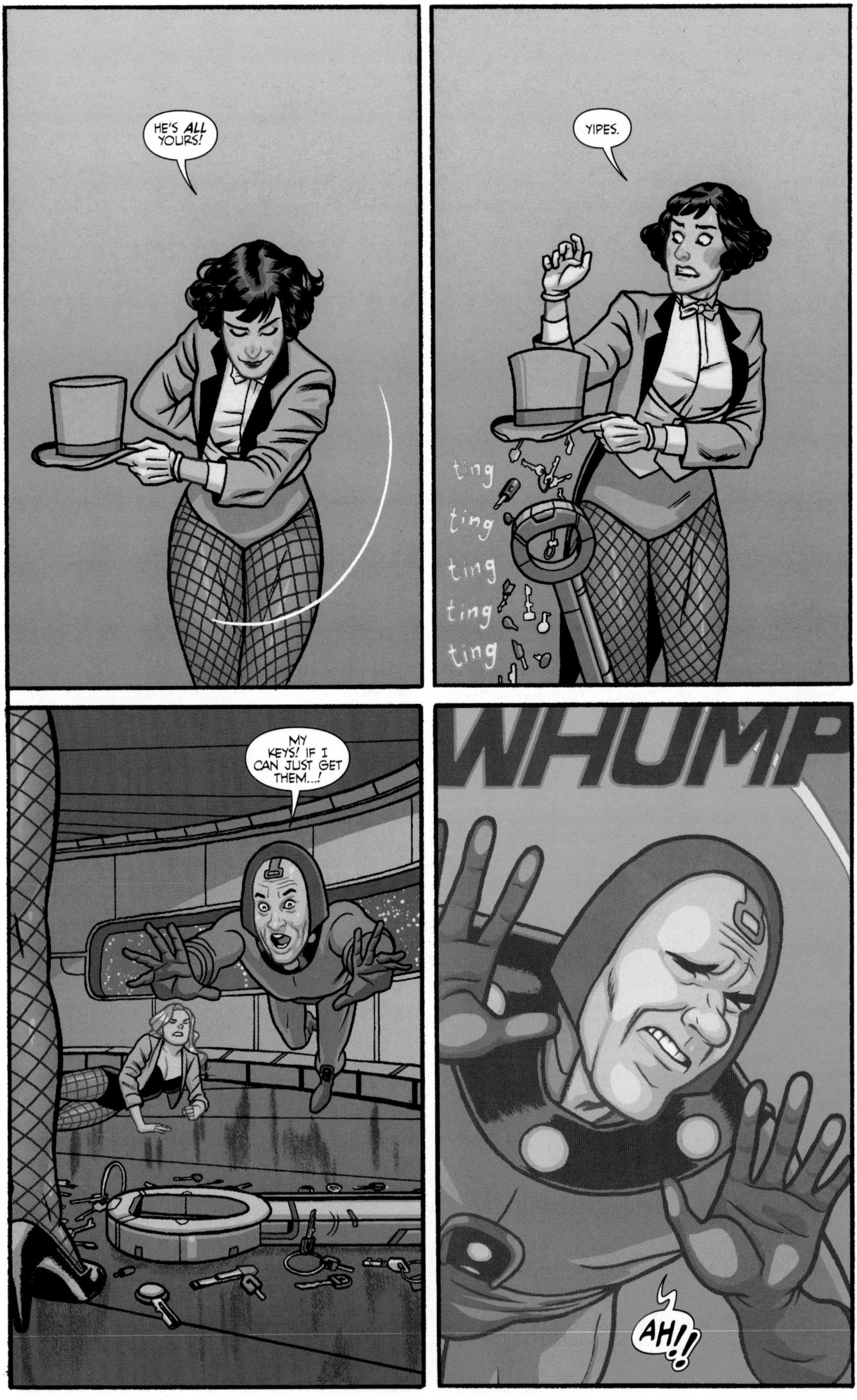
HE'S ALL YOURS!
YIPES.
ting
ting
ting
ting
ting
MY KEYS! IF I CAN JUST GET THEM...!
WHUMP
AH!!

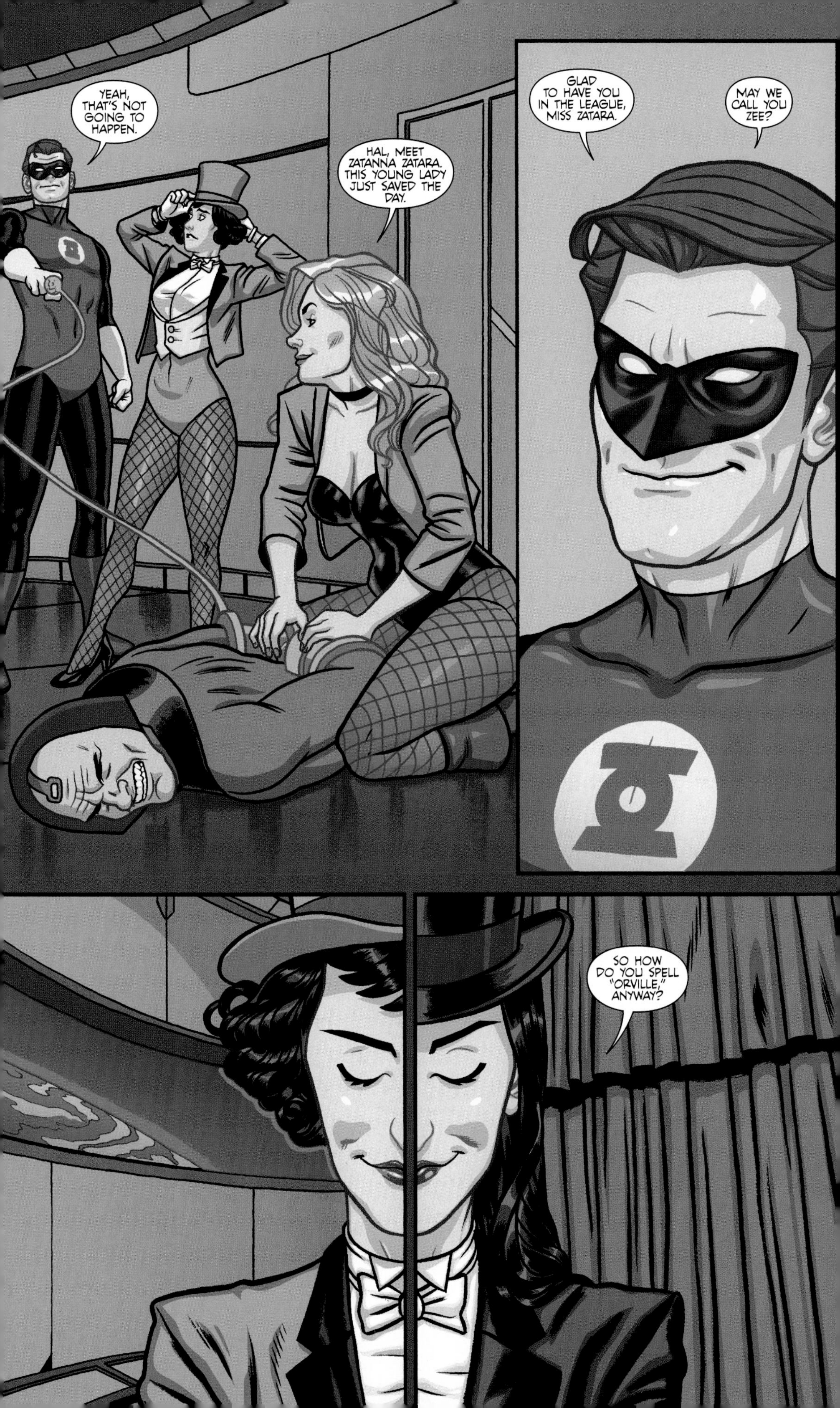
YEAH, THAT'S NOT GOING TO HAPPEN.
HAL, MEET ZATANNA ZATARA. THIS YOUNG LADY JUST SAVED THE DAY.
GLAD TO HAVE YOU IN THE LEAGUE, MISS ZATARA.
MAY WE CALL YOU ZEE?
SO HOW DO YOU SPELL "ORVILLE," ANYWAY?

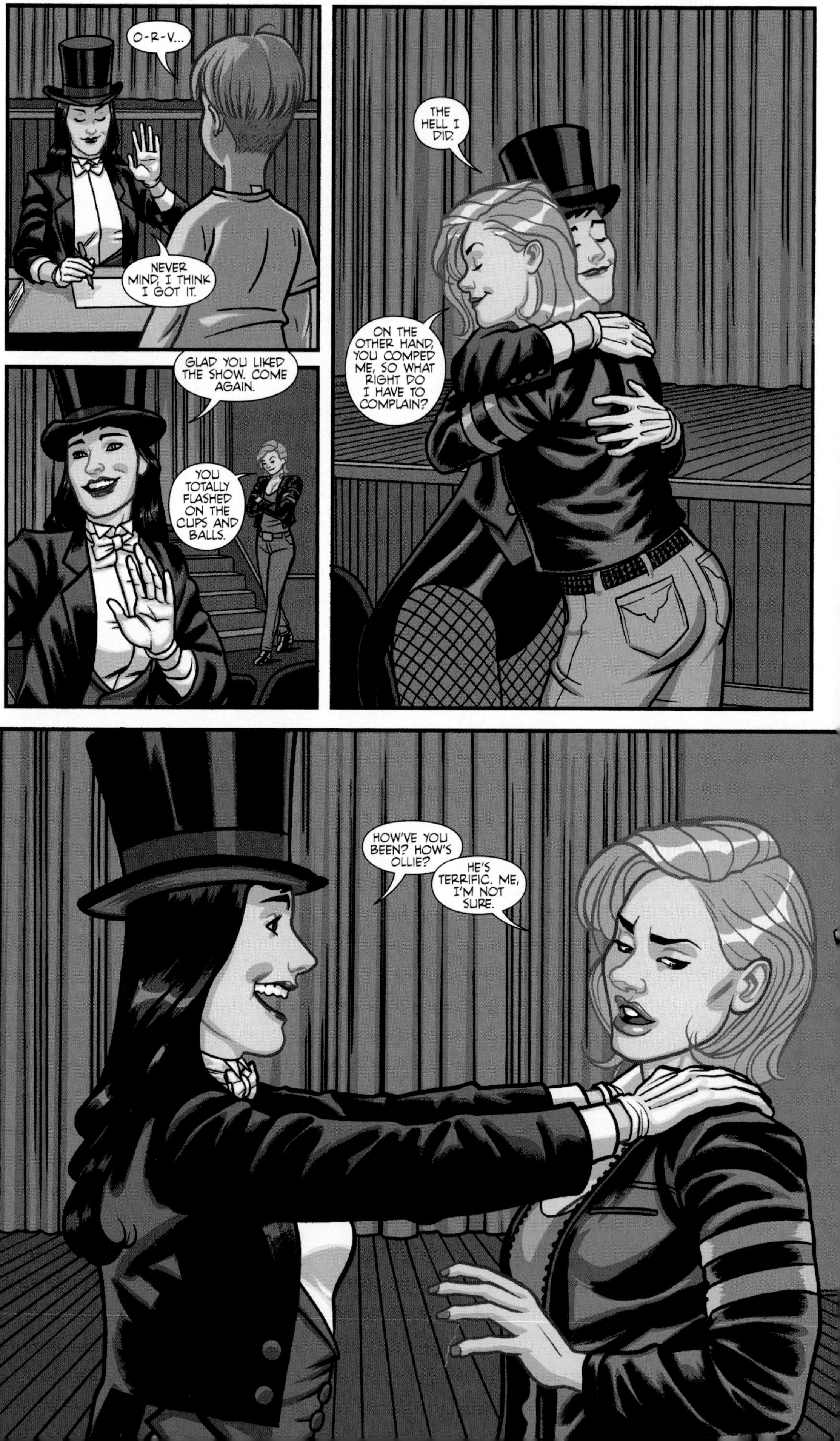
O-R-V...
NEVER MIND, I THINK I GOT IT.
GLAD YOU LIKED THE SHOW. COME AGAIN.
YOU TOTALLY FLASHED ON THE CUPS AND BALLS.
THE HELL I DID.
ON THE OTHER HAND, YOU COMPED ME, SO WHAT RIGHT DO I HAVE TO COMPLAIN?
HOW'VE YOU BEEN? HOW'S OLLIE?
HE'S TERRIFIC. ME, I'M NOT SURE.

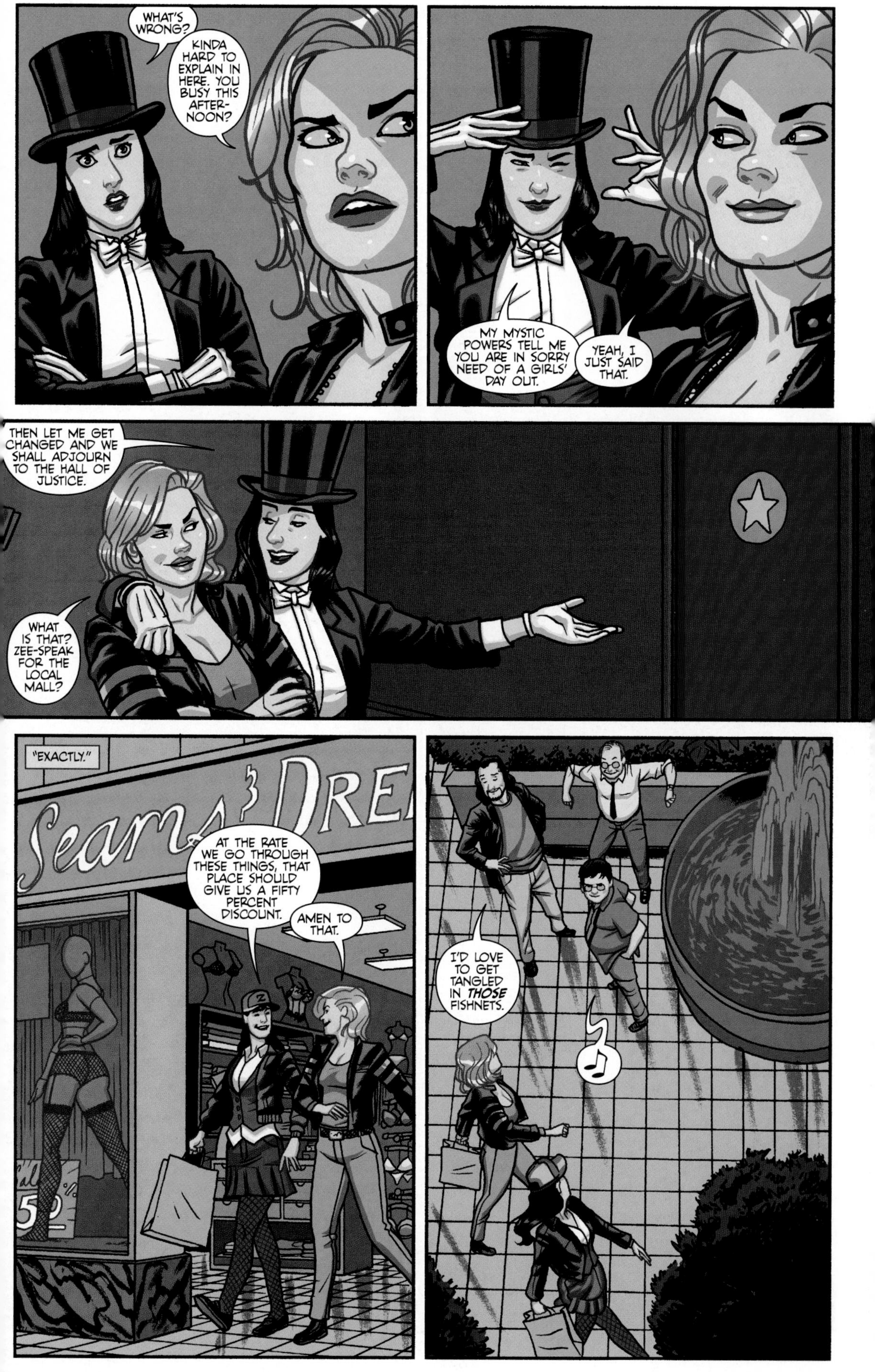

WHAT'S WRONG?
KINDA HARD TO EXPLAIN IN HERE. YOU BUSY THIS AFTER-NOON?
MY MYSTIC POWERS TELL ME YOU ARE IN SORRY NEED OF A GIRLS' DAY OUT.
YEAH, I JUST SAID THAT.
THEN LET ME GET CHANGED AND WE SHALL ADJOURN TO THE HALL OF JUSTICE.
WHAT IS THAT? ZEE-SPEAK FOR THE LOCAL MALL?
"EXACTLY."
Seams & DRE
AT THE RATE WE GO THROUGH THESE THINGS, THAT PLACE SHOULD GIVE US A FIFTY PERCENT DISCOUNT.
AMEN TO THAT.
I'D LOVE TO GET TANGLED IN *THOSE* FISHNETS.

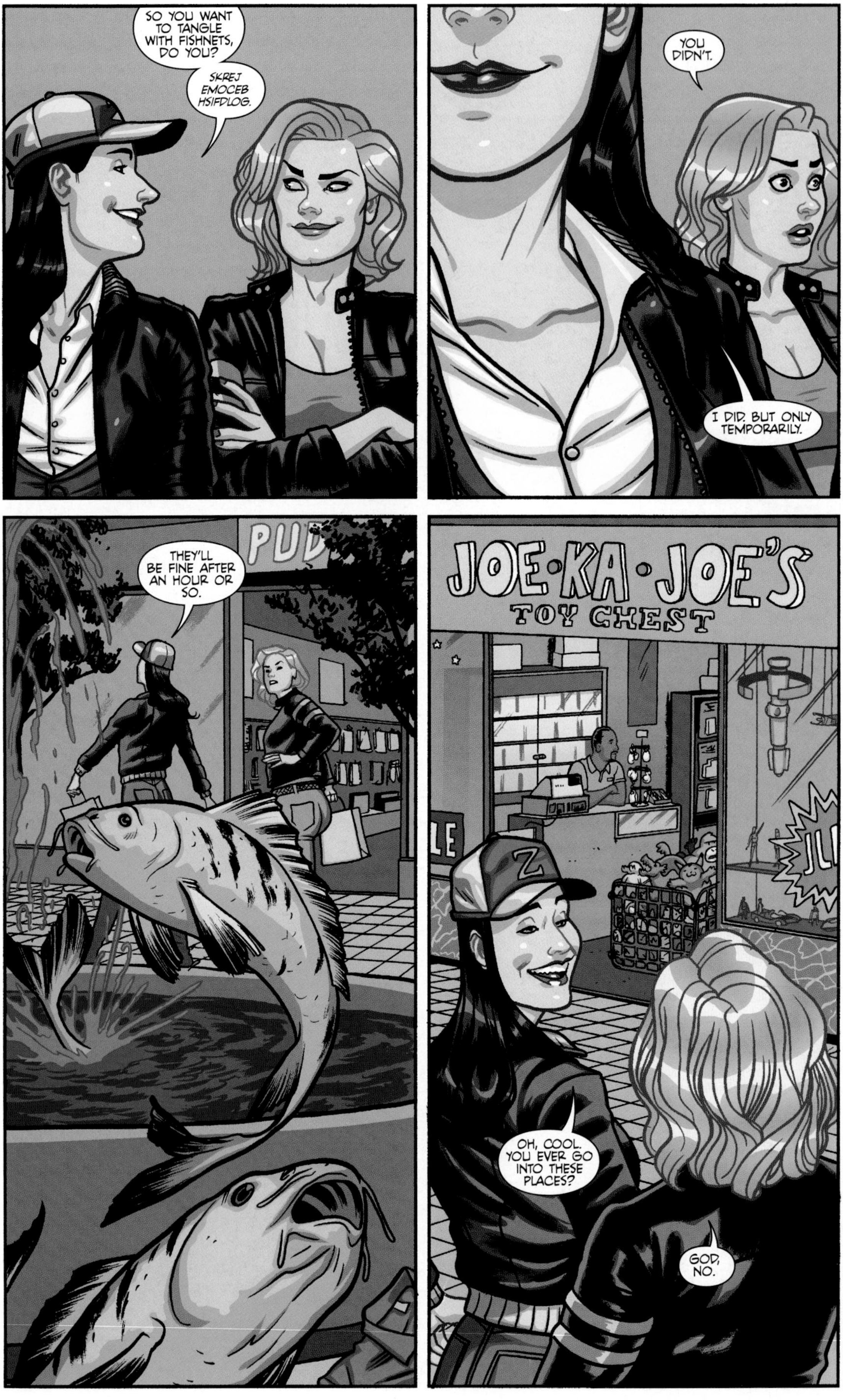
SO YOU WANT TO TANGLE WITH FISHNETS, DO YOU?
SKREJ EMOCEB HSIFDLOG.
YOU DIDN'T.
I DID. BUT ONLY TEMPORARILY.
PUD
THEY'LL BE FINE AFTER AN HOUR OR SO.
JOE-KA-JOE'S
TOY CHEST
OH, COOL. YOU EVER GO INTO THESE PLACES?
GOD, NO.

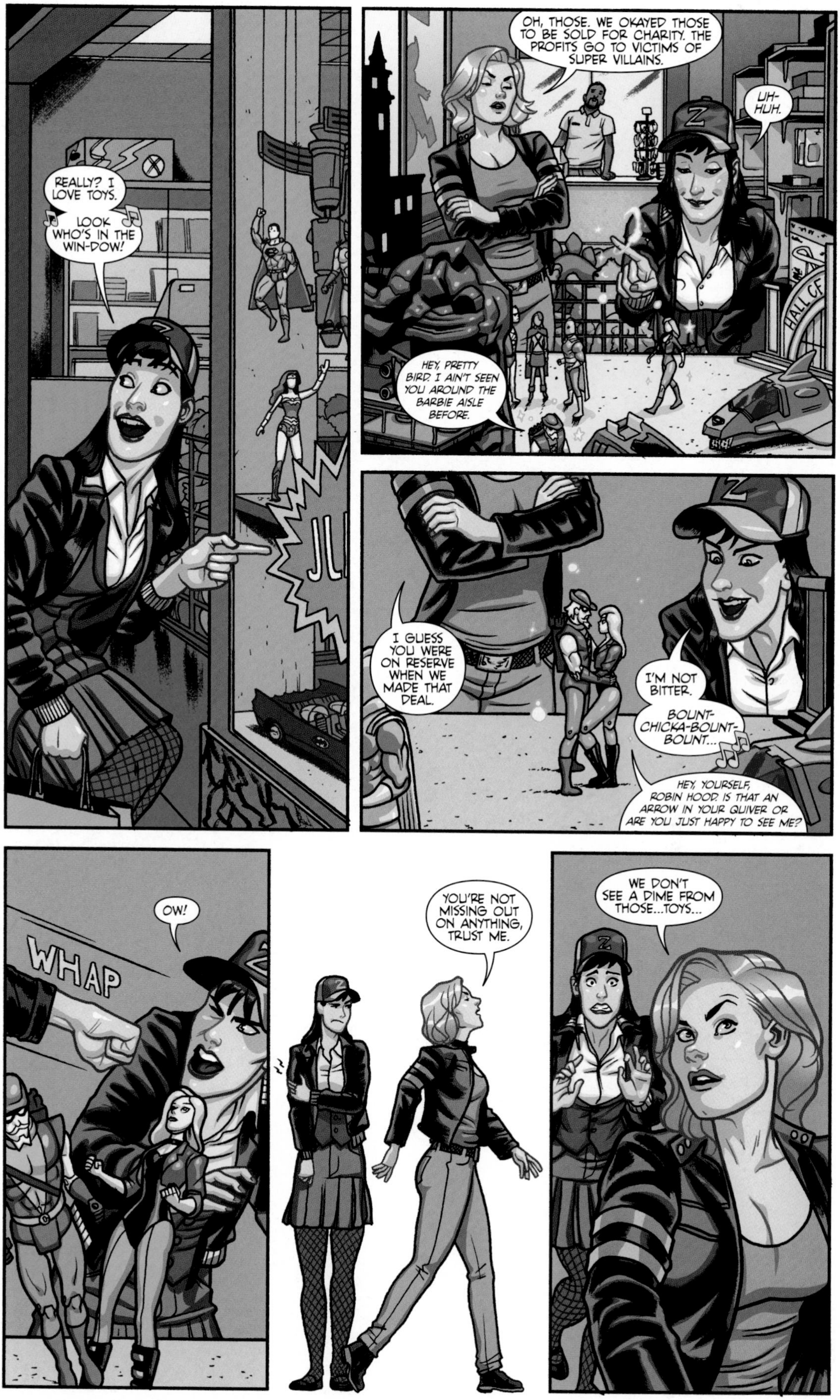
REALLY? I LOVE TOYS.
LOOK WHO'S IN THE WIN-DOW!
OH, THOSE. WE OKAYED THOSE TO BE SOLD FOR CHARITY. THE PROFITS GO TO VICTIMS OF SUPER VILLAINS.
UH-HUH.
HEY, PRETTY BIRD. I AIN'T SEEN YOU AROUND THE BARBIE AISLE BEFORE.
I GUESS YOU WERE ON RESERVE WHEN WE MADE THAT DEAL.
I'M NOT BITTER.
BOUNT-CHICKA-BOUNT-BOUNT...
HEY, YOURSELF, ROBIN HOOD. IS THAT AN ARROW IN YOUR QUIVER OR ARE YOU JUST HAPPY TO SEE ME?
OW!
WHAP
YOU'RE NOT MISSING OUT ON ANYTHING, TRUST ME.
WE DON'T SEE A DIME FROM THOSE...TOYS...

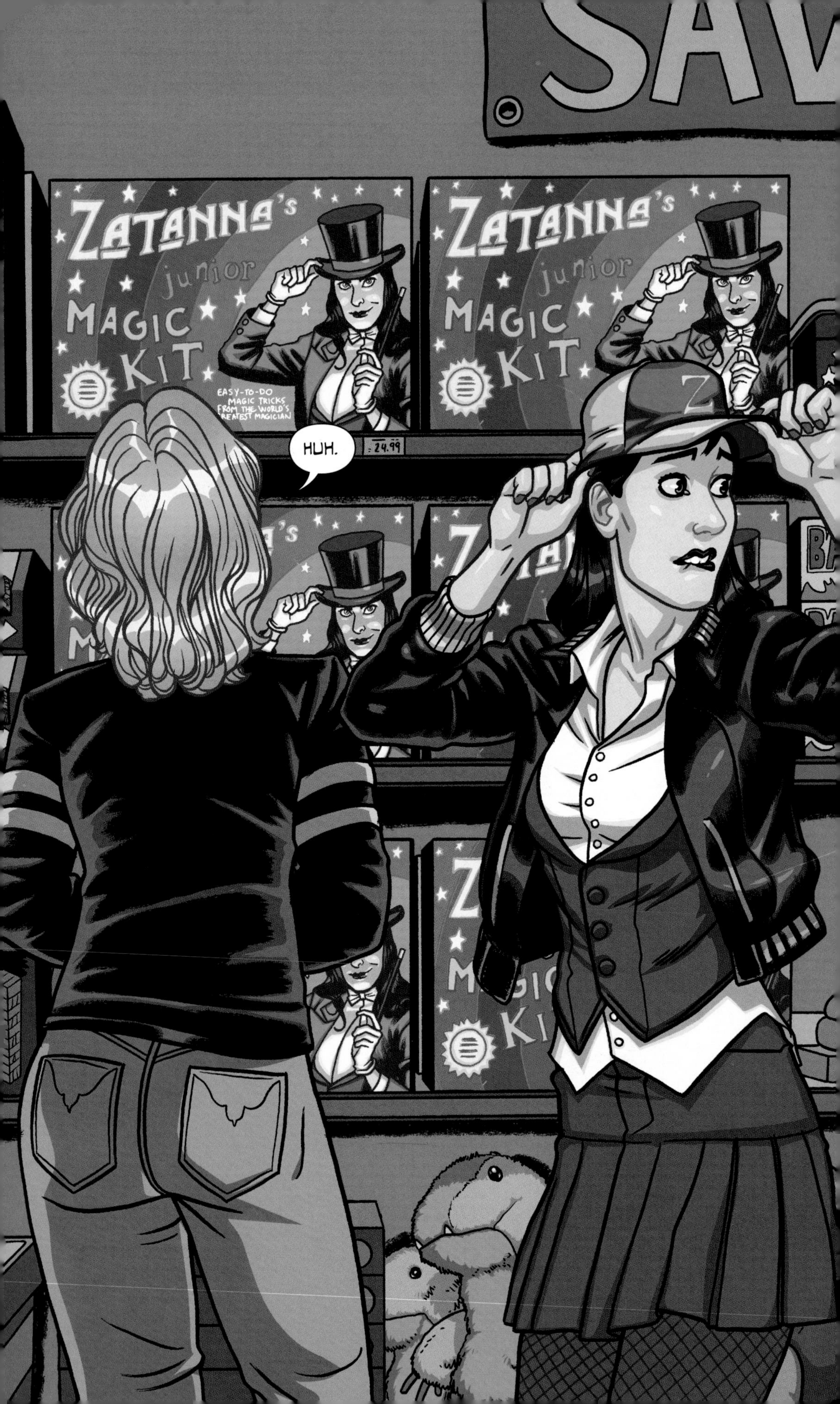
ZATANNA's junior MAGIC KIT
EASY-TO-DO MAGIC TRICKS FROM THE WORLD'S
HUH.
24.99

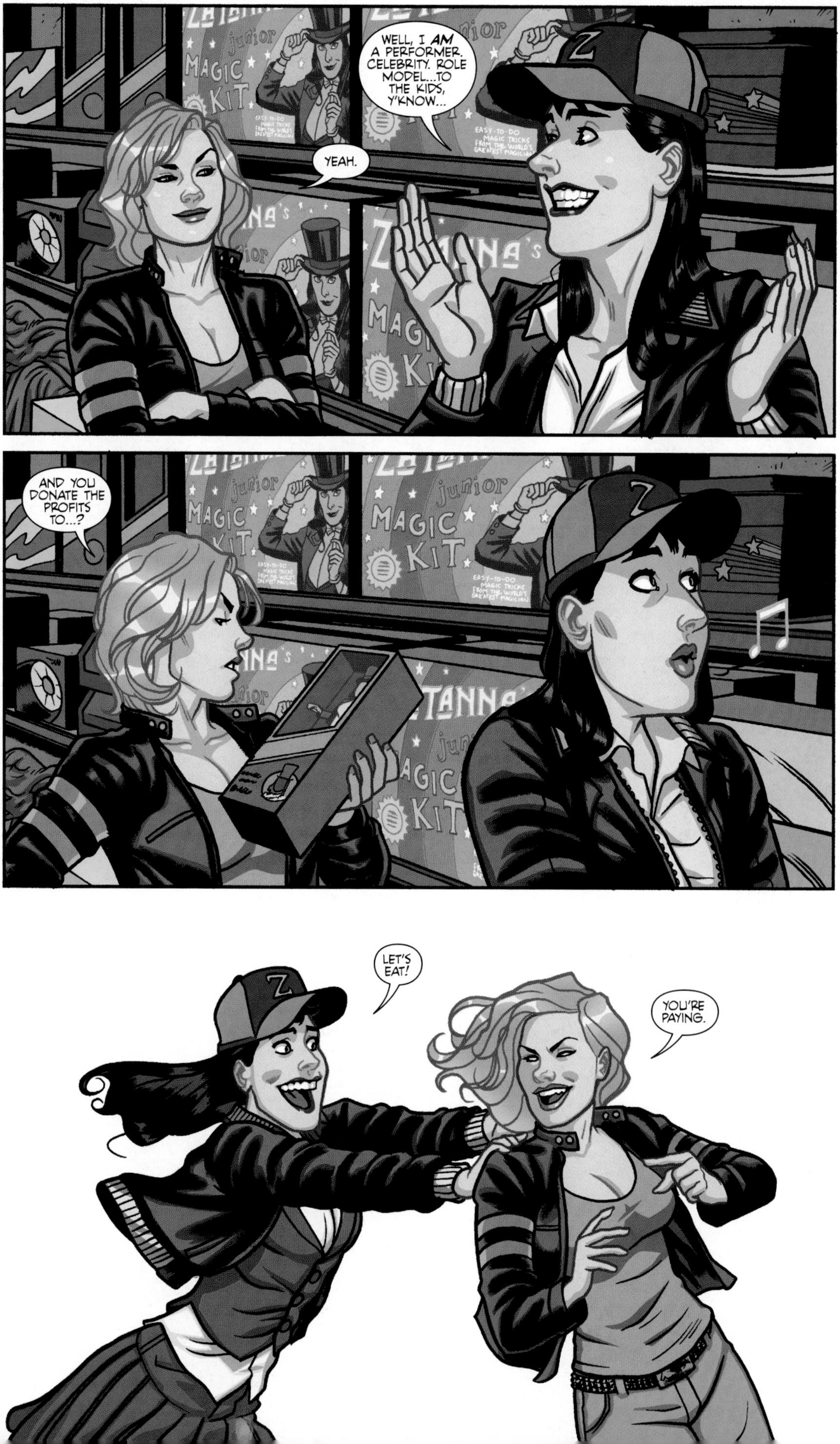
junior
MAGIC KIT
EASY-TO-DO MAGIC TRICKS FROM THE WORLD'S GREATEST MAGICIAN
WELL, I **AM** A PERFORMER. CELEBRITY. ROLE MODEL...TO THE KIDS, Y'KNOW...
YEAH.
AND YOU DONATE THE PROFITS TO...?
LET'S EAT!
YOU'RE PAYING.

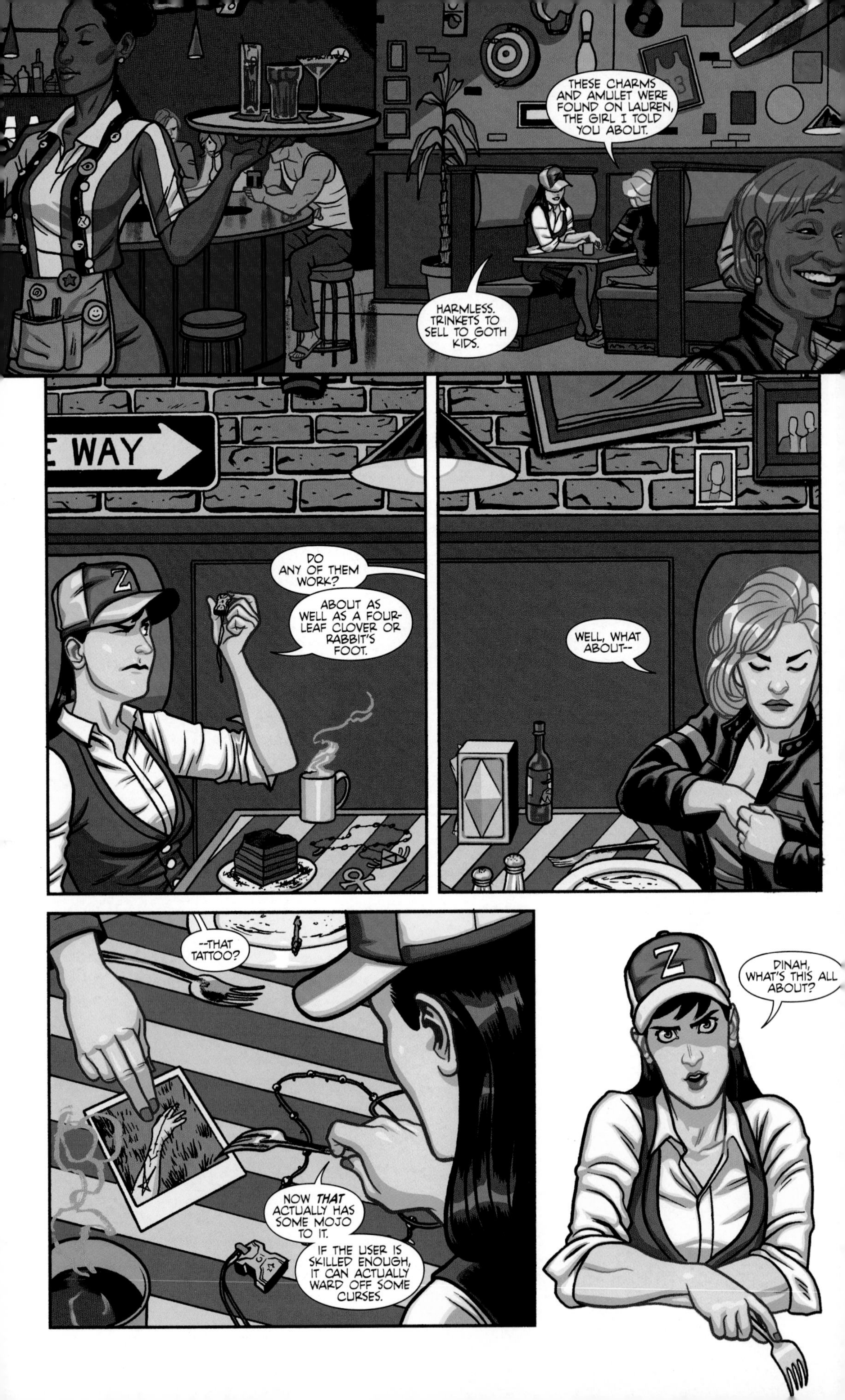
THESE CHARMS AND AMULET WERE FOUND ON LAUREN, THE GIRL I TOLD YOU ABOUT.
HARMLESS. TRINKETS TO SELL TO GOTH KIDS.
E WAY
DO ANY OF THEM WORK?
ABOUT AS WELL AS A FOUR-LEAF CLOVER OR RABBIT'S FOOT.
WELL, WHAT ABOUT--
--THAT TATTOO?
NOW *THAT* ACTUALLY HAS SOME MOJO TO IT.
IF THE USER IS SKILLED ENOUGH, IT CAN ACTUALLY WARD OFF SOME CURSES.
DINAH, WHAT'S THIS ALL ABOUT?

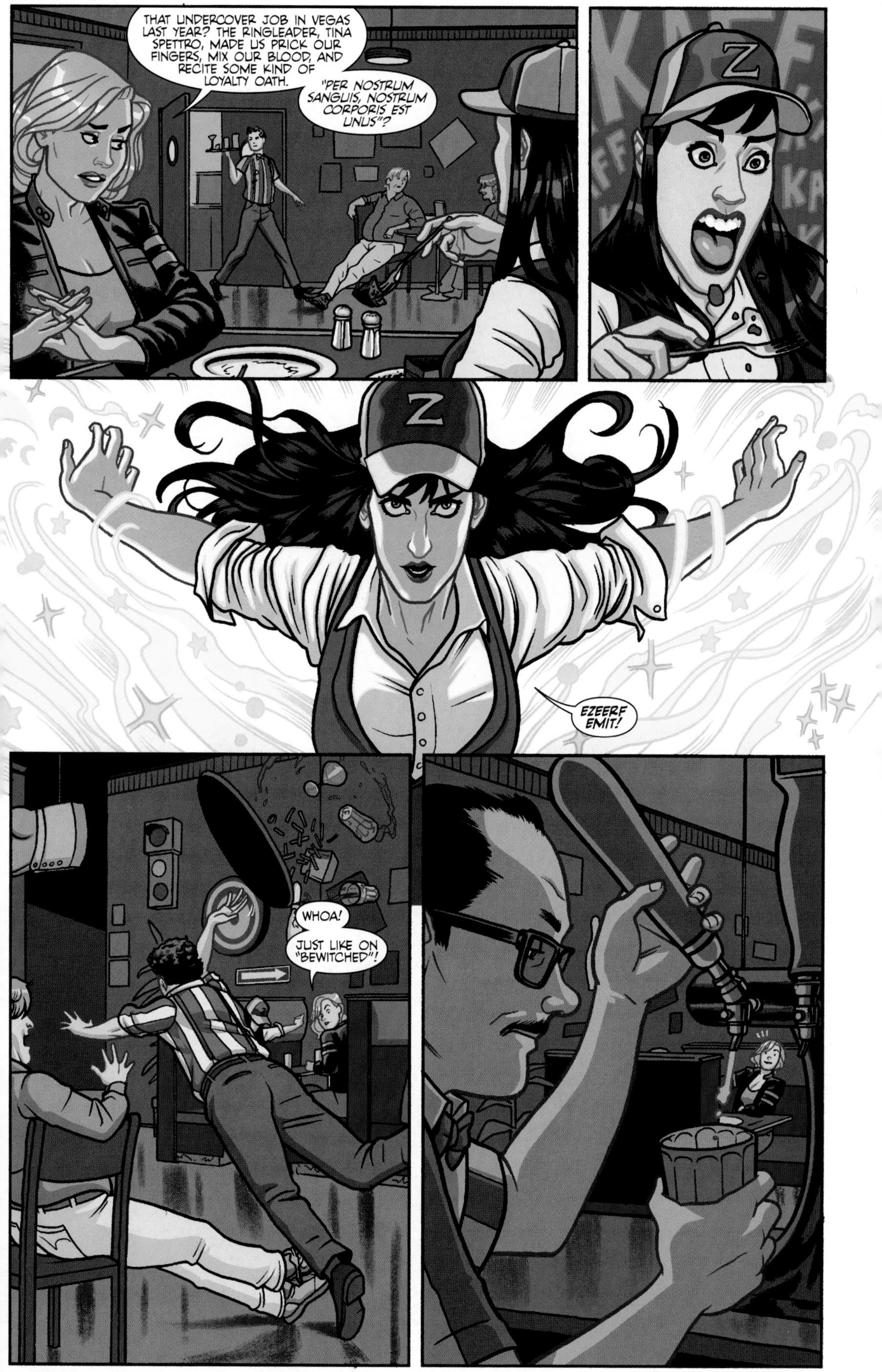
THAT UNDERCOVER JOB IN VEGAS LAST YEAR? THE RINGLEADER, TINA SPETTRO, MADE US PRICK OUR FINGERS, MIX OUR BLOOD, AND RECITE SOME KIND OF LOYALTY OATH.
"PER NOSTRUM SANGUIS, NOSTRUM CORPORIS EST UNUS"?
EZEERF EMIT!
WHOA!
JUST LIKE ON "BEWITCHED"!

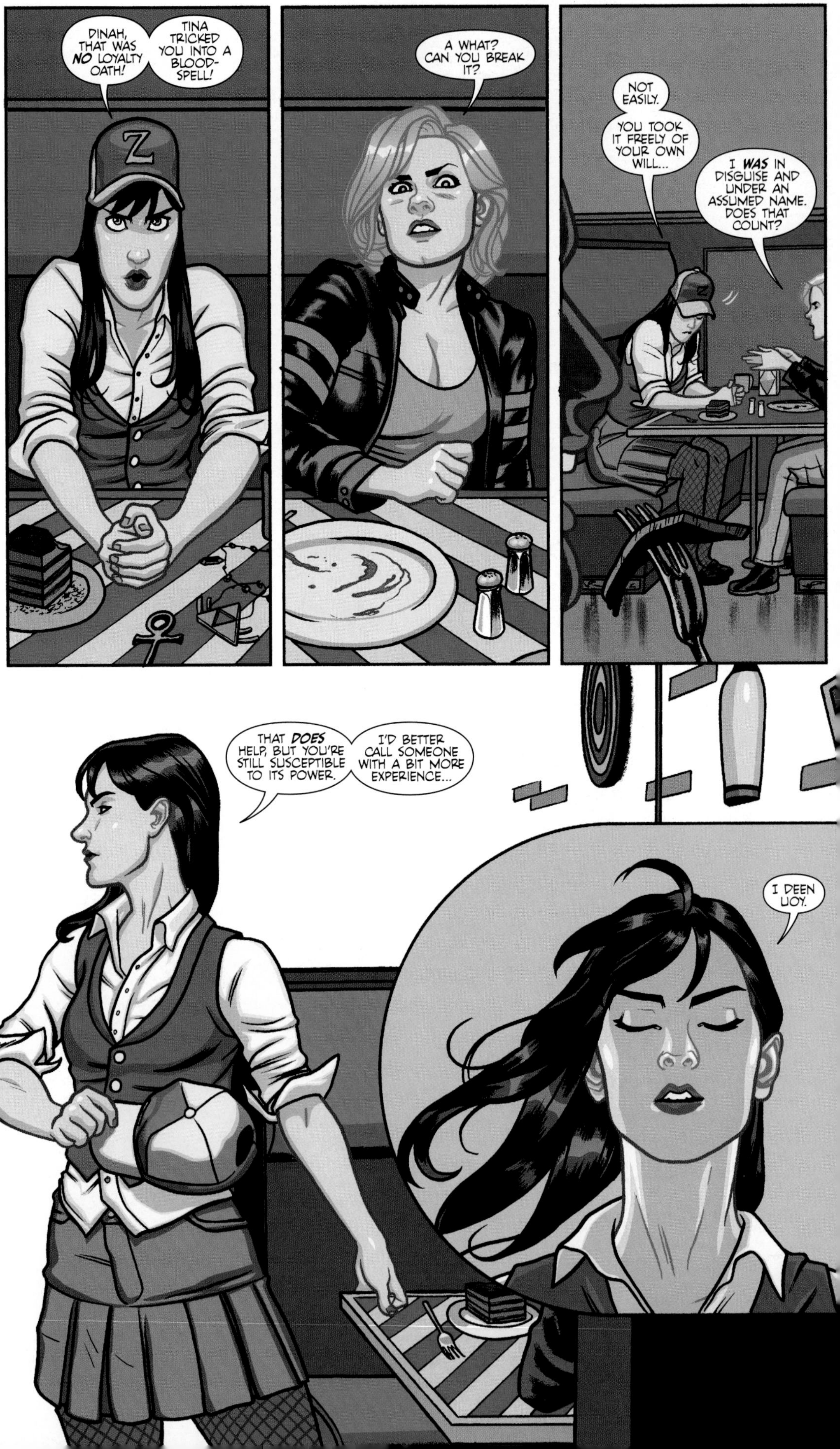

DINAH, THAT WAS NO LOYALTY OATH!
TINA TRICKED YOU INTO A BLOOD-SPELL!
A WHAT? CAN YOU BREAK IT?
NOT EASILY.
YOU TOOK IT FREELY OF YOUR OWN WILL...
I WAS IN DISGUISE AND UNDER AN ASSUMED NAME. DOES THAT COUNT?
THAT DOES HELP, BUT YOU'RE STILL SUSCEPTIBLE TO ITS POWER.
I'D BETTER CALL SOMEONE WITH A BIT MORE EXPERIENCE...
I DEEN UOY.

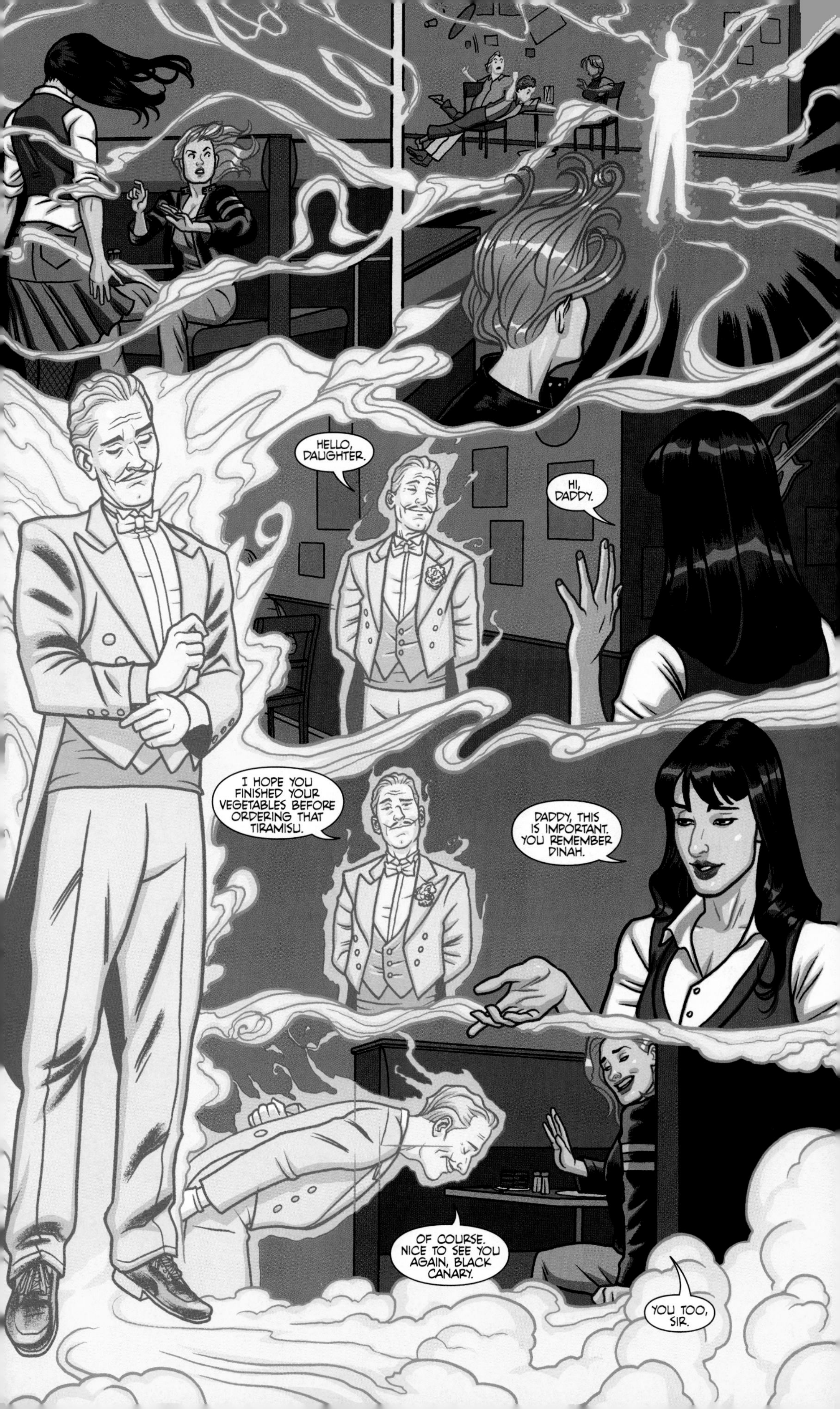
HELLO, DAUGHTER.
HI, DADDY.
I HOPE YOU FINISHED YOUR VEGETABLES BEFORE ORDERING THAT TIRAMISU.
DADDY, THIS IS IMPORTANT. YOU REMEMBER DINAH.
OF COURSE. NICE TO SEE YOU AGAIN, BLACK CANARY.
YOU TOO, SIR.

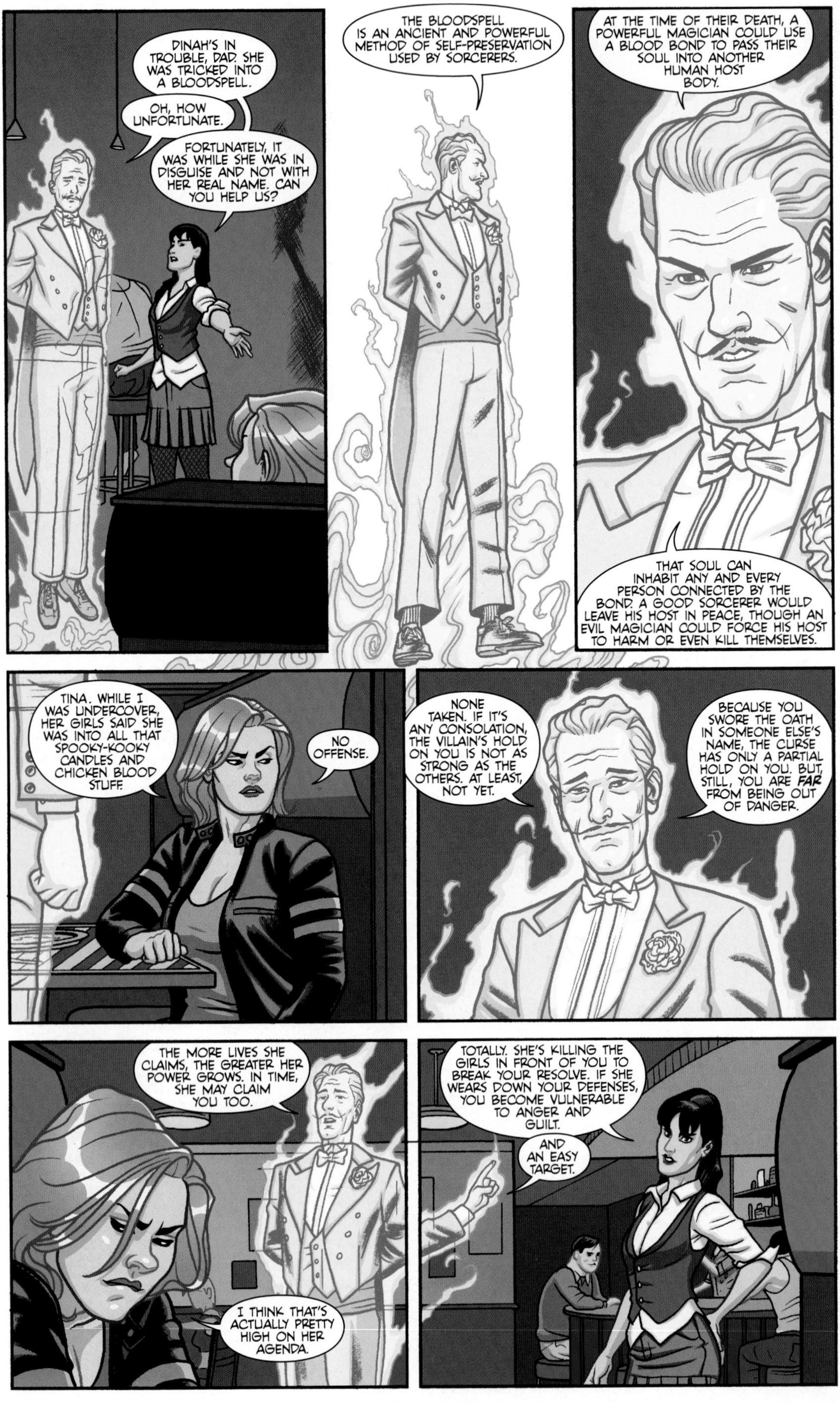
DINAH'S IN TROUBLE, DAD. SHE WAS TRICKED INTO A BLOODSPELL.
OH, HOW UNFORTUNATE.
FORTUNATELY, IT WAS WHILE SHE WAS IN DISGUISE AND NOT WITH HER REAL NAME. CAN YOU HELP US?
THE BLOODSPELL IS AN ANCIENT AND POWERFUL METHOD OF SELF-PRESERVATION USED BY SORCERERS.
AT THE TIME OF THEIR DEATH, A POWERFUL MAGICIAN COULD USE A BLOOD BOND TO PASS THEIR SOUL INTO ANOTHER HUMAN HOST BODY.
THAT SOUL CAN INHABIT ANY AND EVERY PERSON CONNECTED BY THE BOND. A GOOD SORCERER WOULD LEAVE HIS HOST IN PEACE, THOUGH AN EVIL MAGICIAN COULD FORCE HIS HOST TO HARM OR EVEN KILL THEMSELVES.
TINA. WHILE I WAS UNDERCOVER, HER GIRLS SAID SHE WAS INTO ALL THAT SPOOKY-KOOKY CANDLES AND CHICKEN BLOOD STUFF.
NO OFFENSE.
NONE TAKEN. IF IT'S ANY CONSOLATION, THE VILLAIN'S HOLD ON YOU IS NOT AS STRONG AS THE OTHERS. AT LEAST, NOT YET.
BECAUSE YOU SWORE THE OATH IN SOMEONE ELSE'S NAME, THE CURSE HAS ONLY A PARTIAL HOLD ON YOU. BUT, STILL, YOU ARE *FAR* FROM BEING OUT OF DANGER.
THE MORE LIVES SHE CLAIMS, THE GREATER HER POWER GROWS. IN TIME, SHE MAY CLAIM YOU TOO.
I THINK THAT'S ACTUALLY PRETTY HIGH ON HER AGENDA.
TOTALLY. SHE'S KILLING THE GIRLS IN FRONT OF YOU TO BREAK YOUR RESOLVE. IF SHE WEARS DOWN YOUR DEFENSES, YOU BECOME VULNERABLE TO ANGER AND GUILT.
AND AN EASY TARGET.

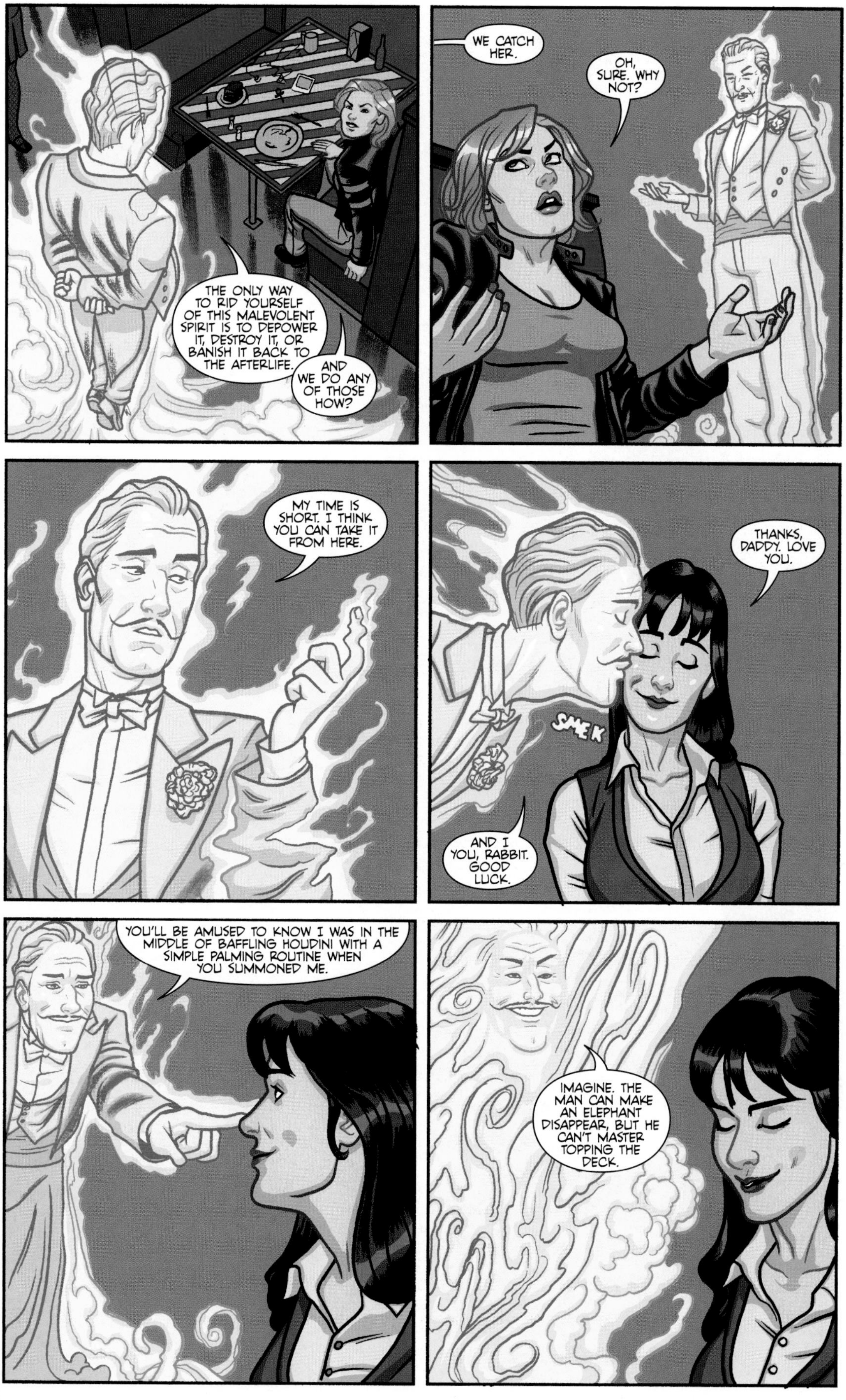
THE ONLY WAY TO RID YOURSELF OF THIS MALEVOLENT SPIRIT IS TO DEPOWER IT, DESTROY IT, OR BANISH IT BACK TO THE AFTERLIFE.
AND WE DO ANY OF THOSE HOW?
WE CATCH HER.
OH, SURE. WHY NOT?
MY TIME IS SHORT. I THINK YOU CAN TAKE IT FROM HERE.
THANKS, DADDY. LOVE YOU.
SMEK
AND I YOU, RABBIT. GOOD LUCK.
YOU'LL BE AMUSED TO KNOW I WAS IN THE MIDDLE OF BAFFLING HOUDINI WITH A SIMPLE PALMING ROUTINE WHEN YOU SUMMONED ME.
IMAGINE. THE MAN CAN MAKE AN ELEPHANT DISAPPEAR, BUT HE CAN'T MASTER TOPPING THE DECK.

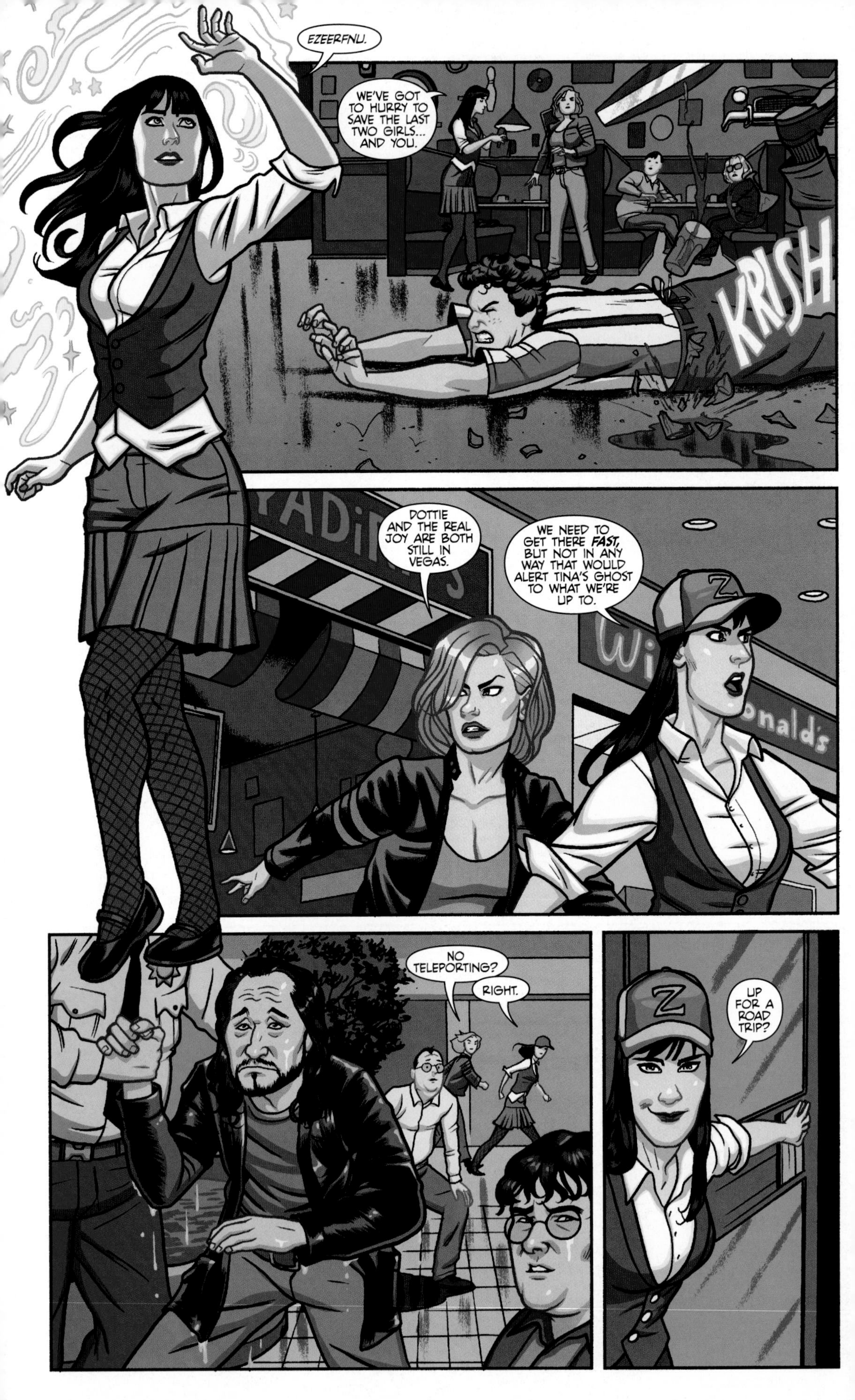

EZEERFNU.
WE'VE GOT TO HURRY TO SAVE THE LAST TWO GIRLS... AND YOU.
KRISH
DOTTIE AND THE REAL JOY ARE BOTH STILL IN VEGAS.
WE NEED TO GET THERE FAST, BUT NOT IN ANY WAY THAT WOULD ALERT TINA'S GHOST TO WHAT WE'RE UP TO.
NO TELEPORTING?
RIGHT.
UP FOR A ROAD TRIP?

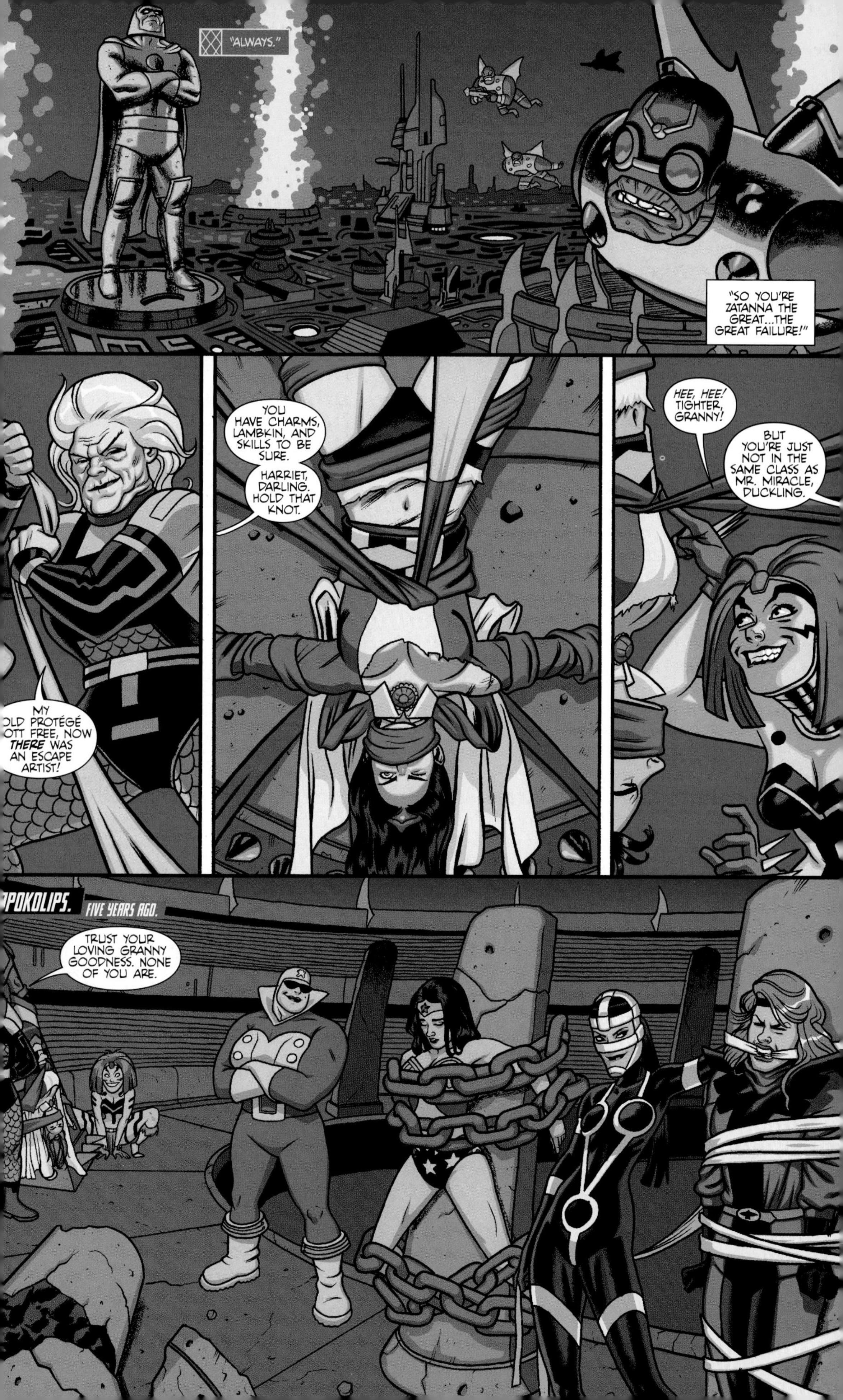
"ALWAYS."
"SO YOU'RE ZATANNA THE GREAT...THE GREAT FAILURE!"
YOU HAVE CHARMS, LAMBKIN, AND SKILLS TO BE SURE.
HARRIET, DARLING. HOLD THAT KNOT.
HEE, HEE! TIGHTER, GRANNY!
BUT YOU'RE JUST NOT IN THE SAME CLASS AS MR. MIRACLE, DUCKLING.
MY OLD PROTÉGÉ OTT FREE, NOW THERE WAS AN ESCAPE ARTIST!
POKOLIPS. FIVE YEARS AGO.
TRUST YOUR LOVING GRANNY GOODNESS. NONE OF YOU ARE.

ALTHOUGH IT WILL BE AMUSING TO WATCH YOU TRY TO FREE YOURSELVES.

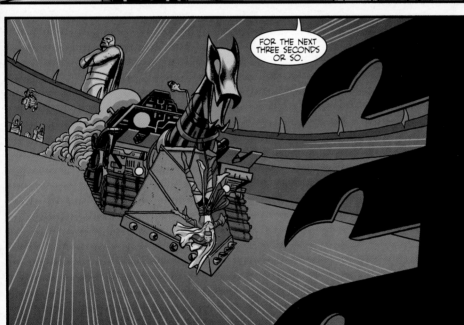

FOR THE NEXT THREE SECONDS OR SO.

A TOAST, MY LOVELY FURIES.

TO A VALIANT, BUT WOEFULLY INFERIOR...

...ADVERSARY?

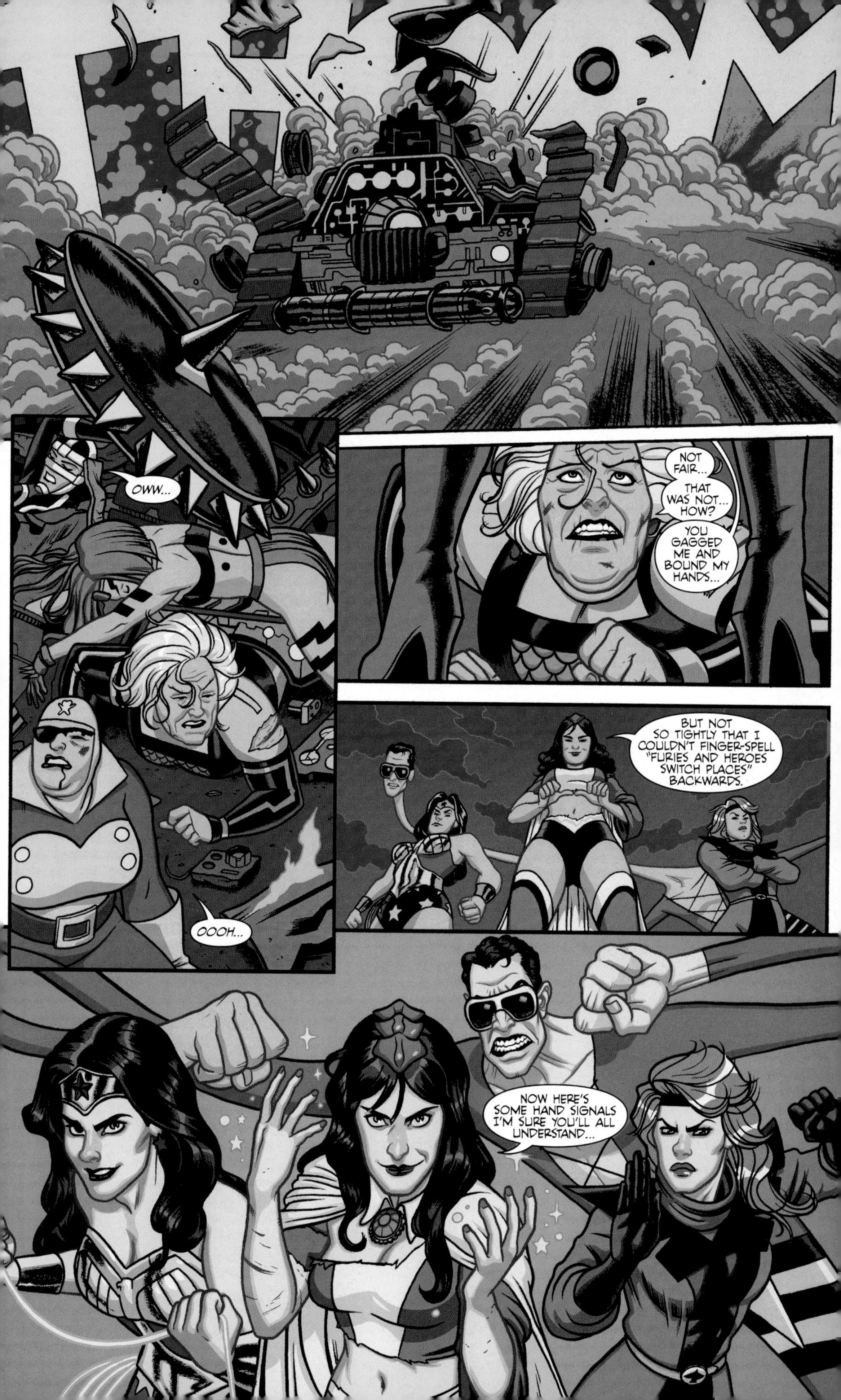
OWW...
OOOH...
NOT FAIR...
THAT WAS NOT... HOW?
YOU GAGGED ME AND BOUND MY HANDS...
BUT NOT SO TIGHTLY THAT I COULDN'T FINGER-SPELL "FURIES AND HEROES SWITCH PLACES" BACKWARDS.
NOW HERE'S SOME HAND SIGNALS I'M SURE YOU'LL ALL UNDERSTAND...

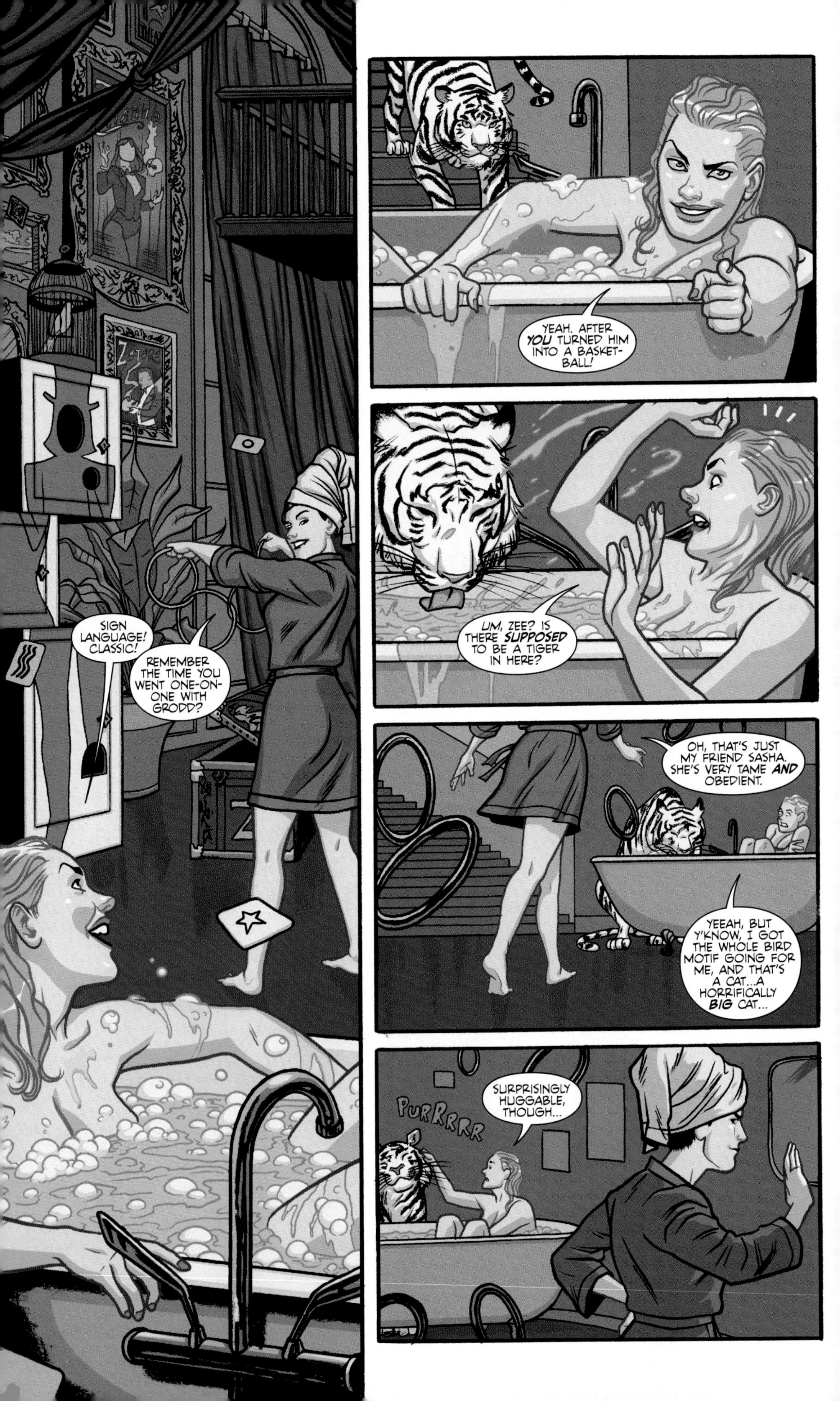

SIGN LANGUAGE! CLASSIC!
REMEMBER THE TIME YOU WENT ONE-ON-ONE WITH GRODD?
YEAH. AFTER YOU TURNED HIM INTO A BASKET-BALL!
UM, ZEE? IS THERE SUPPOSED TO BE A TIGER IN HERE?
OH, THAT'S JUST MY FRIEND SASHA. SHE'S VERY TAME AND OBEDIENT.
YEEAH, BUT Y'KNOW, I GOT THE WHOLE BIRD MOTIF GOING FOR ME, AND THAT'S A CAT...A HORRIFICALLY BIG CAT...
PURRRRR
SURPRISINGLY HUGGABLE, THOUGH...

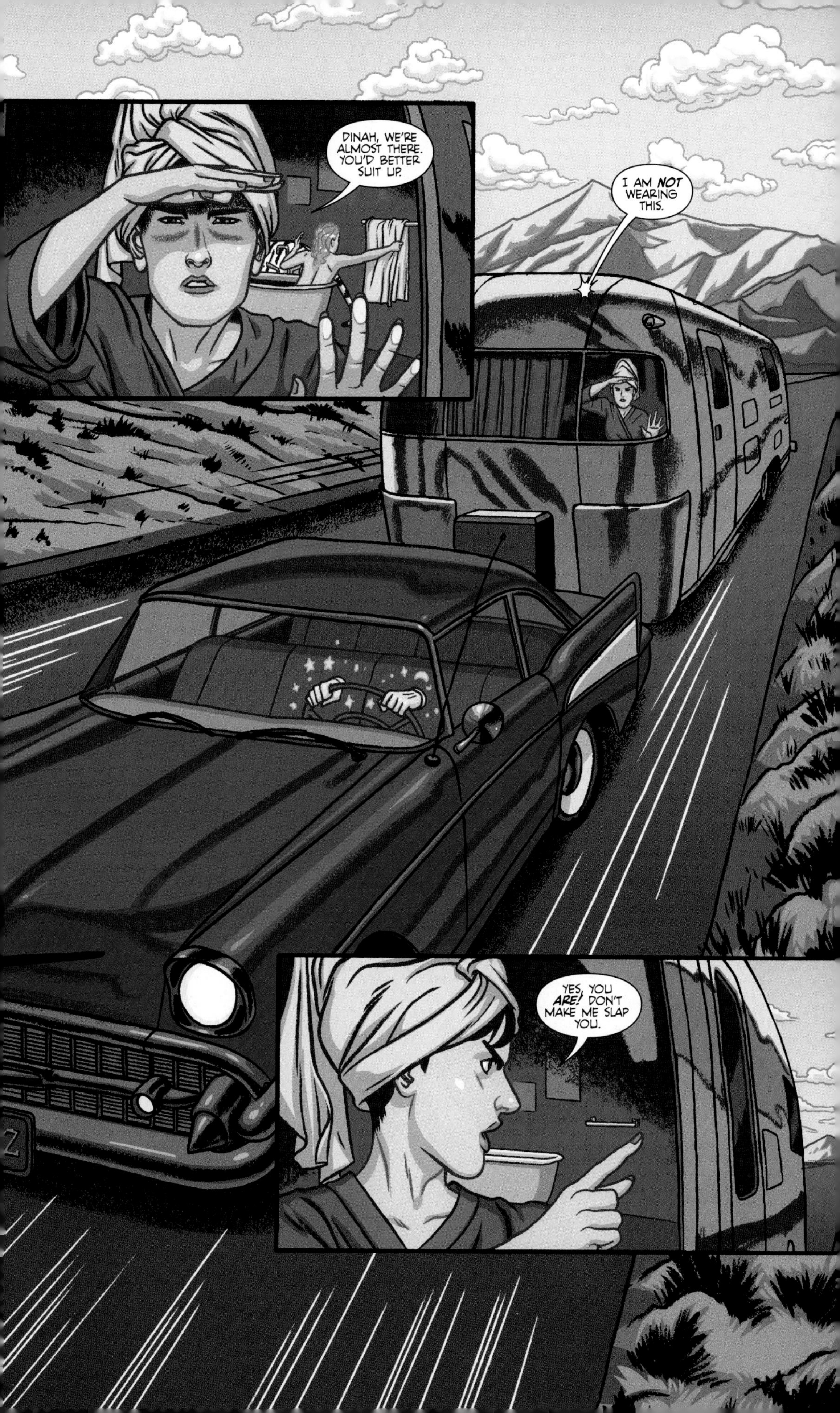
DINAH, WE'RE ALMOST THERE. YOU'D BETTER SUIT UP.
I AM **NOT** WEARING THIS.
YES, YOU **ARE!** DON'T MAKE ME SLAP YOU.

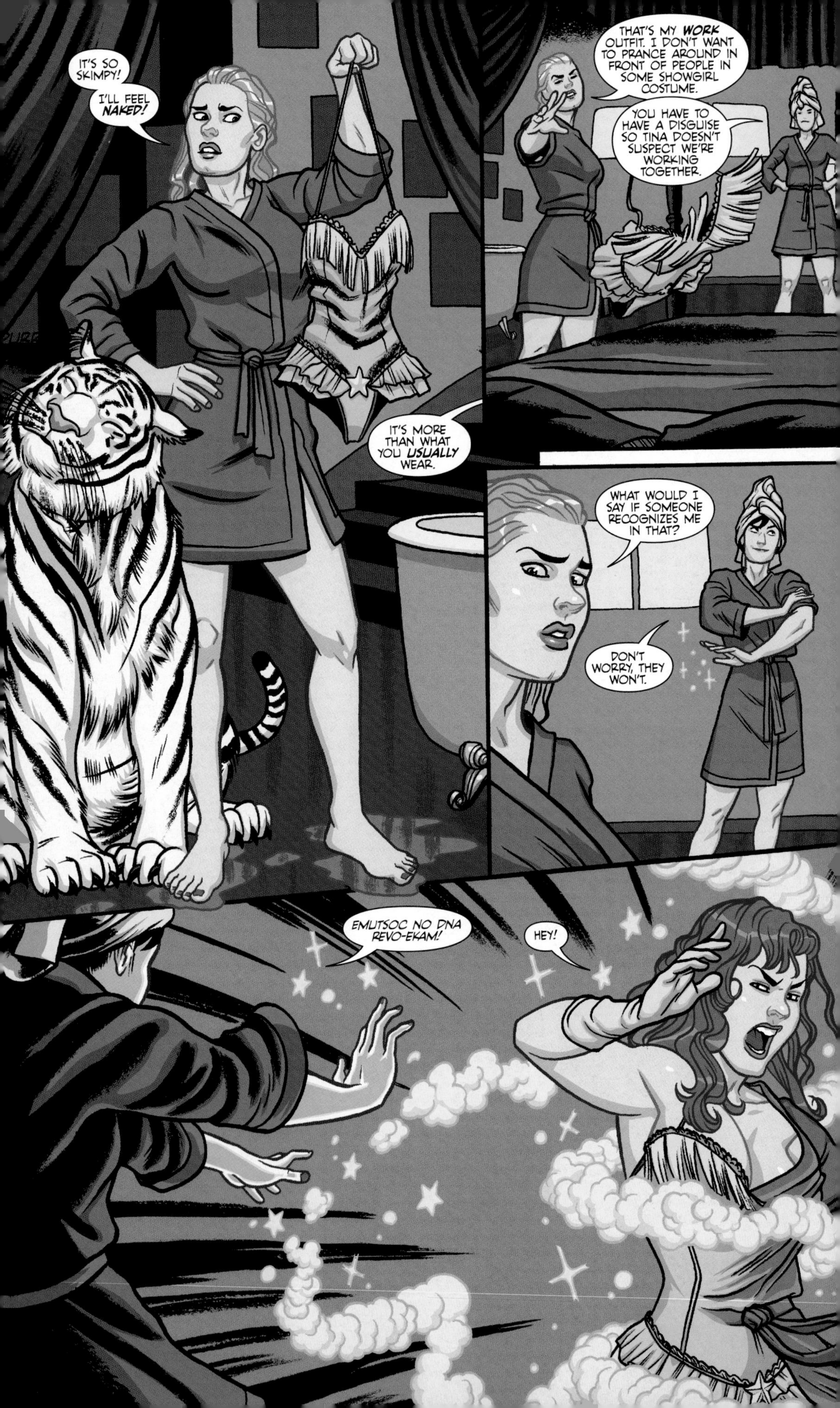
IT'S SO SKIMPY!
I'LL FEEL NAKED!
IT'S MORE THAN WHAT YOU USUALLY WEAR.
THAT'S MY WORK OUTFIT. I DON'T WANT TO PRANCE AROUND IN FRONT OF PEOPLE IN SOME SHOWGIRL COSTUME.
YOU HAVE TO HAVE A DISGUISE SO TINA DOESN'T SUSPECT WE'RE WORKING TOGETHER.
WHAT WOULD I SAY IF SOMEONE RECOGNIZES ME IN THAT?
DON'T WORRY, THEY WON'T.
EMUTSOC NO DNA REVO-EKAM!
HEY!

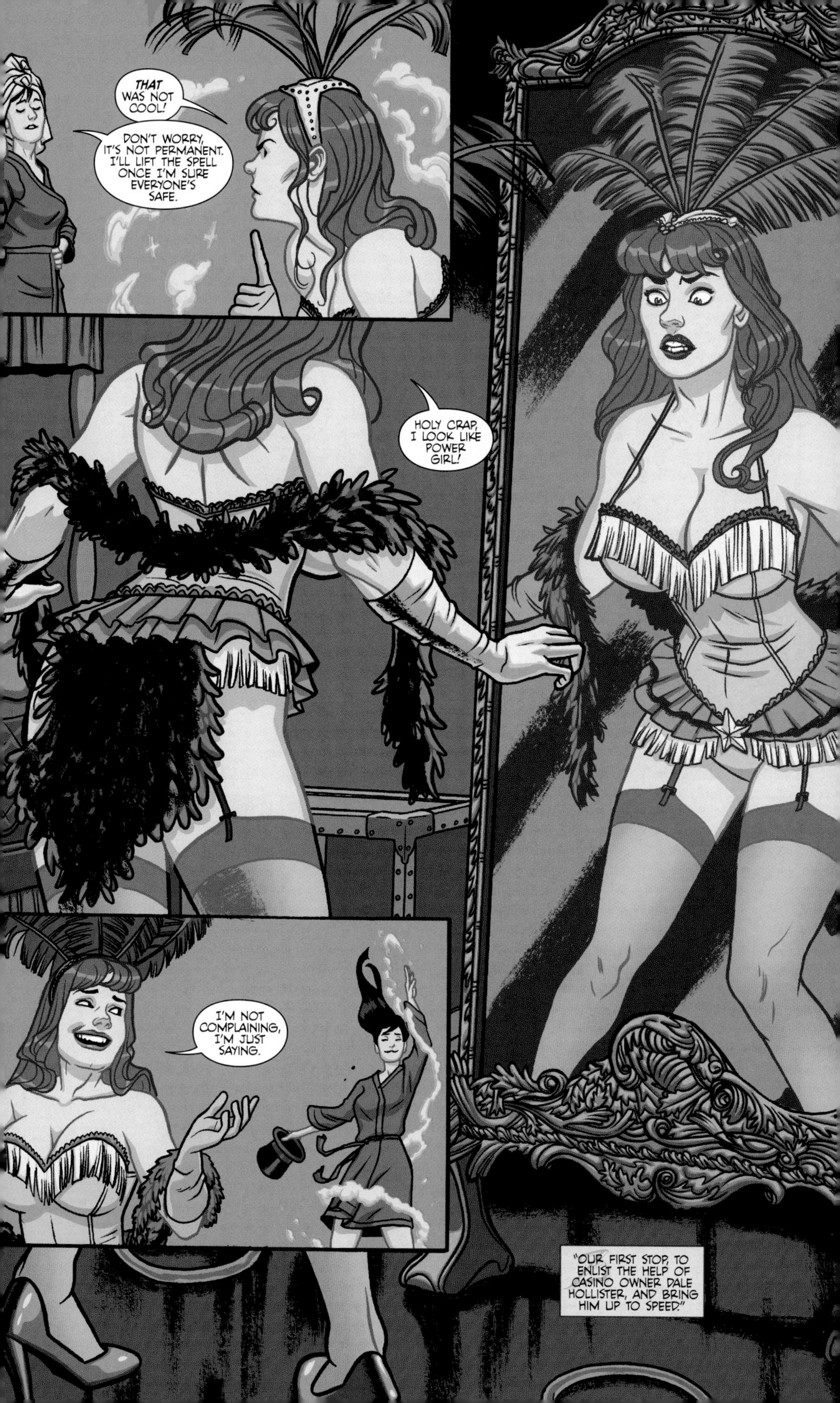
THAT WAS NOT COOL!
DON'T WORRY, IT'S NOT PERMANENT. I'LL LIFT THE SPELL ONCE I'M SURE EVERYONE'S SAFE.
HOLY CRAP, I LOOK LIKE POWER GIRL!
I'M NOT COMPLAINING, I'M JUST SAYING.
"OUR FIRST STOP, TO ENLIST THE HELP OF CASINO OWNER DALE HOLLISTER, AND BRING HIM UP TO SPEED."

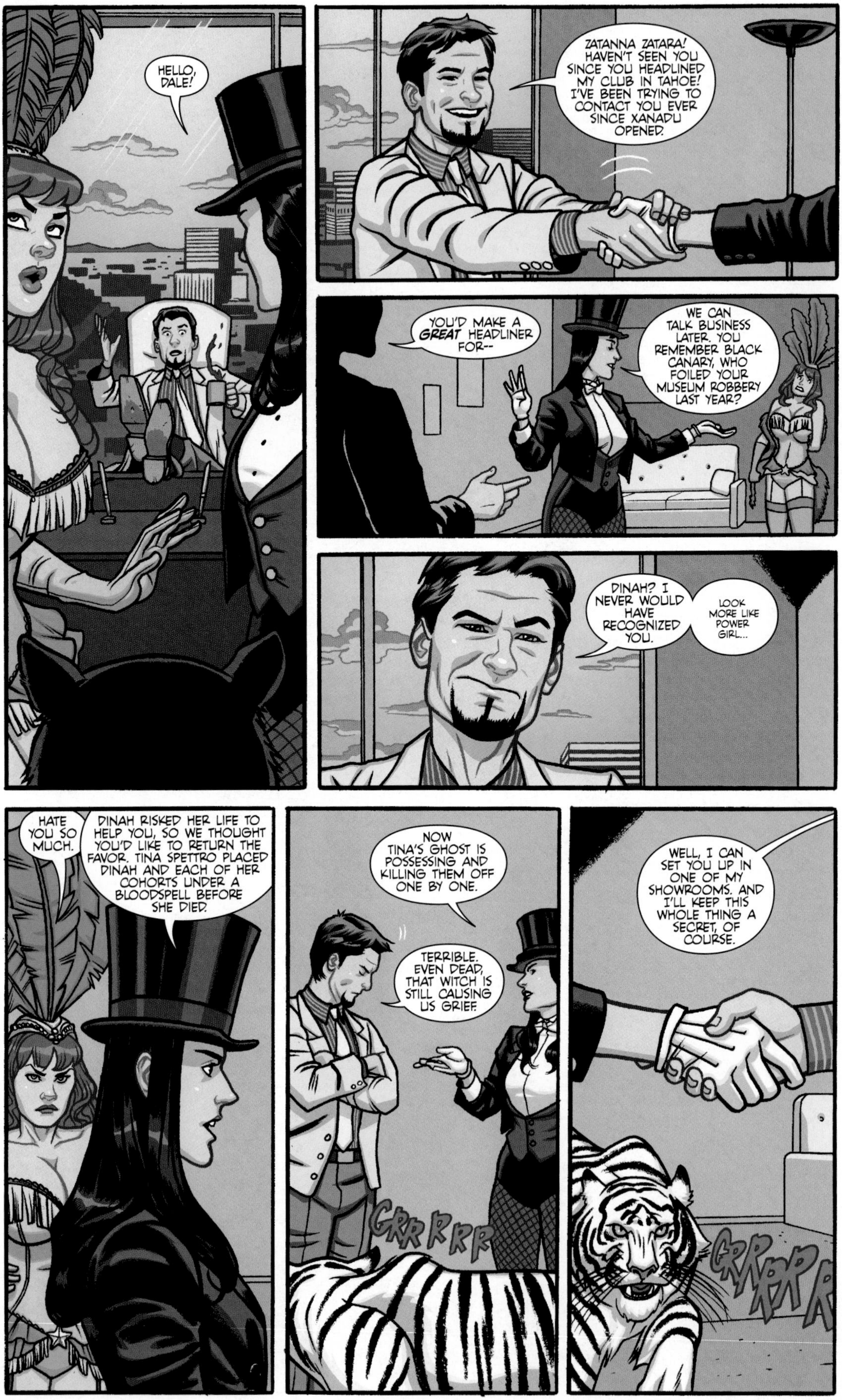
HELLO, DALE!
ZATANNA ZATARA! HAVEN'T SEEN YOU SINCE YOU HEADLINED MY CLUB IN TAHOE! I'VE BEEN TRYING TO CONTACT YOU EVER SINCE XANADU OPENED.
YOU'D MAKE A GREAT HEADLINER FOR--
WE CAN TALK BUSINESS LATER. YOU REMEMBER BLACK CANARY, WHO FOILED YOUR MUSEUM ROBBERY LAST YEAR?
DINAH? I NEVER WOULD HAVE RECOGNIZED YOU.
LOOK MORE LIKE POWER GIRL...
HATE YOU SO MUCH.
DINAH RISKED HER LIFE TO HELP YOU, SO WE THOUGHT YOU'D LIKE TO RETURN THE FAVOR. TINA SPETTRO PLACED DINAH AND EACH OF HER COHORTS UNDER A BLOODSPELL BEFORE SHE DIED.
NOW TINA'S GHOST IS POSSESSING AND KILLING THEM OFF ONE BY ONE.
TERRIBLE. EVEN DEAD, THAT WITCH IS STILL CAUSING US GRIEF.
GRRRRR
WELL, I CAN SET YOU UP IN ONE OF MY SHOWROOMS. AND I'LL KEEP THIS WHOLE THING A SECRET, OF COURSE.
GRRRRR

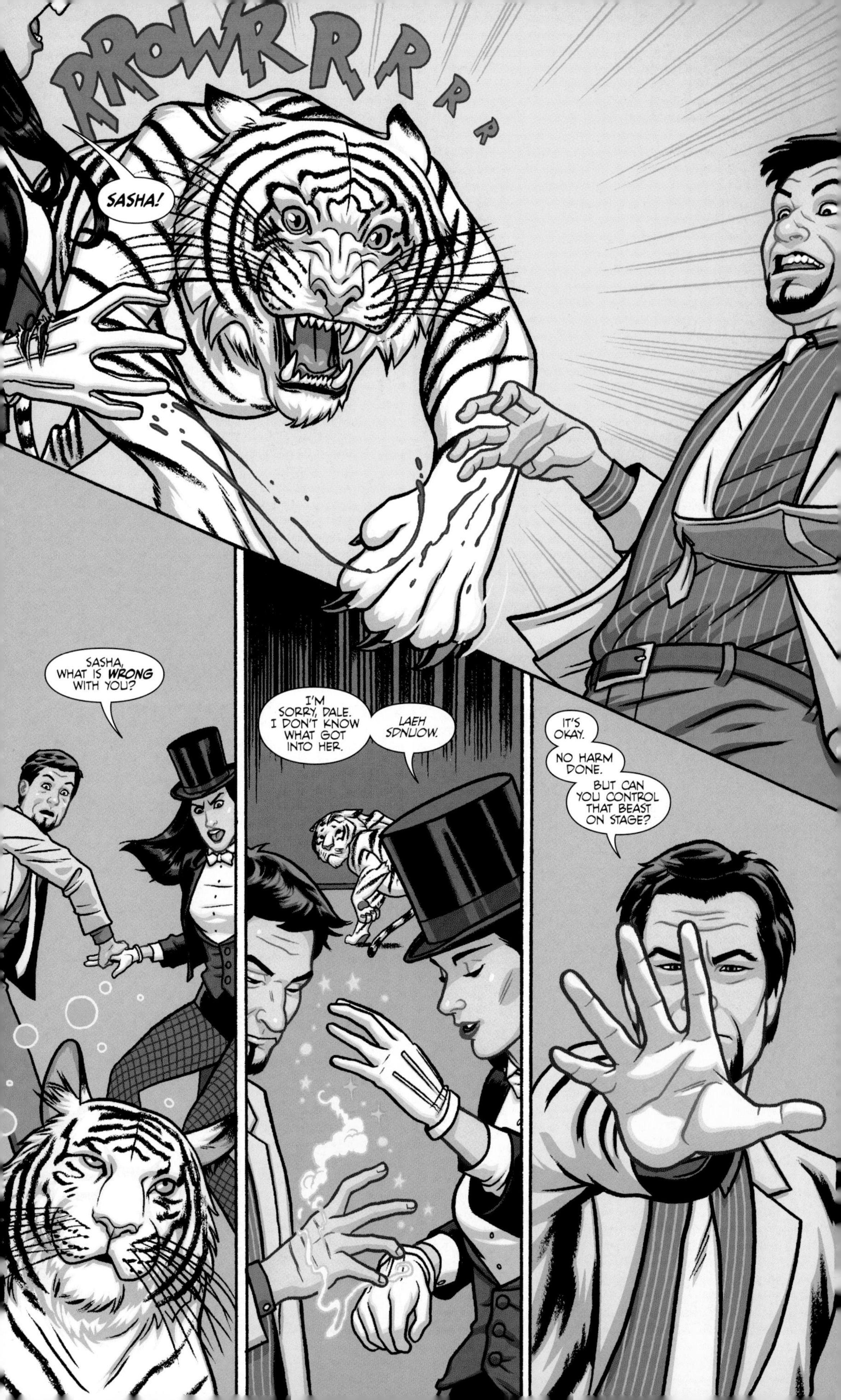
RROWRRRRRR
SASHA!
SASHA, WHAT IS **WRONG** WITH YOU?
I'M SORRY, DALE. I DON'T KNOW WHAT GOT INTO HER.
LAEH SDNUOW.
IT'S OKAY.
NO HARM DONE.
BUT CAN YOU CONTROL THAT BEAST ON STAGE?

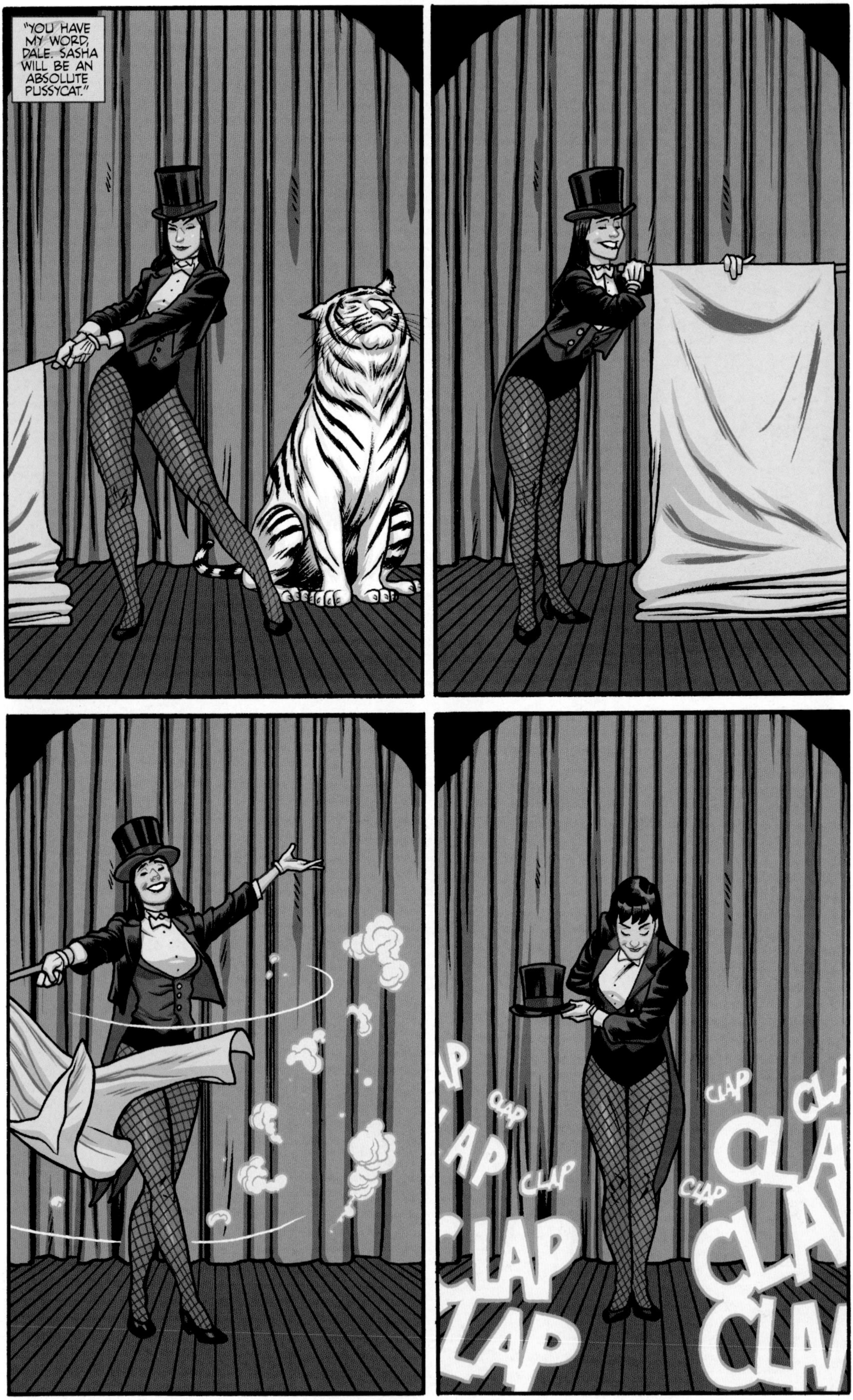
"YOU HAVE MY WORD, DALE. SASHA WILL BE AN ABSOLUTE PUSSYCAT."
CLAP
CLAP
CLAP
CLAP

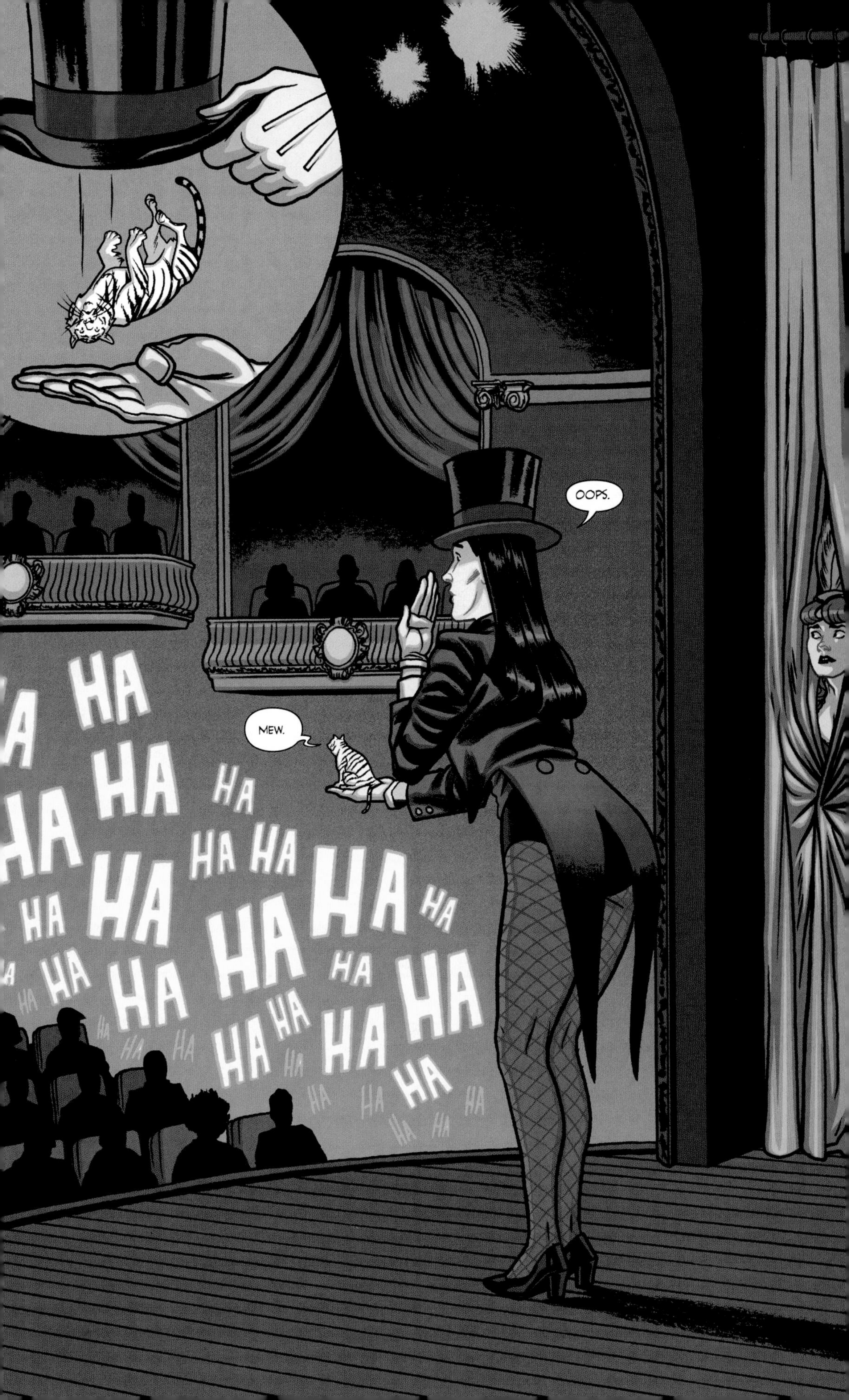
OOPS.
MEW.
HA HA HA HA HA HA HA HA HA HA HA HA HA HA HA HA HA HA HA HA HA HA HA HA HA HA HA HA

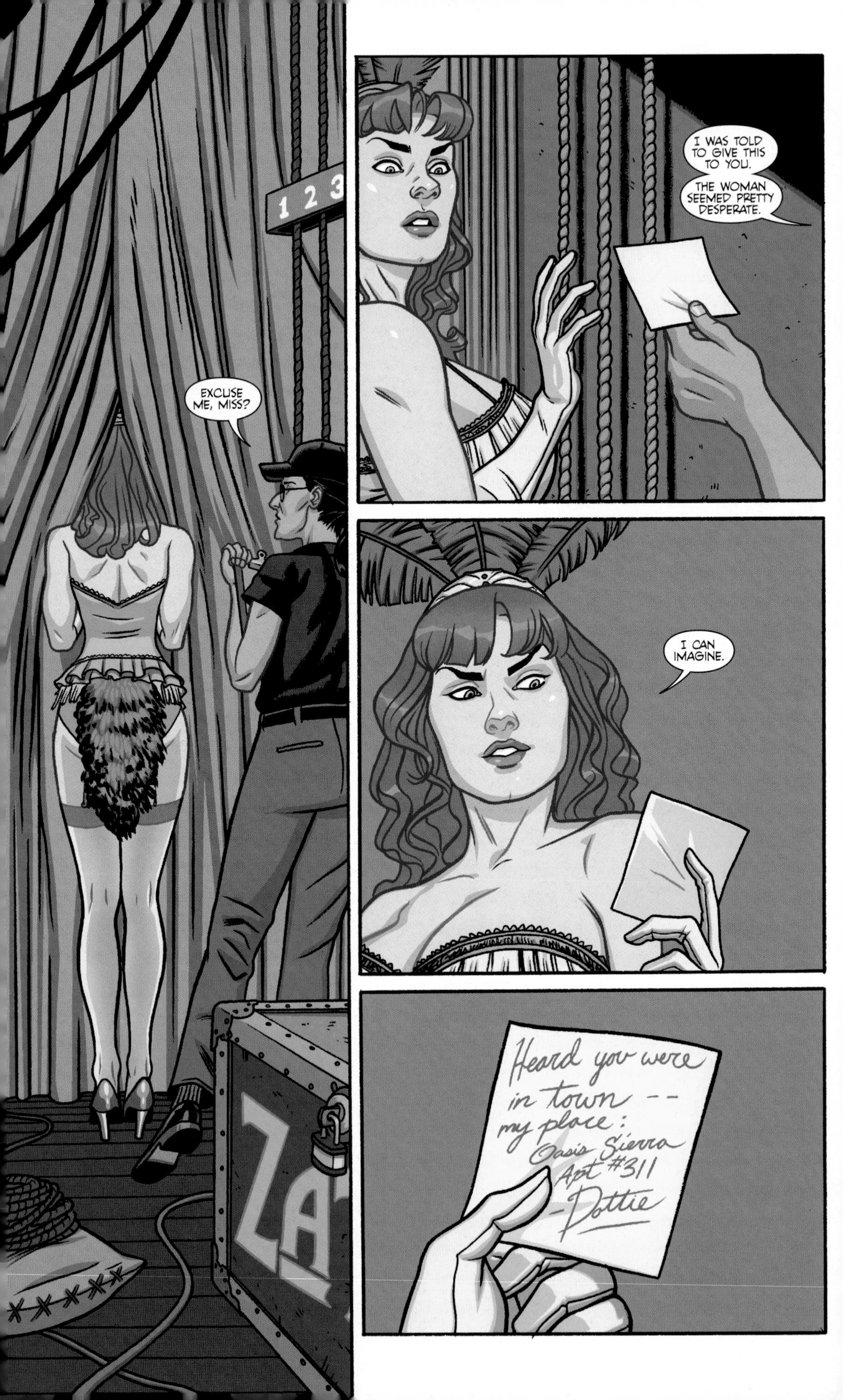
EXCUSE ME, MISS?
I WAS TOLD TO GIVE THIS TO YOU.
THE WOMAN SEEMED PRETTY DESPERATE.
I CAN IMAGINE.
Heard you were in town -- my place: Oasis Sierra Apt #311 -Dottie

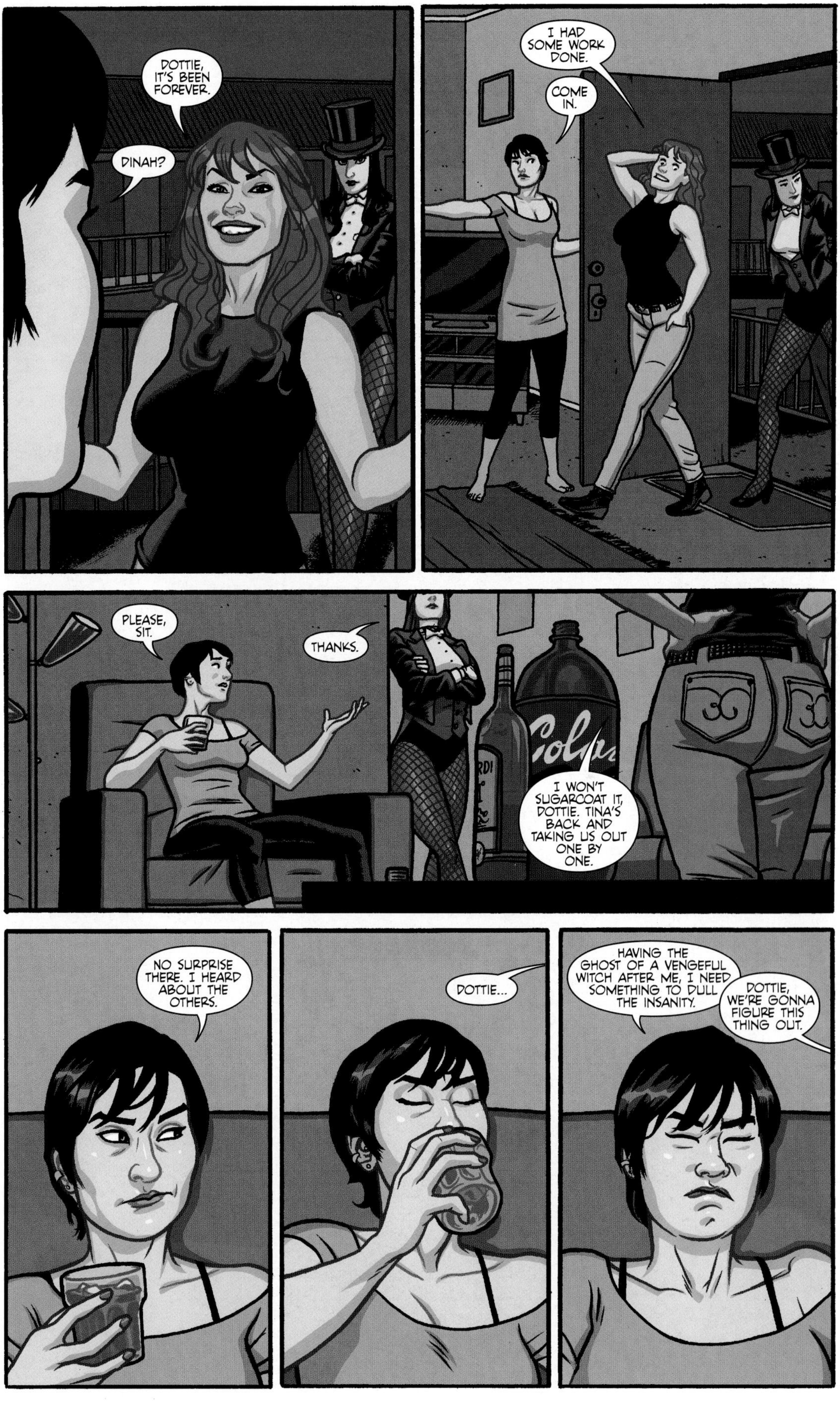
DOTTIE, IT'S BEEN FOREVER.
DINAH?
I HAD SOME WORK DONE.
COME IN.
PLEASE, SIT.
THANKS.
I WON'T SUGARCOAT IT, DOTTIE. TINA'S BACK AND TAKING US OUT ONE BY ONE.
NO SURPRISE THERE. I HEARD ABOUT THE OTHERS.
DOTTIE...
HAVING THE GHOST OF A VENGEFUL WITCH AFTER ME, I NEED SOMETHING TO DULL THE INSANITY.
DOTTIE, WE'RE GONNA FIGURE THIS THING OUT.

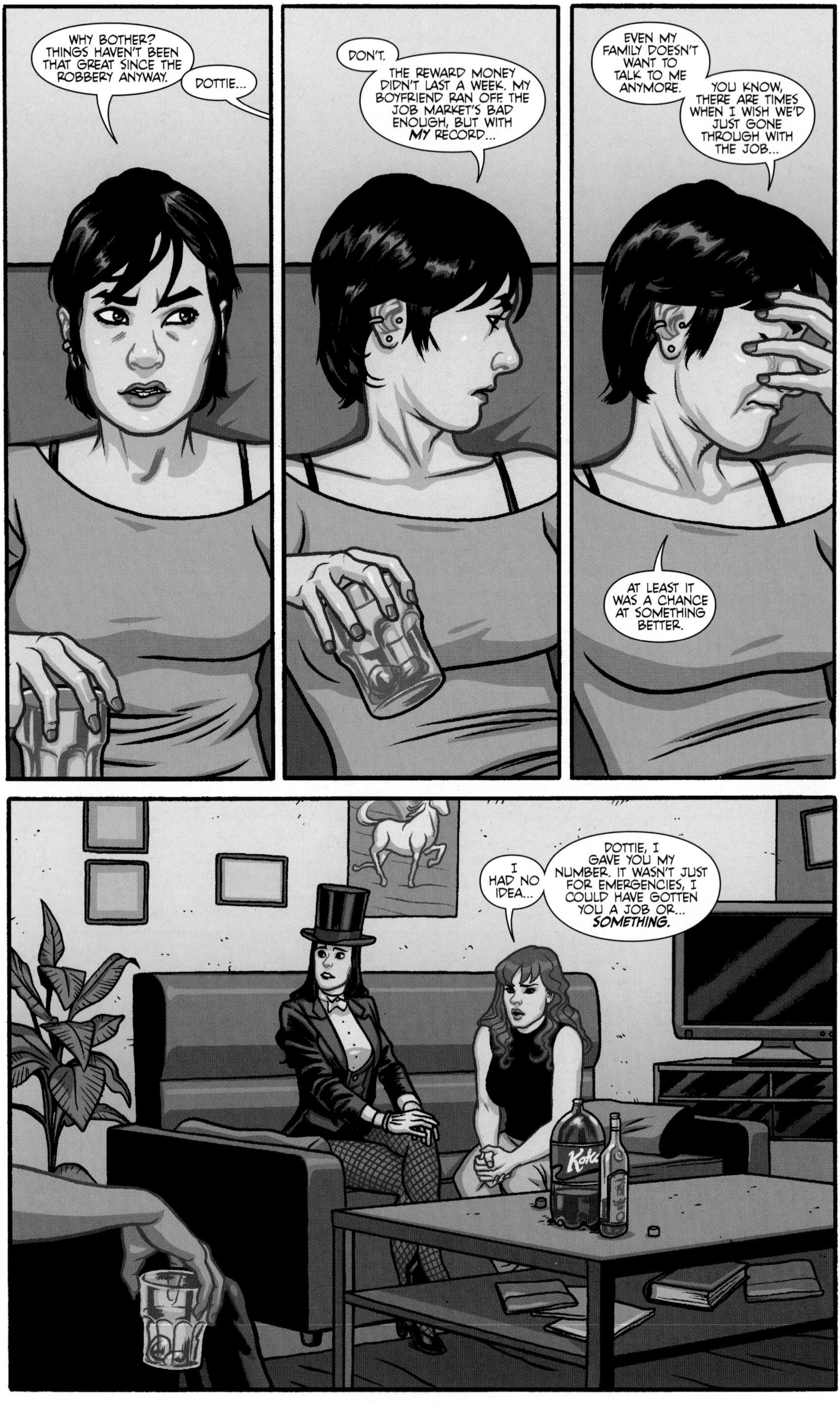
WHY BOTHER? THINGS HAVEN'T BEEN THAT GREAT SINCE THE ROBBERY ANYWAY.
DOTTIE...
DON'T.
THE REWARD MONEY DIDN'T LAST A WEEK. MY BOYFRIEND RAN OFF. THE JOB MARKET'S BAD ENOUGH, BUT WITH *MY* RECORD...
EVEN MY FAMILY DOESN'T WANT TO TALK TO ME ANYMORE.
YOU KNOW, THERE ARE TIMES WHEN I WISH WE'D JUST GONE THROUGH WITH THE JOB...
AT LEAST IT WAS A CHANCE AT SOMETHING BETTER.
I HAD NO IDEA...
DOTTIE, I GAVE YOU MY NUMBER. IT WASN'T JUST FOR EMERGENCIES, I COULD HAVE GOTTEN YOU A JOB OR... *SOMETHING.*

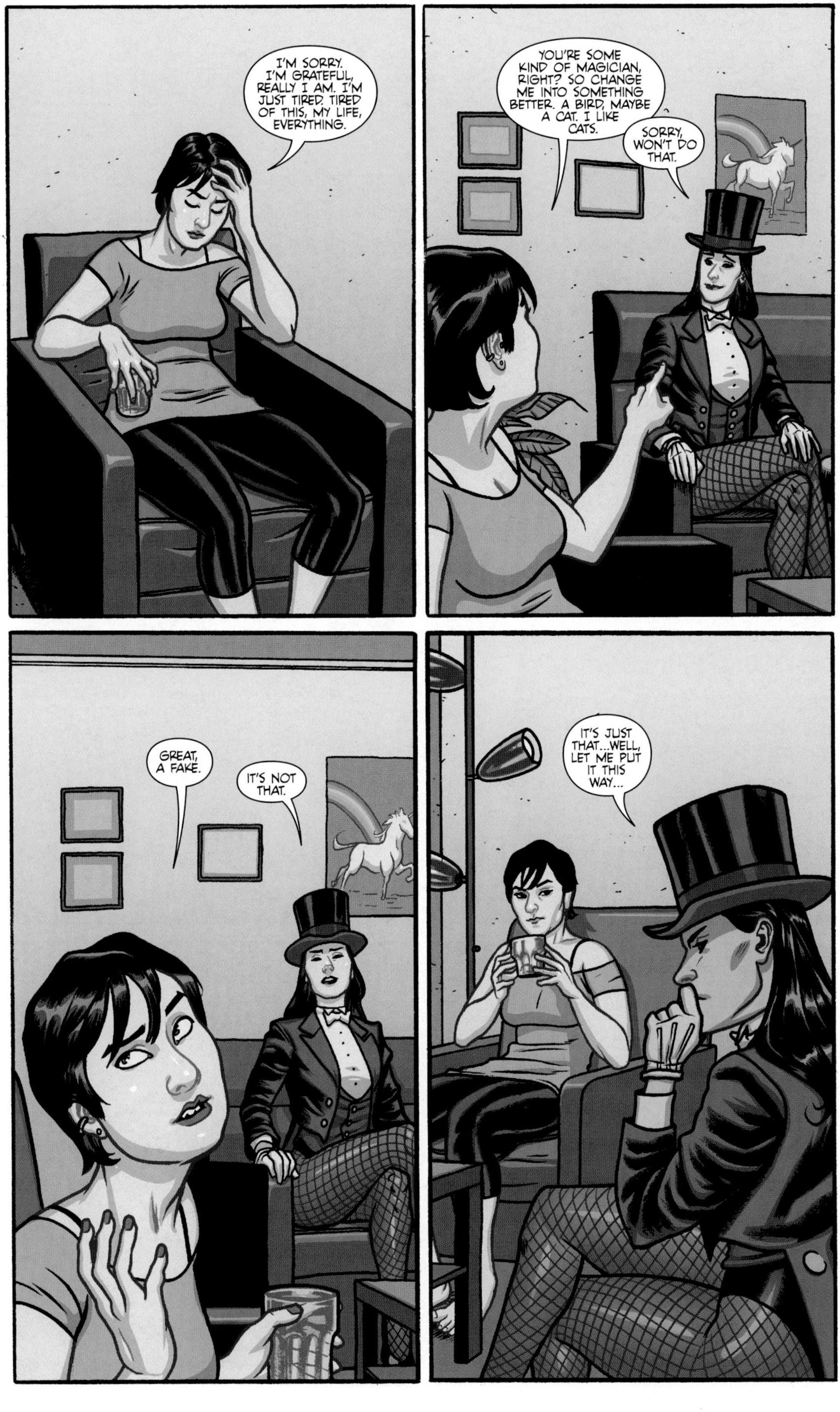
I'M SORRY. I'M GRATEFUL, REALLY I AM. I'M JUST TIRED. TIRED OF THIS, MY LIFE, EVERYTHING.
YOU'RE SOME KIND OF MAGICIAN, RIGHT? SO CHANGE ME INTO SOMETHING BETTER. A BIRD, MAYBE A CAT. I LIKE CATS.
SORRY, WON'T DO THAT.
GREAT, A FAKE.
IT'S NOT THAT.
IT'S JUST THAT...WELL, LET ME PUT IT THIS WAY...

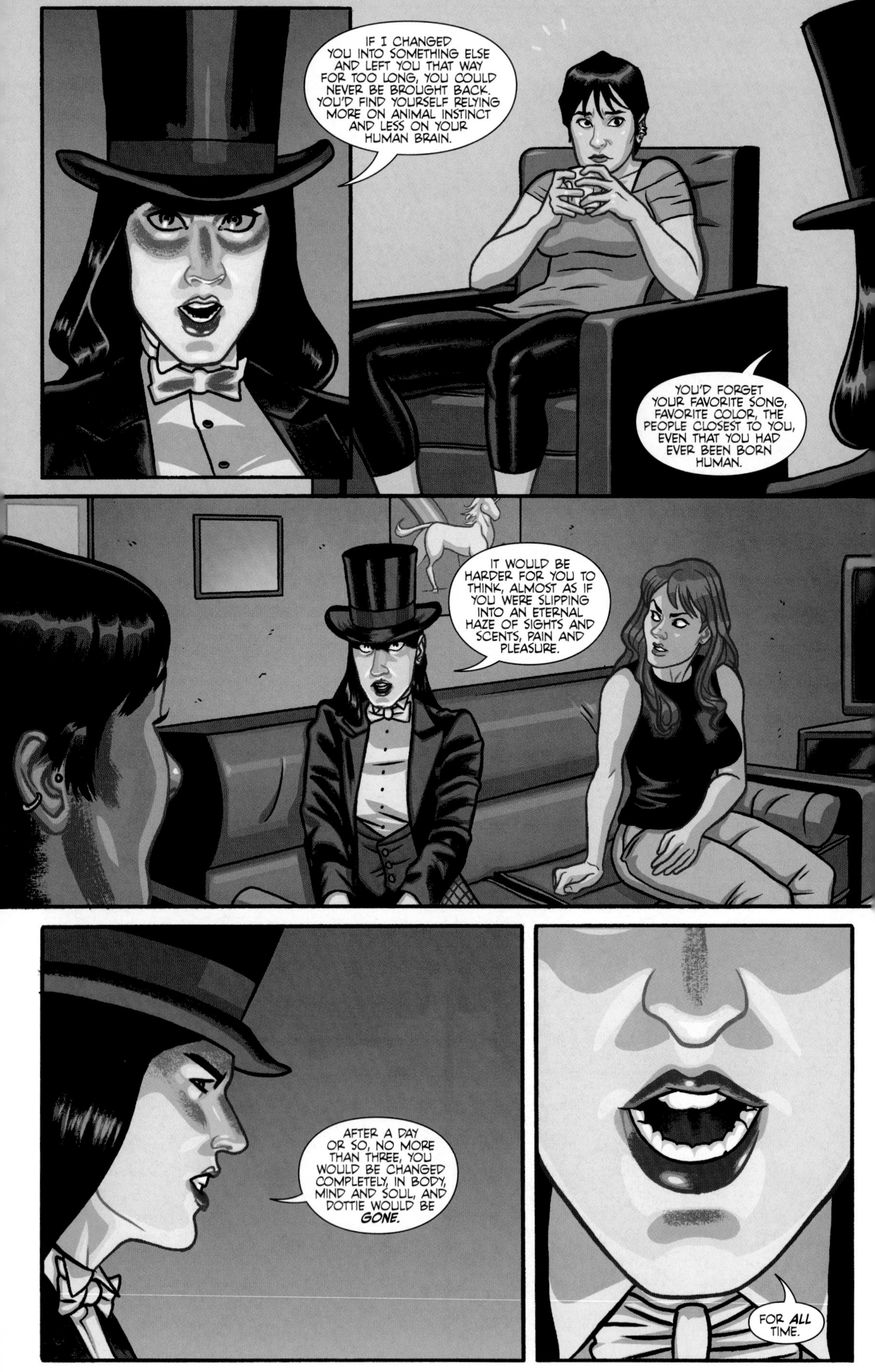
IF I CHANGED YOU INTO SOMETHING ELSE AND LEFT YOU THAT WAY FOR TOO LONG, YOU COULD NEVER BE BROUGHT BACK. YOU'D FIND YOURSELF RELYING MORE ON ANIMAL INSTINCT AND LESS ON YOUR HUMAN BRAIN.
YOU'D FORGET YOUR FAVORITE SONG, FAVORITE COLOR, THE PEOPLE CLOSEST TO YOU, EVEN THAT YOU HAD EVER BEEN BORN HUMAN.
IT WOULD BE HARDER FOR YOU TO THINK, ALMOST AS IF YOU WERE SLIPPING INTO AN ETERNAL HAZE OF SIGHTS AND SCENTS, PAIN AND PLEASURE.
AFTER A DAY OR SO, NO MORE THAN THREE, YOU WOULD BE CHANGED COMPLETELY, IN BODY, MIND AND SOUL, AND DOTTIE WOULD BE *GONE.*
FOR *ALL* TIME.

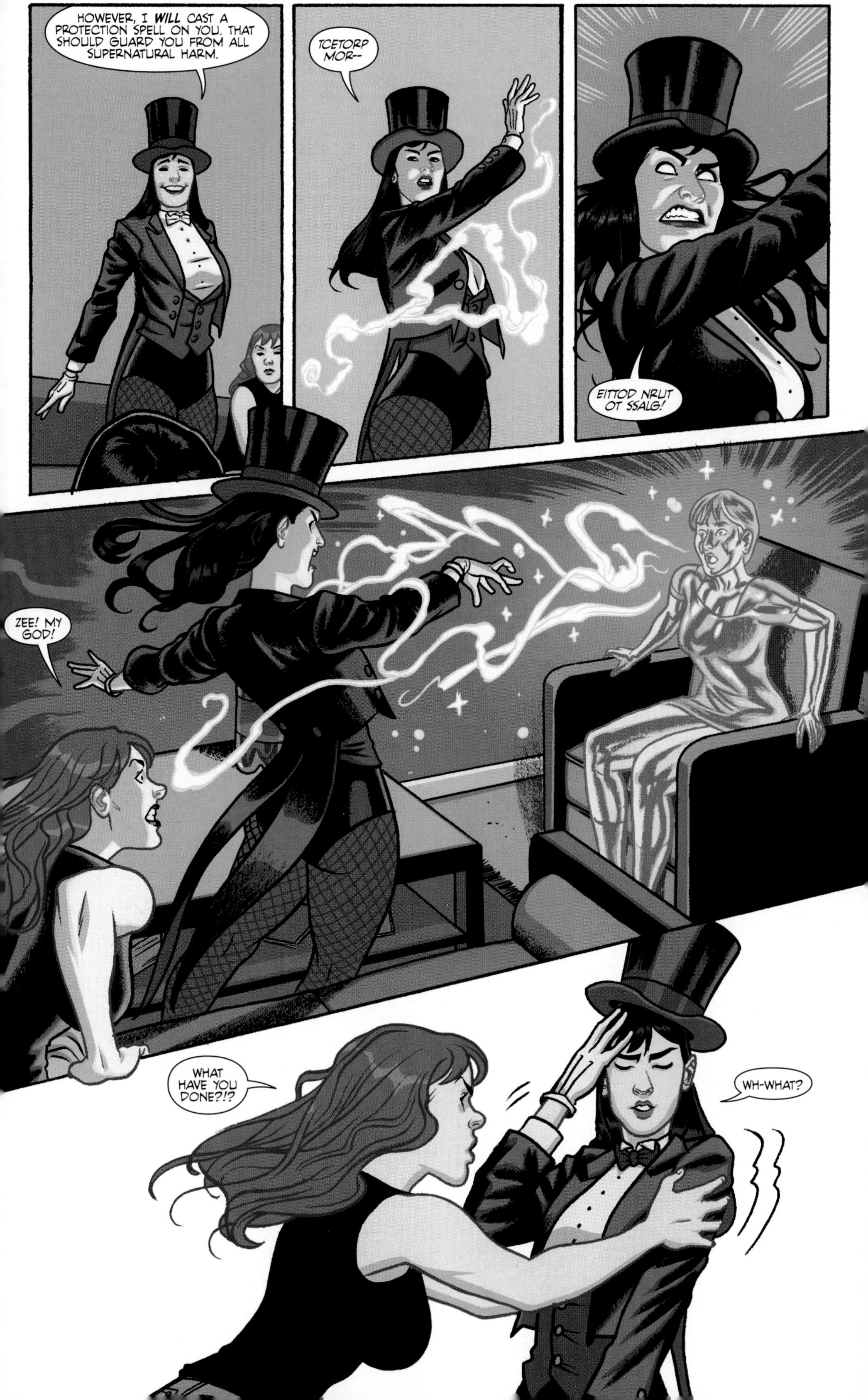
HOWEVER, I WILL CAST A PROTECTION SPELL ON YOU. THAT SHOULD GUARD YOU FROM ALL SUPERNATURAL HARM.
TCETORP MOR--
EITTOD NRUT OT SSALG!
ZEE! MY GOD!
WHAT HAVE YOU DONE?!?
WH-WHAT?

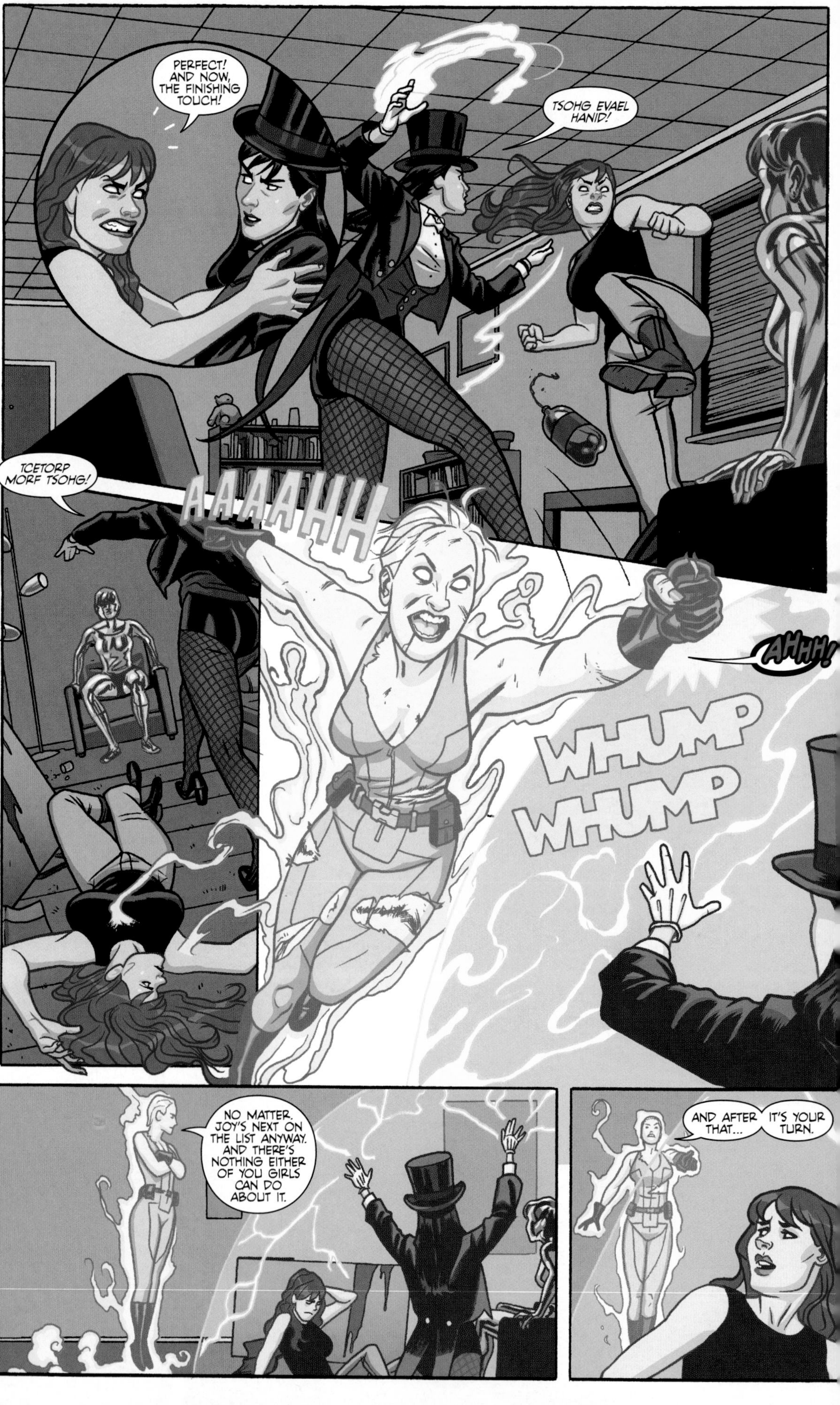

PERFECT! AND NOW, THE FINISHING TOUCH!
TSOHG EVAEL HANID!
TCETORP MORF TSOHG!
AAAAAHH
AHHH!
WHUMP WHUMP
NO MATTER. JOY'S NEXT ON THE LIST ANYWAY. AND THERE'S NOTHING EITHER OF YOU GIRLS CAN DO ABOUT IT.
AND AFTER THAT...
IT'S YOUR TURN.

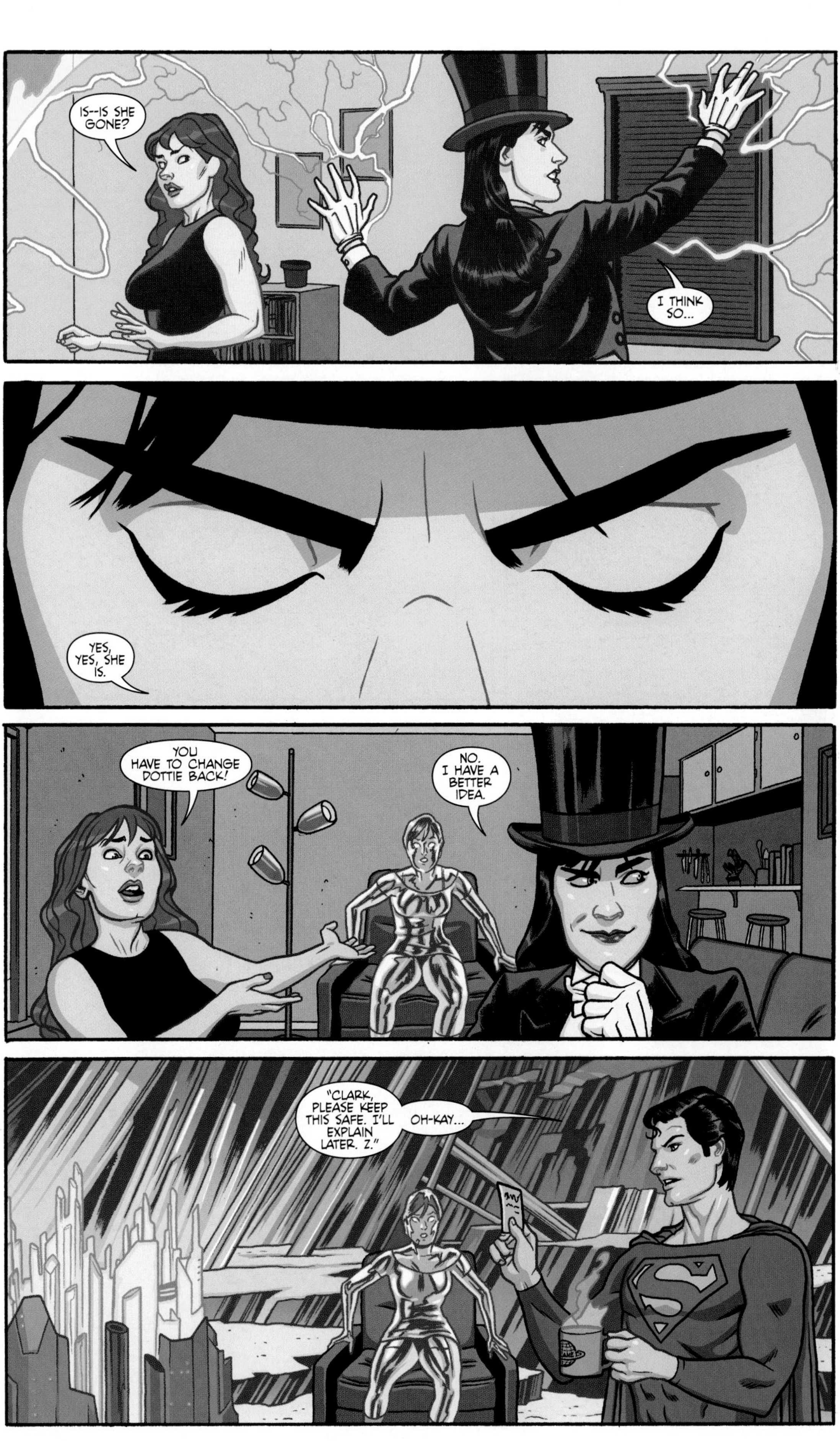
IS--IS SHE GONE?
I THINK SO...
YES, YES, SHE IS.
YOU HAVE TO CHANGE DOTTIE BACK!
NO. I HAVE A BETTER IDEA.
"CLARK, PLEASE KEEP THIS SAFE. I'LL EXPLAIN LATER. Z."
OH-KAY...

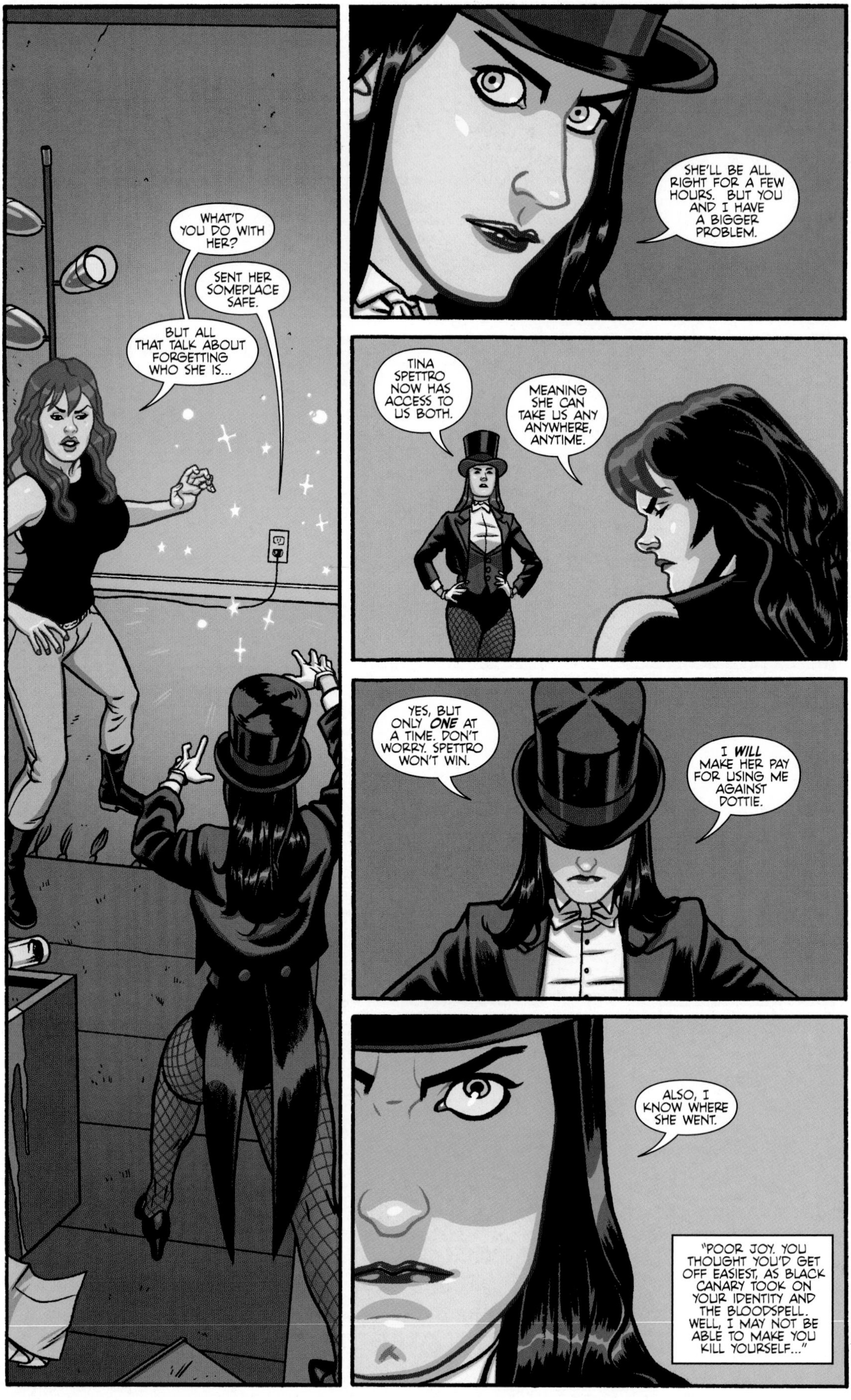
WHAT'D YOU DO WITH HER?
SENT HER SOMEPLACE SAFE.
BUT ALL THAT TALK ABOUT FORGETTING WHO SHE IS...
SHE'LL BE ALL RIGHT FOR A FEW HOURS. BUT YOU AND I HAVE A BIGGER PROBLEM.
TINA SPETTRO NOW HAS ACCESS TO US BOTH.
MEANING SHE CAN TAKE US ANY ANYWHERE, ANYTIME.
YES, BUT ONLY ONE AT A TIME. DON'T WORRY. SPETTRO WON'T WIN.
I WILL MAKE HER PAY FOR USING ME AGAINST DOTTIE.
ALSO, I KNOW WHERE SHE WENT.
"POOR JOY. YOU THOUGHT YOU'D GET OFF EASIEST, AS BLACK CANARY TOOK ON YOUR IDENTITY AND THE BLOODSPELL. WELL, I MAY NOT BE ABLE TO MAKE YOU KILL YOURSELF..."

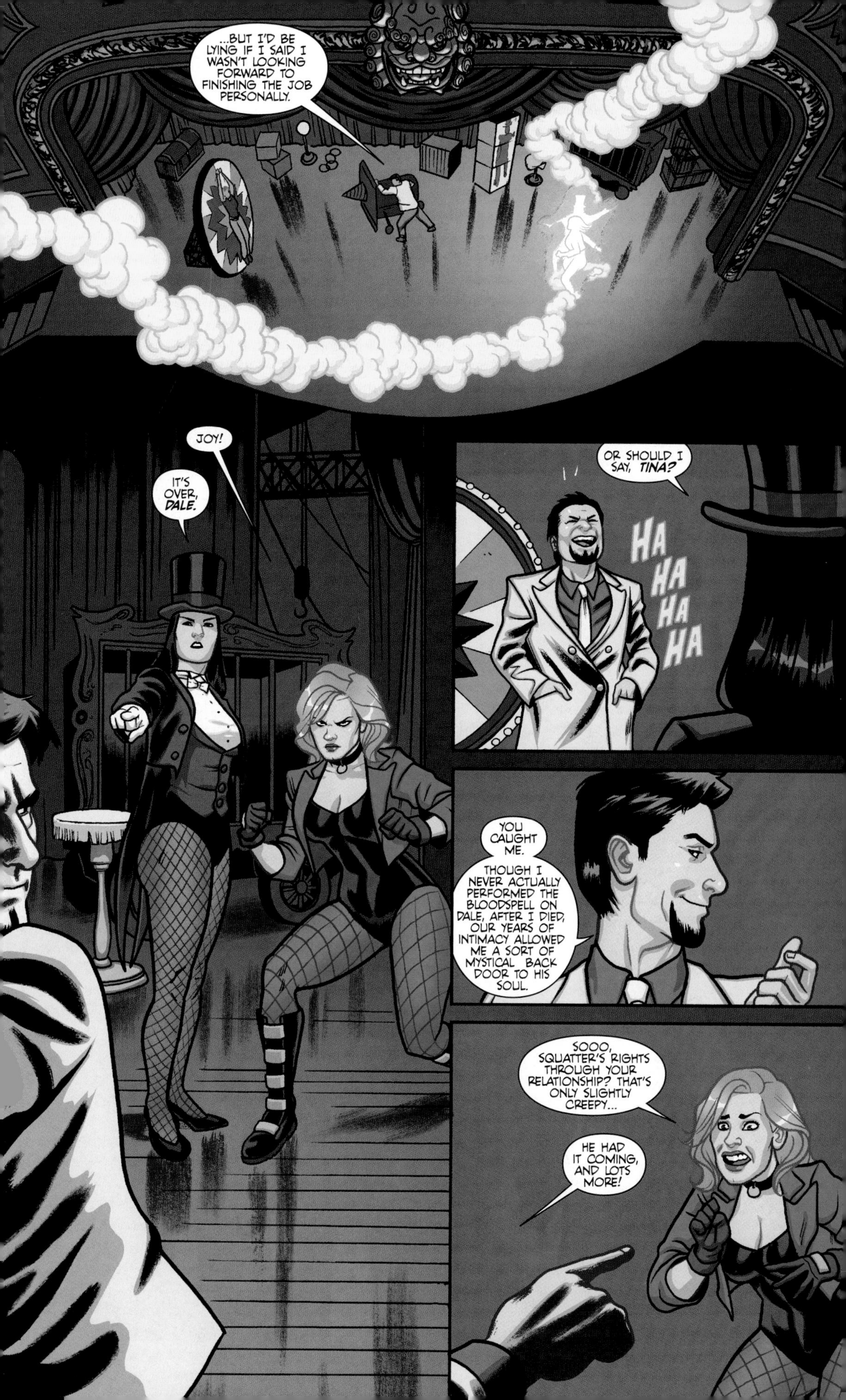
...BUT I'D BE LYING IF I SAID I WASN'T LOOKING FORWARD TO FINISHING THE JOB PERSONALLY.
JOY!
IT'S OVER, DALE.
OR SHOULD I SAY, TINA?
HA HA HA HA
YOU CAUGHT ME.
THOUGH I NEVER ACTUALLY PERFORMED THE BLOODSPELL ON DALE, AFTER I DIED, OUR YEARS OF INTIMACY ALLOWED ME A SORT OF MYSTICAL BACK DOOR TO HIS SOUL.
SOOO, SQUATTER'S RIGHTS THROUGH YOUR RELATIONSHIP? THAT'S ONLY SLIGHTLY CREEPY...
HE HAD IT COMING, AND LOTS MORE!

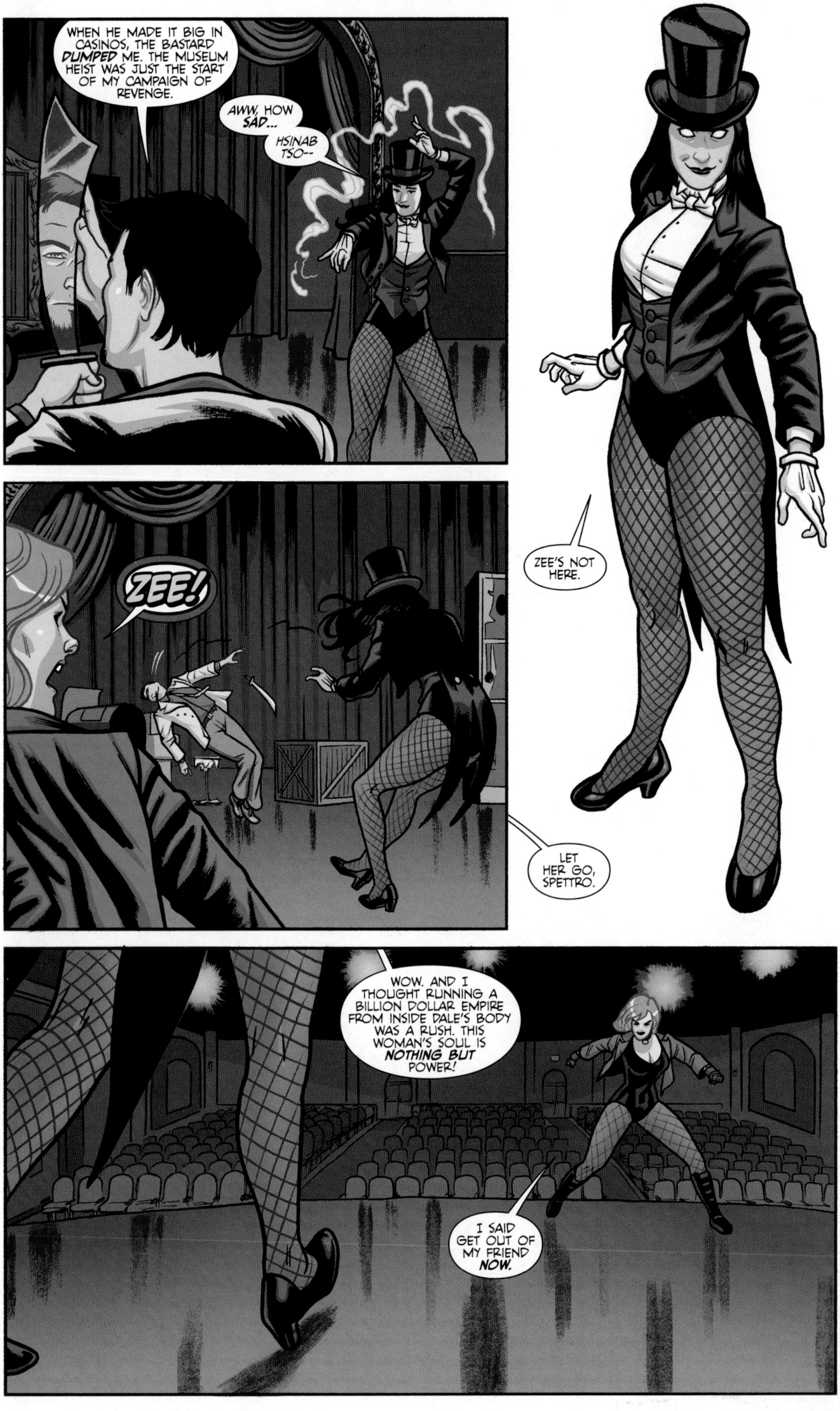

WHEN HE MADE IT BIG IN CASINOS, THE BASTARD *DUMPED* ME. THE MUSEUM HEIST WAS JUST THE START OF MY CAMPAIGN OF REVENGE.
AWW, HOW *SAD...*
HSINAB TSO--
ZEE!
ZEE'S NOT HERE.
LET HER GO, SPETTRO.
WOW. AND I THOUGHT RUNNING A BILLION DOLLAR EMPIRE FROM INSIDE DALE'S BODY WAS A RUSH. THIS WOMAN'S SOUL IS *NOTHING BUT* POWER!
I SAID GET OUT OF MY FRIEND *NOW.*

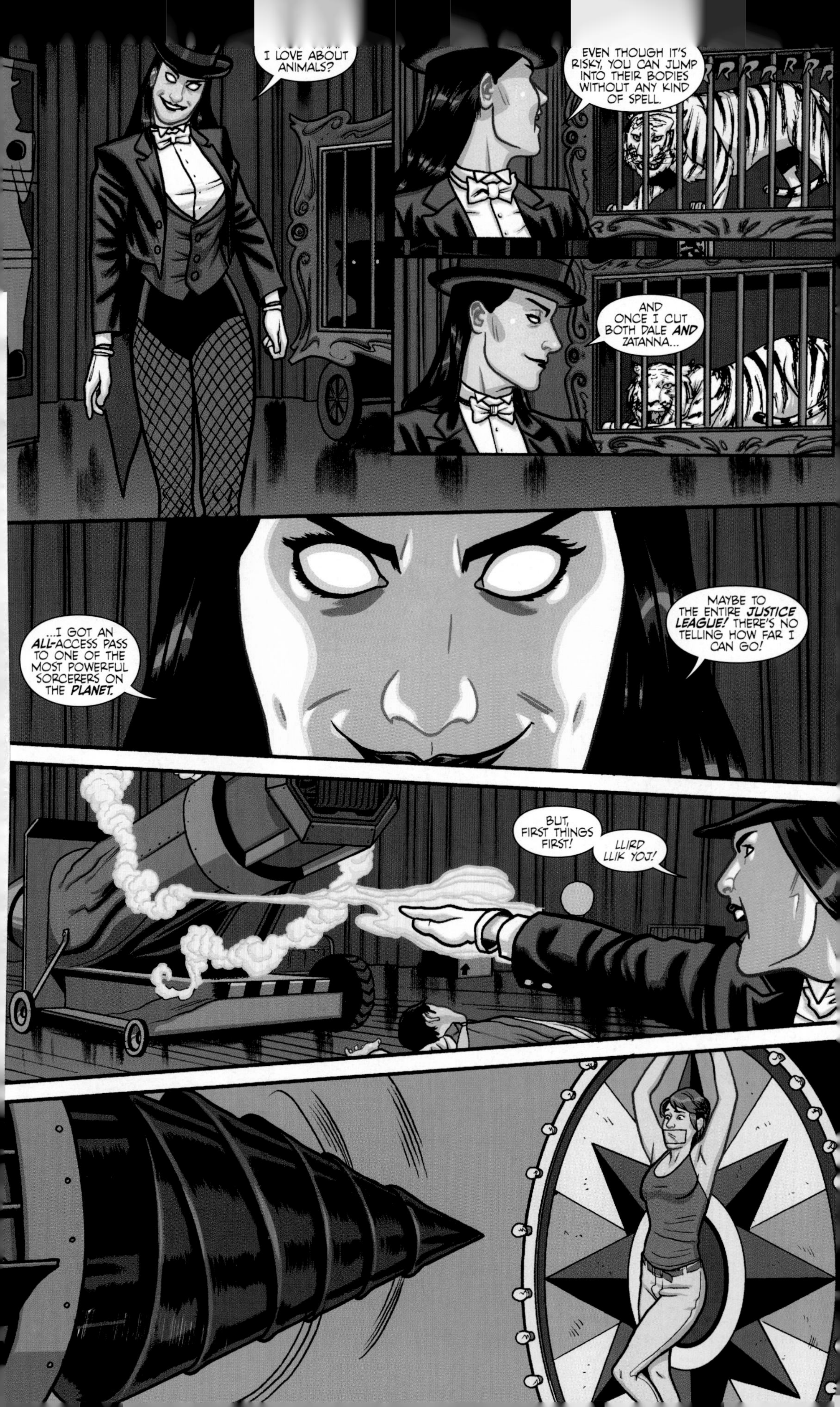
I LOVE ABOUT ANIMALS?
EVEN THOUGH IT'S RISKY, YOU CAN JUMP INTO THEIR BODIES WITHOUT ANY KIND OF SPELL.
RRRRRR
AND ONCE I CUT BOTH DALE AND ZATANNA...
...I GOT AN ALL-ACCESS PASS TO ONE OF THE MOST POWERFUL SORCERERS ON THE PLANET.
MAYBE TO THE ENTIRE JUSTICE LEAGUE! THERE'S NO TELLING HOW FAR I CAN GO!
BUT, FIRST THINGS FIRST!
LLIRD LLIK YOJ!

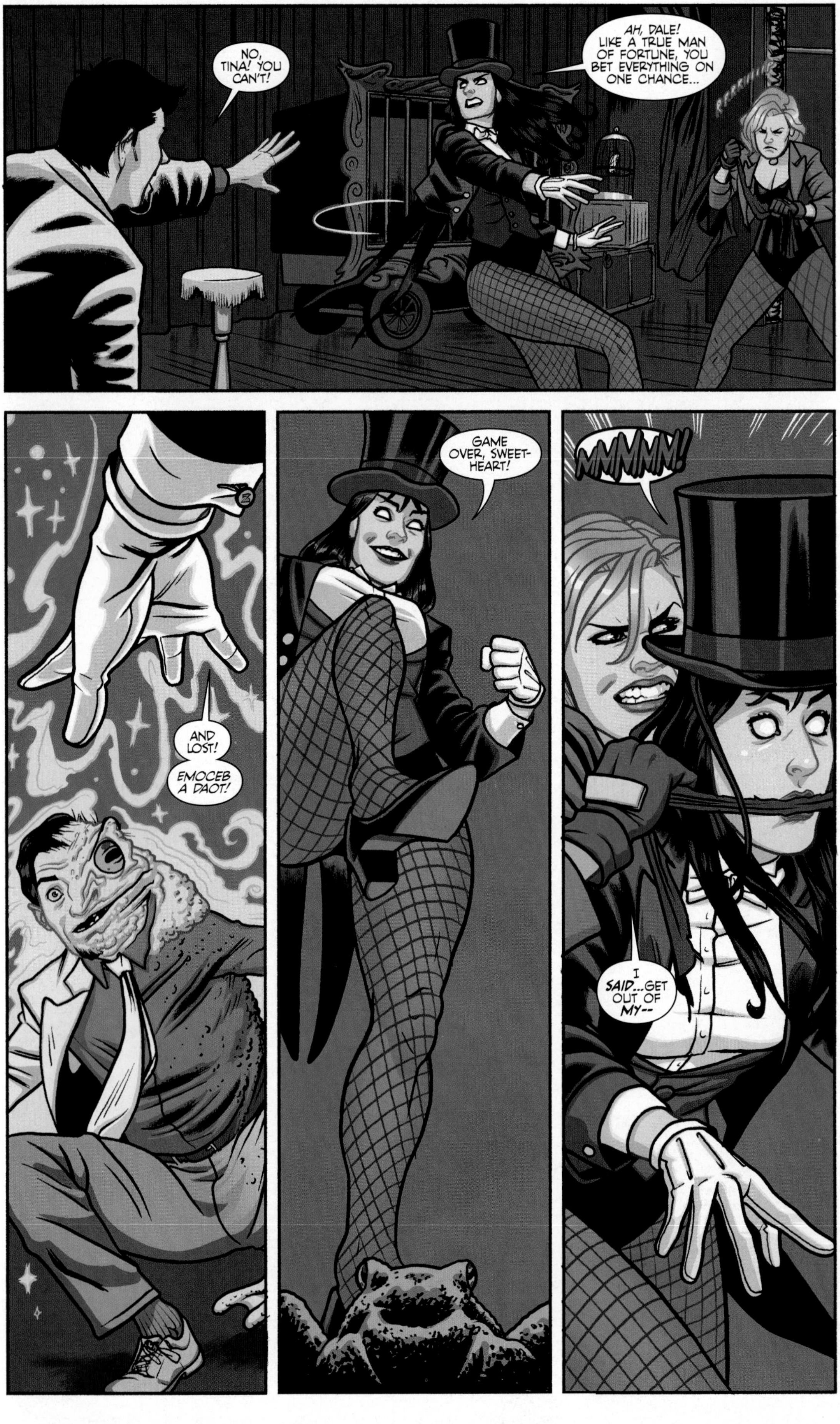
NO, TINA! YOU CAN'T!
AH, DALE! LIKE A TRUE MAN OF FORTUNE, YOU BET EVERYTHING ON ONE CHANCE...
RRRRIIIIIP
AND LOST!
EMOCEB A DAOT!
GAME OVER, SWEET-HEART!
MMMMM!
I SAID...GET OUT OF MY--

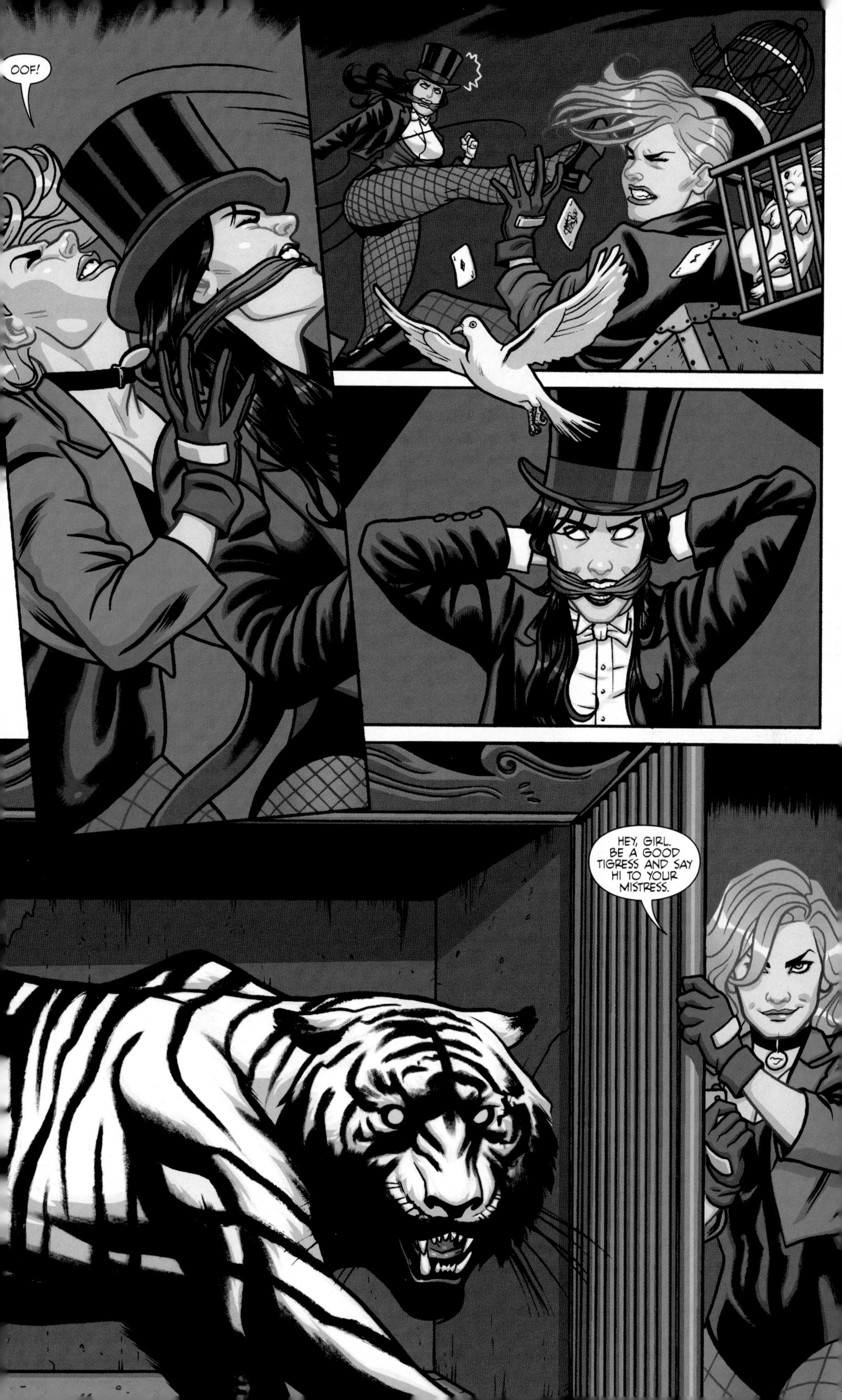
OOF!
HEY, GIRL. BE A GOOD TIGRESS AND SAY HI TO YOUR MISTRESS.

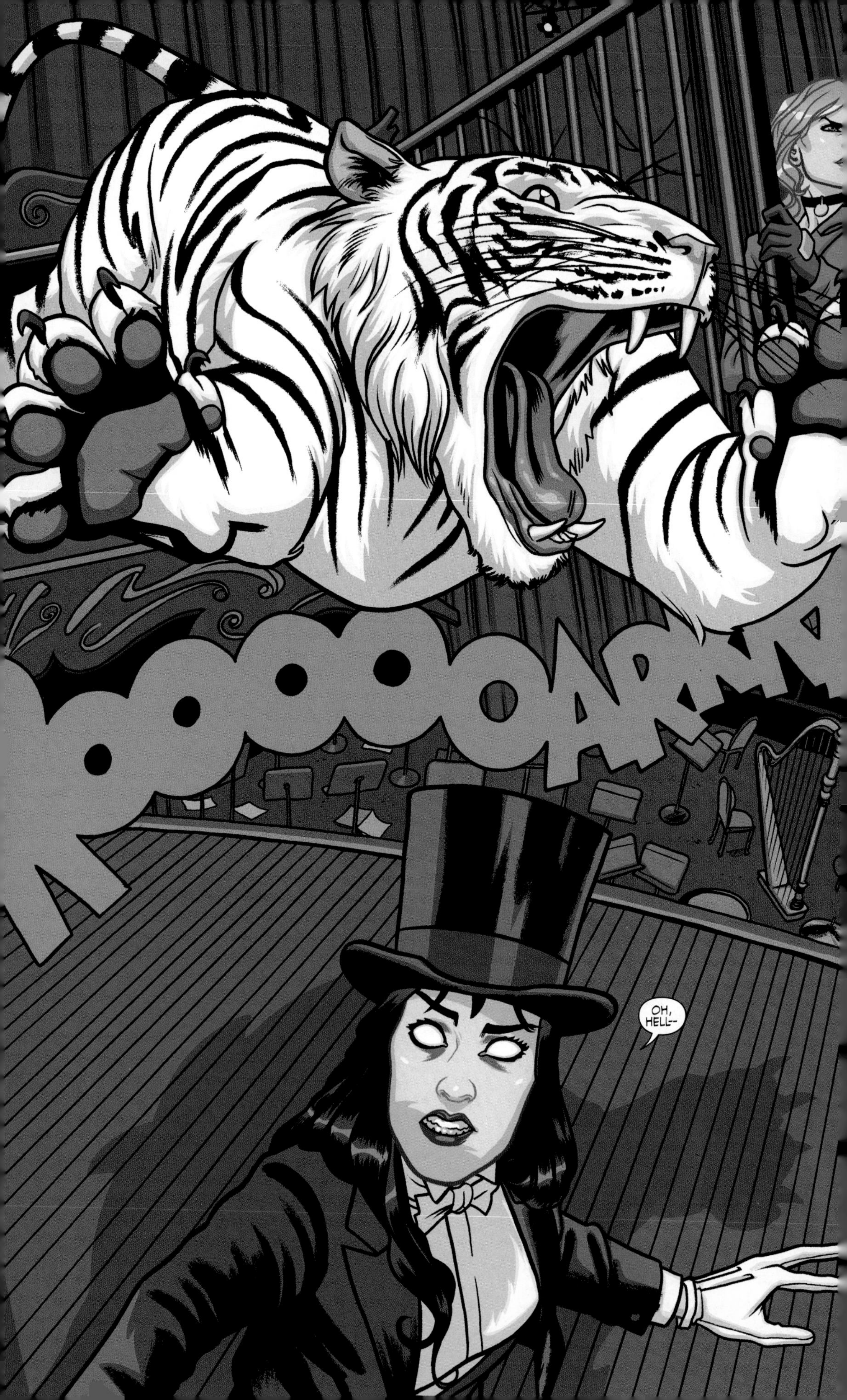
OH, HELL--

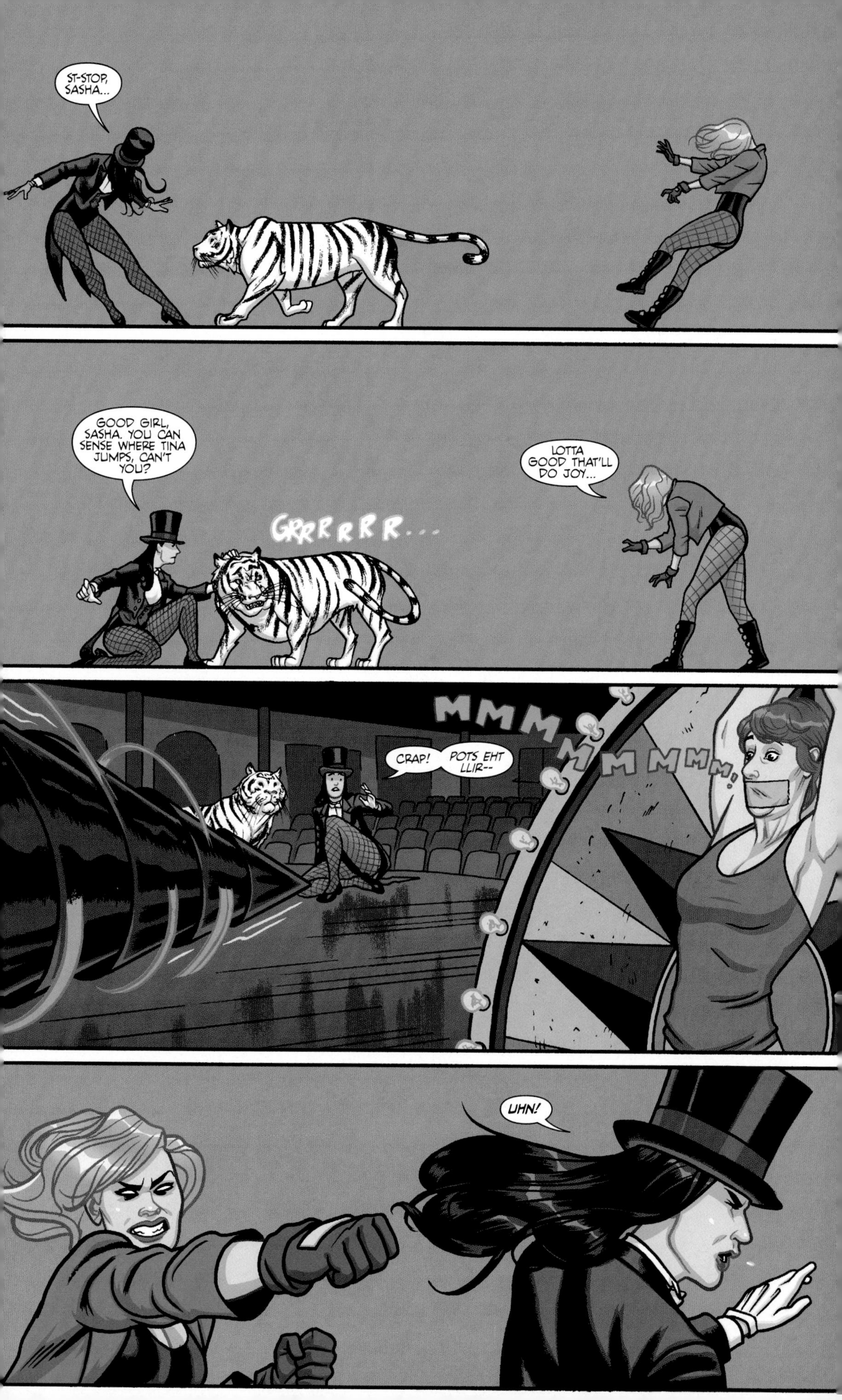

ST-STOP, SASHA...
GOOD GIRL, SASHA. YOU CAN SENSE WHERE TINA JUMPS, CAN'T YOU?
GRRRRRR...
LOTTA GOOD THAT'LL DO JOY...
MMMMMMMMMM!
CRAP!
POTS EHT LLIR--
UHN!

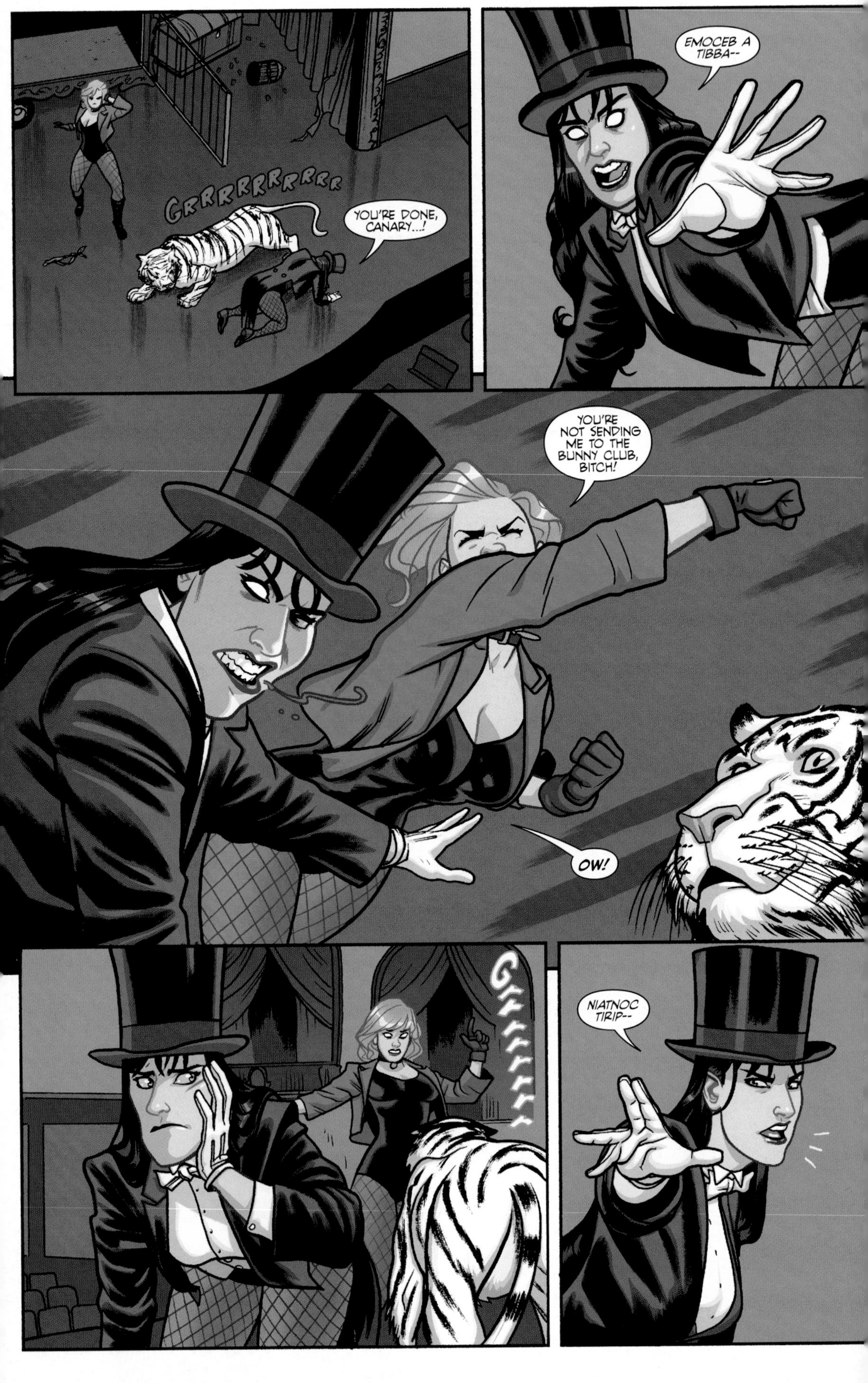

GRRRRRRRRRR
YOU'RE DONE, CANARY...!
EMOCEB A TIBBA--
YOU'RE NOT SENDING ME TO THE BUNNY CLUB, BITCH!
OW!
GRRRRRRRR
NIATNOC TIRIP--

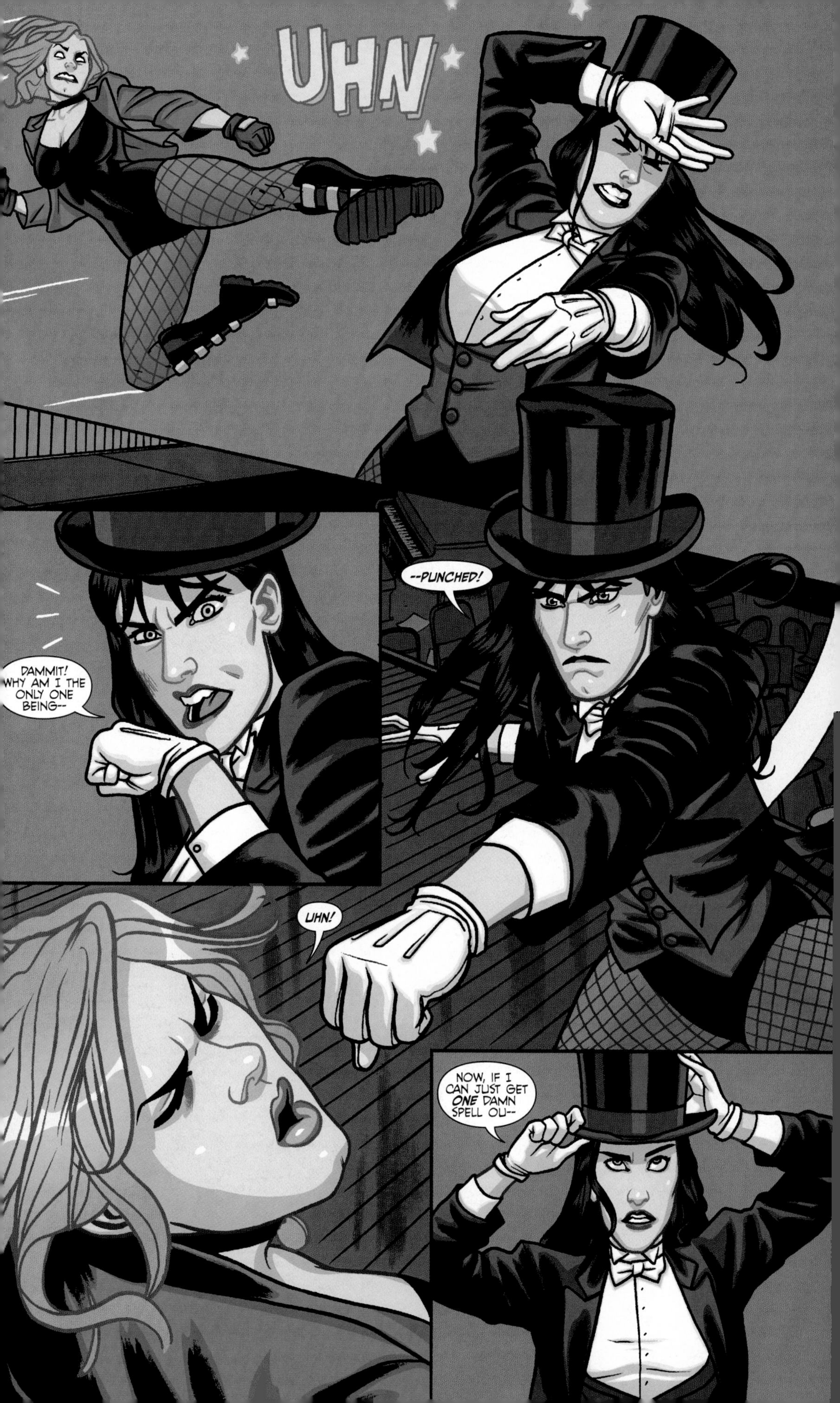
UHN
DAMMIT! WHY AM I THE ONLY ONE BEING--
--PUNCHED!
UHN!
NOW, IF I CAN JUST GET *ONE* DAMN SPELL OU--

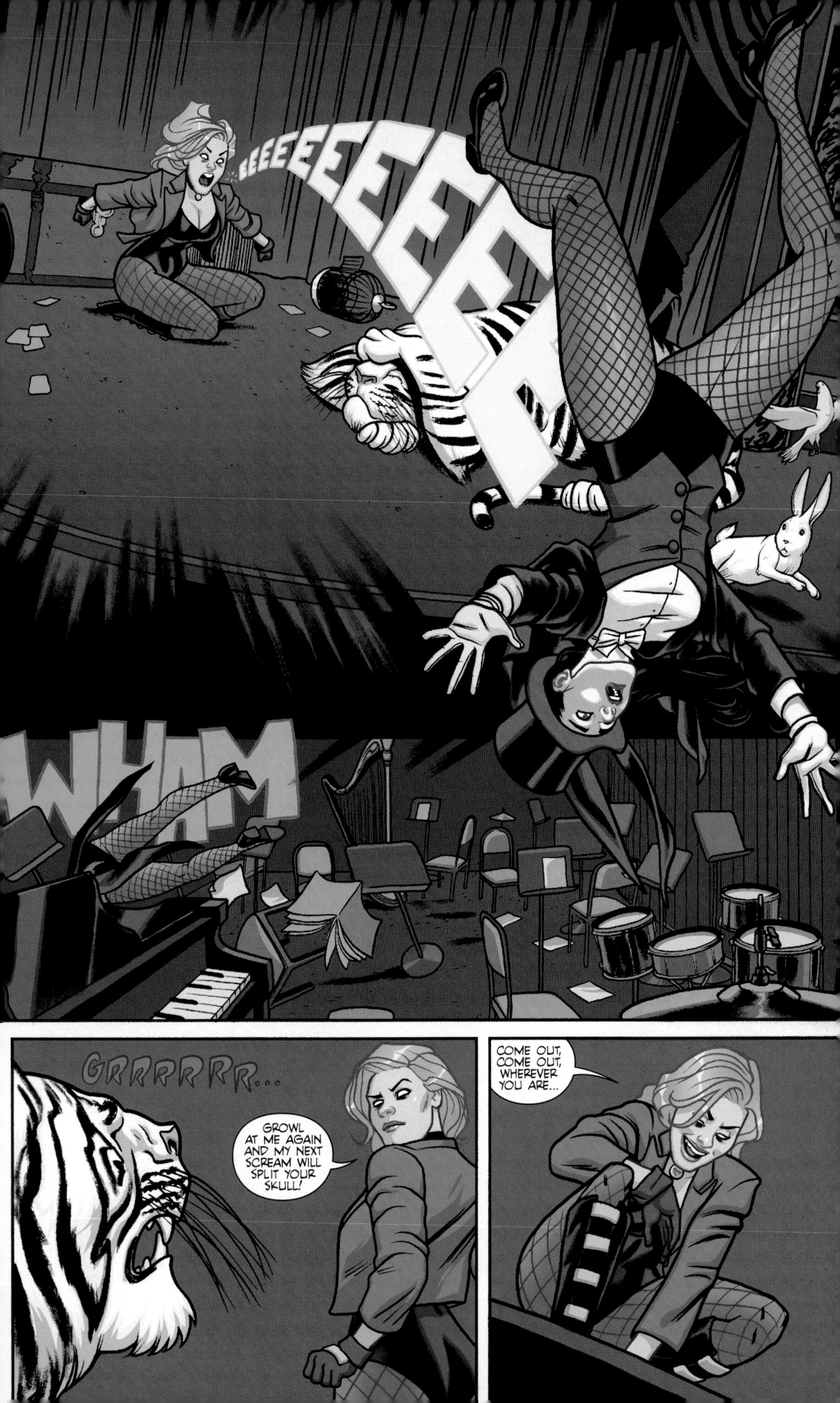

EEEEEEEEEEE
WHAM
GRRRRRRR...
GROWL AT ME AGAIN AND MY NEXT SCREAM WILL SPLIT YOUR SKULL!
COME OUT, COME OUT, WHEREVER YOU ARE...

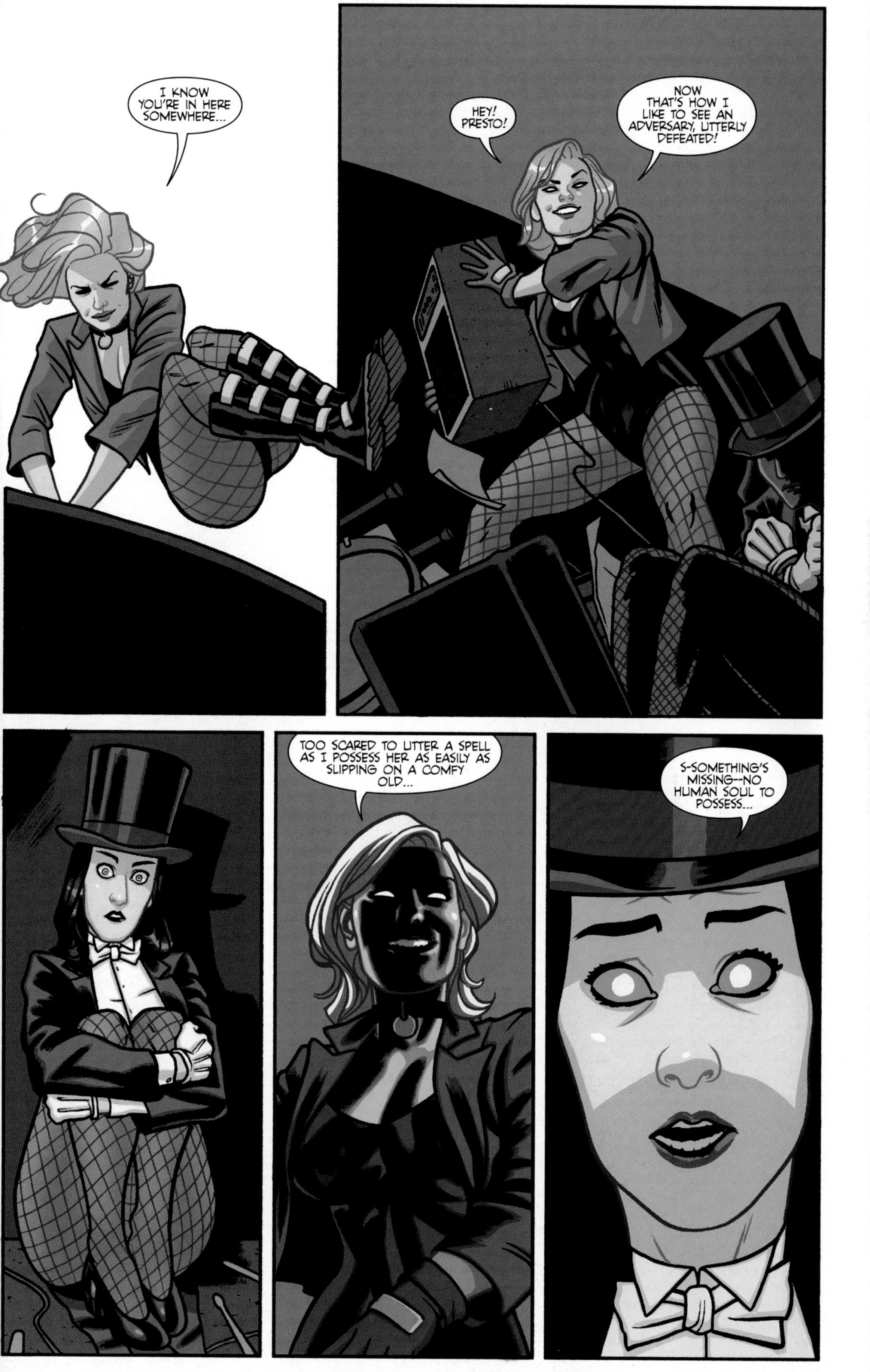
I KNOW YOU'RE IN HERE SOMEWHERE...
HEY! PRESTO!
NOW THAT'S HOW I LIKE TO SEE AN ADVERSARY, UTTERLY DEFEATED!
TOO SCARED TO UTTER A SPELL AS I POSSESS HER AS EASILY AS SLIPPING ON A COMFY OLD...
S-SOMETHING'S MISSING--NO HUMAN SOUL TO POSSESS...

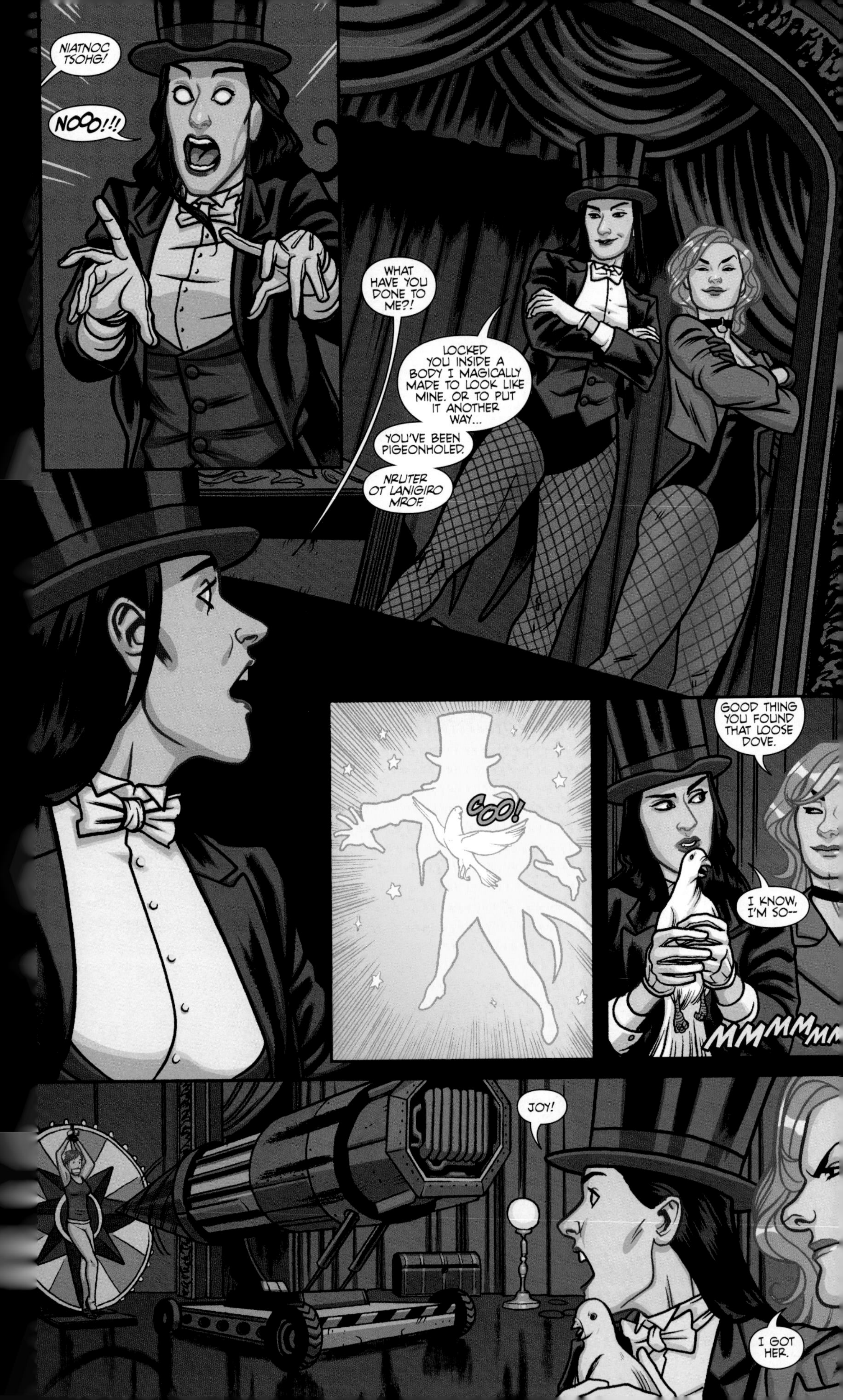
NIATNOC TSOHG!
NOOO!!!
WHAT HAVE YOU DONE TO ME?!
LOCKED YOU INSIDE A BODY I MAGICALLY MADE TO LOOK LIKE MINE. OR TO PUT IT ANOTHER WAY...
YOU'VE BEEN PIGEONHOLED.
NRUTER OT LANIGIRO MROF.
COO!
GOOD THING YOU FOUND THAT LOOSE DOVE.
I KNOW, I'M SO--
MMMMMMA
JOY!
I GOT HER.

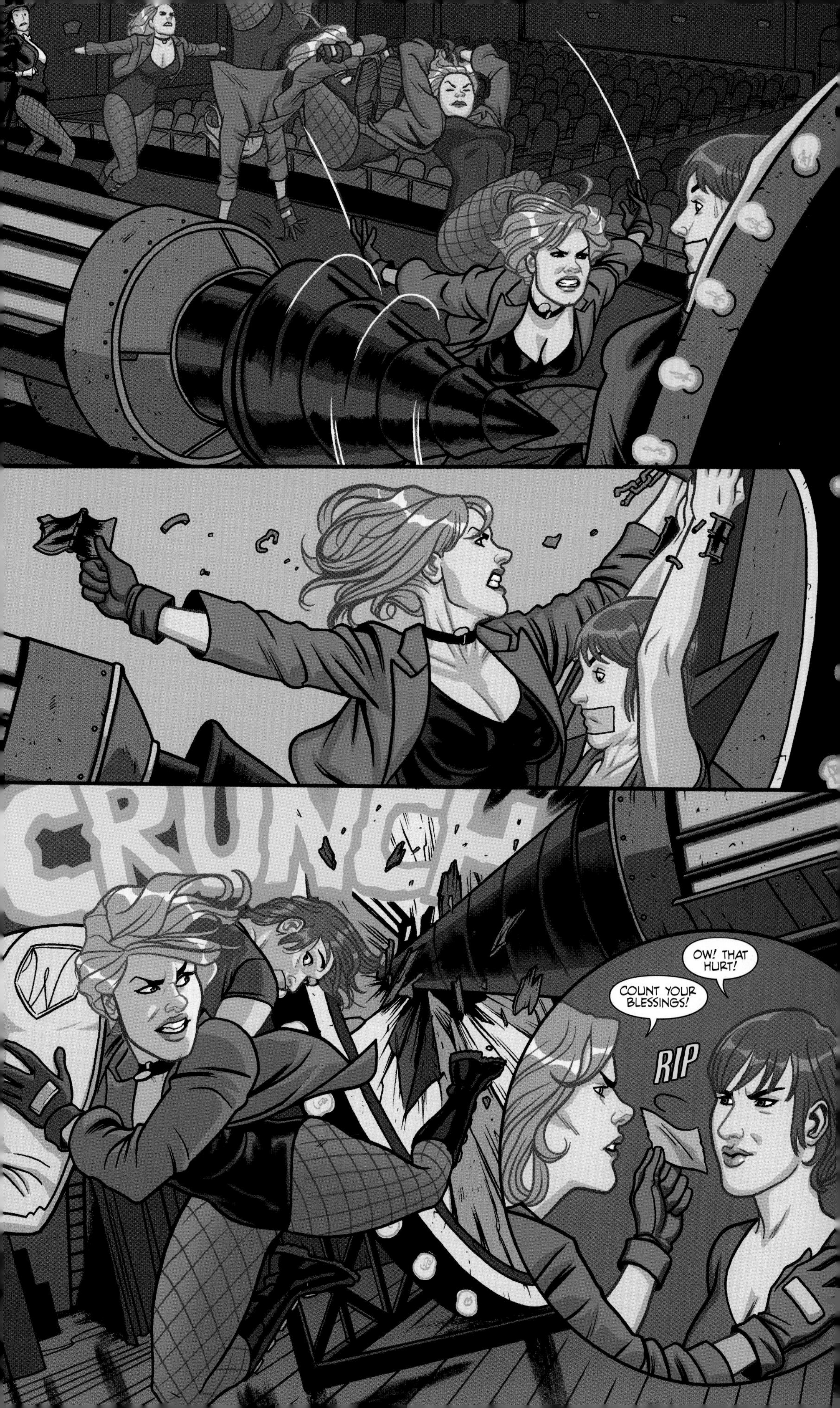
CRUNCH
OW! THAT HURT!
COUNT YOUR BLESSINGS!
RIP

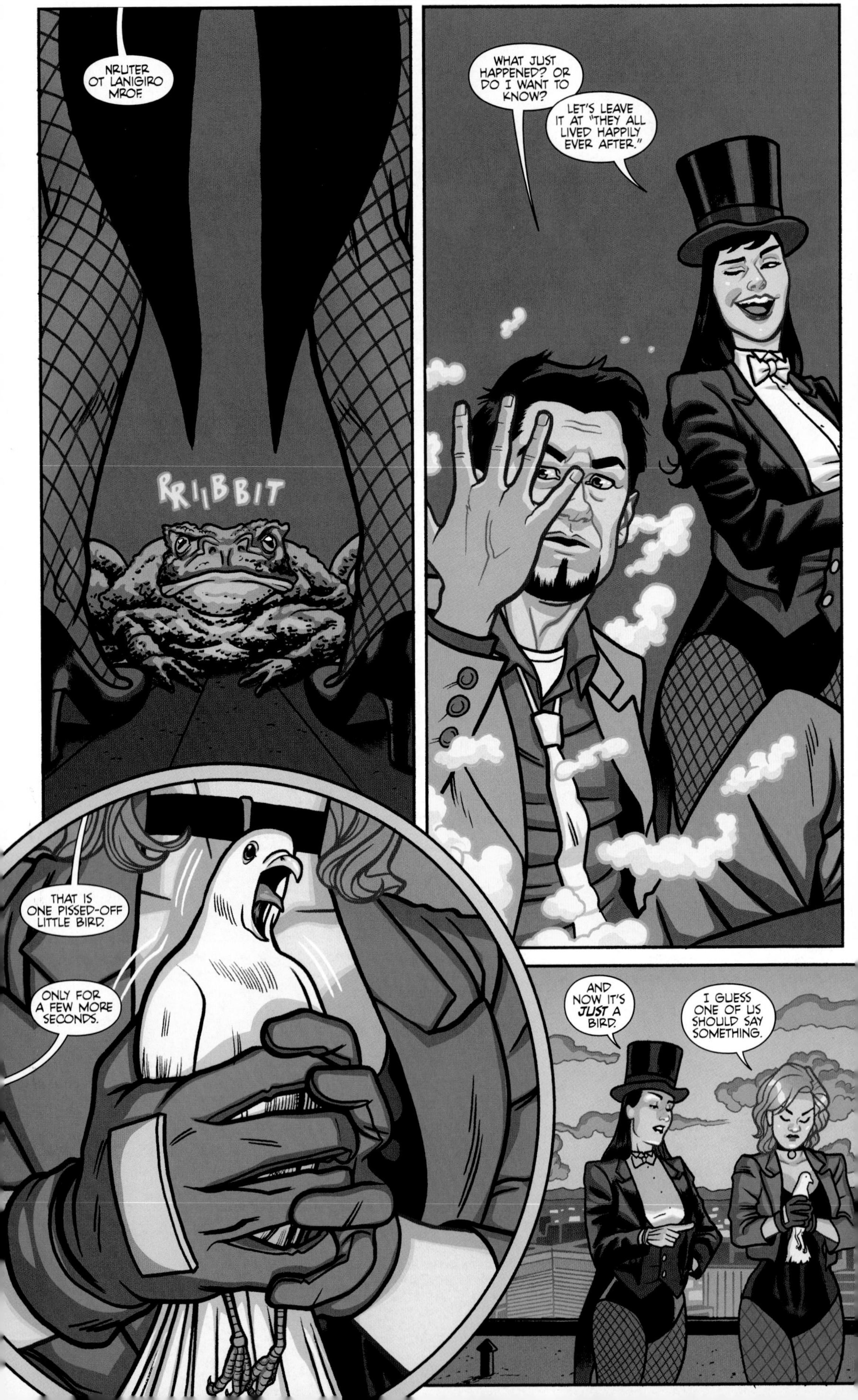
NRUTER OT LANIGIRO MROF.
RRIBBIT
WHAT JUST HAPPENED? OR DO I WANT TO KNOW?
LET'S LEAVE IT AT "THEY ALL LIVED HAPPILY EVER AFTER."
THAT IS ONE PISSED-OFF LITTLE BIRD.
ONLY FOR A FEW MORE SECONDS.
AND NOW IT'S *JUST* A BIRD.
I GUESS ONE OF US SHOULD SAY SOMETHING.

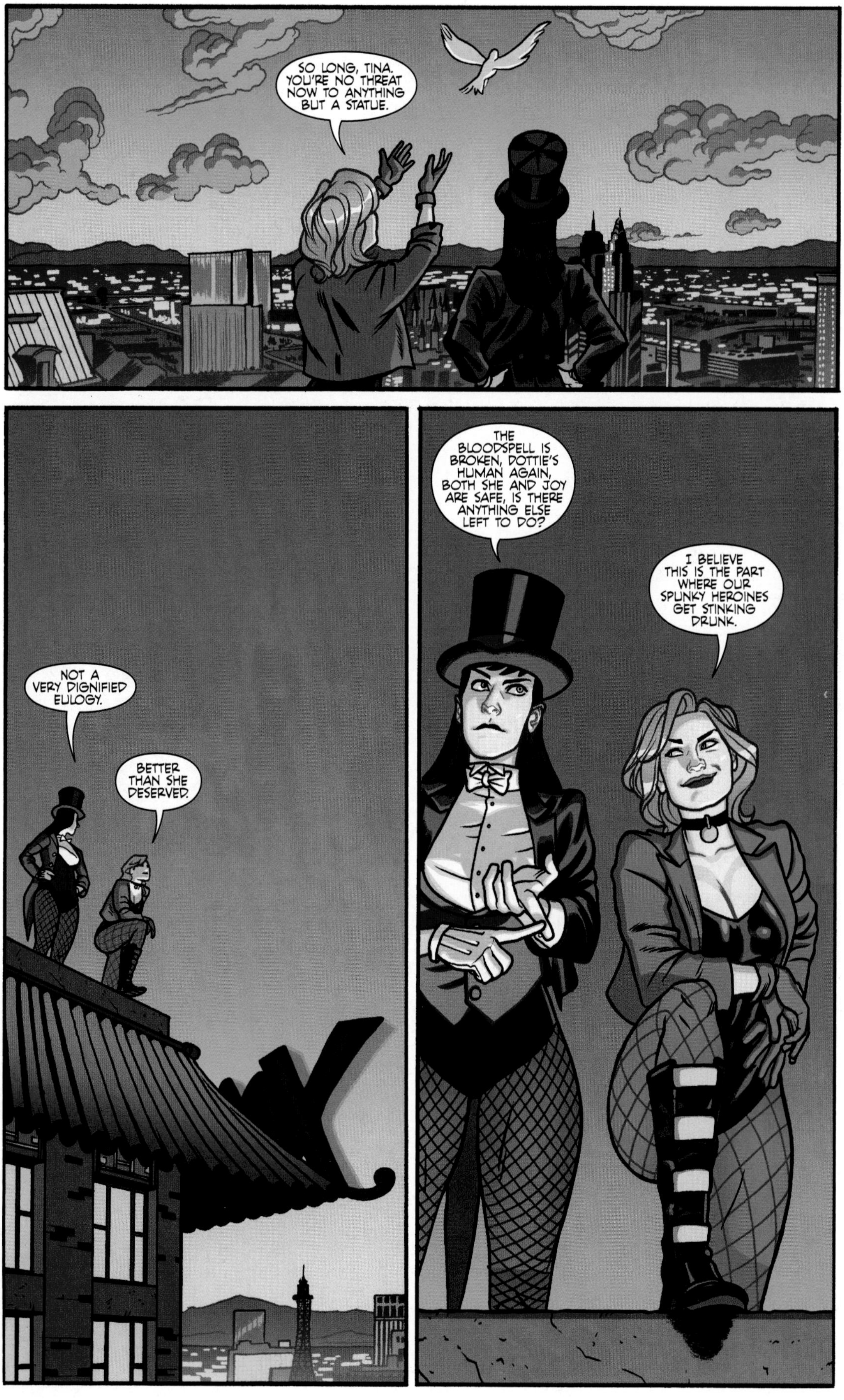
SO LONG, TINA. YOU'RE NO THREAT NOW TO ANYTHING BUT A STATUE.
NOT A VERY DIGNIFIED EULOGY.
BETTER THAN SHE DESERVED.
THE BLOODSPELL IS BROKEN, DOTTIE'S HUMAN AGAIN, BOTH SHE AND JOY ARE SAFE, IS THERE ANYTHING ELSE LEFT TO DO?
I BELIEVE THIS IS THE PART WHERE OUR SPUNKY HEROINES GET STINKING DRUNK.

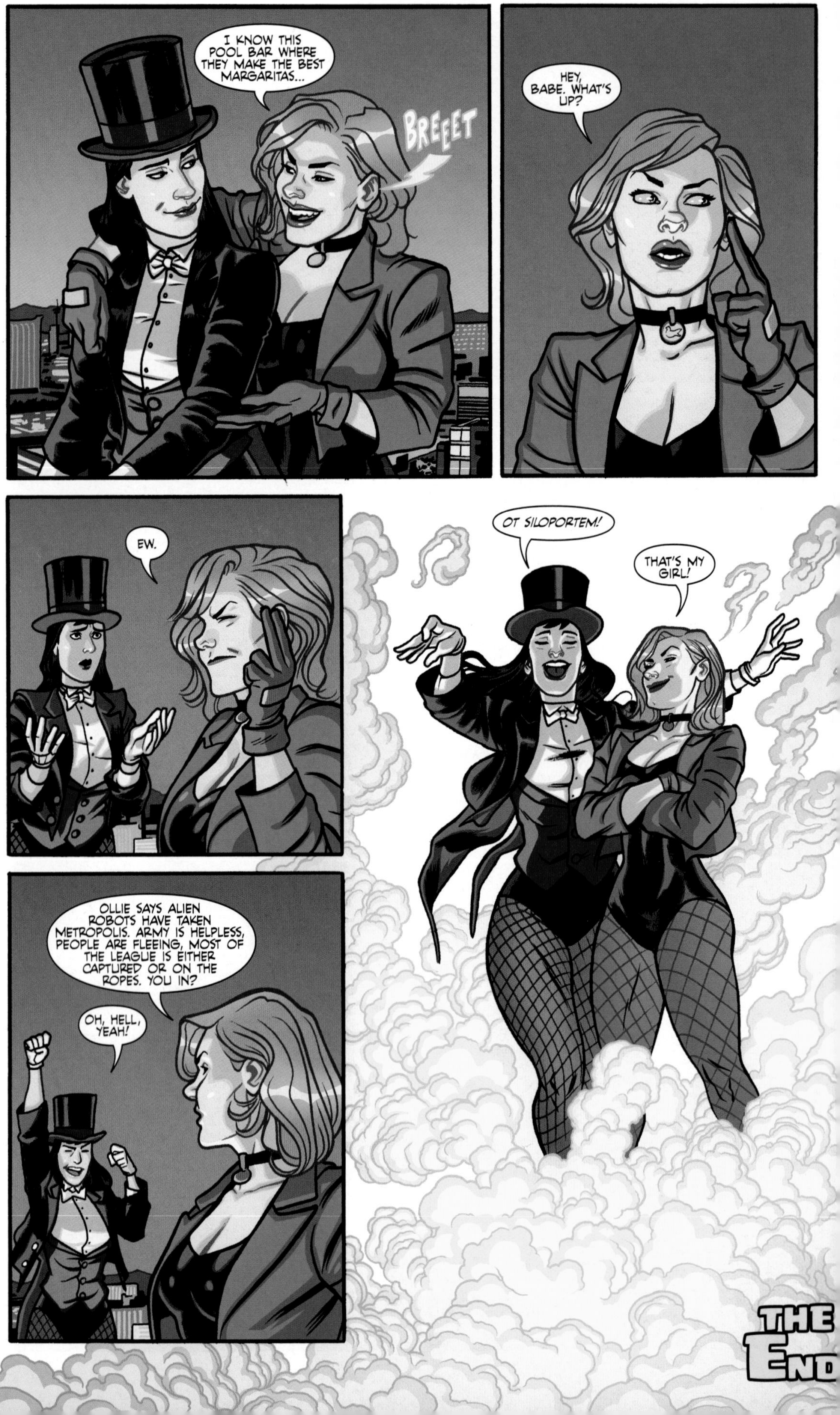
I KNOW THIS POOL BAR WHERE THEY MAKE THE BEST MARGARITAS...
BREEET
HEY, BABE. WHAT'S UP?
EW.
OLLIE SAYS ALIEN ROBOTS HAVE TAKEN METROPOLIS. ARMY IS HELPLESS, PEOPLE ARE FLEEING, MOST OF THE LEAGUE IS EITHER CAPTURED OR ON THE ROPES. YOU IN?
OH, HELL, YEAH!
OT SILOPORTEM!
THAT'S MY GIRL!
THE END

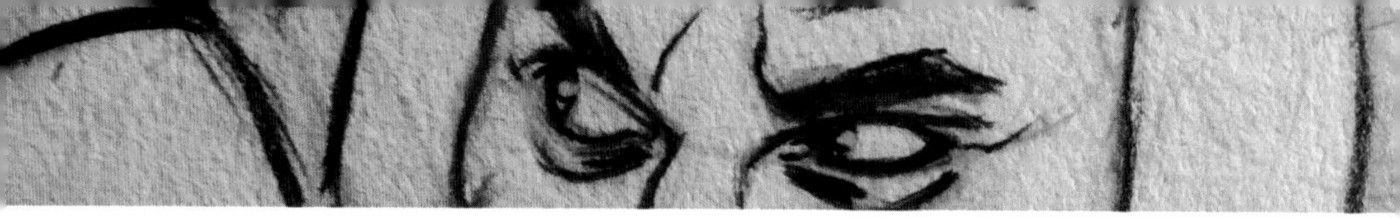

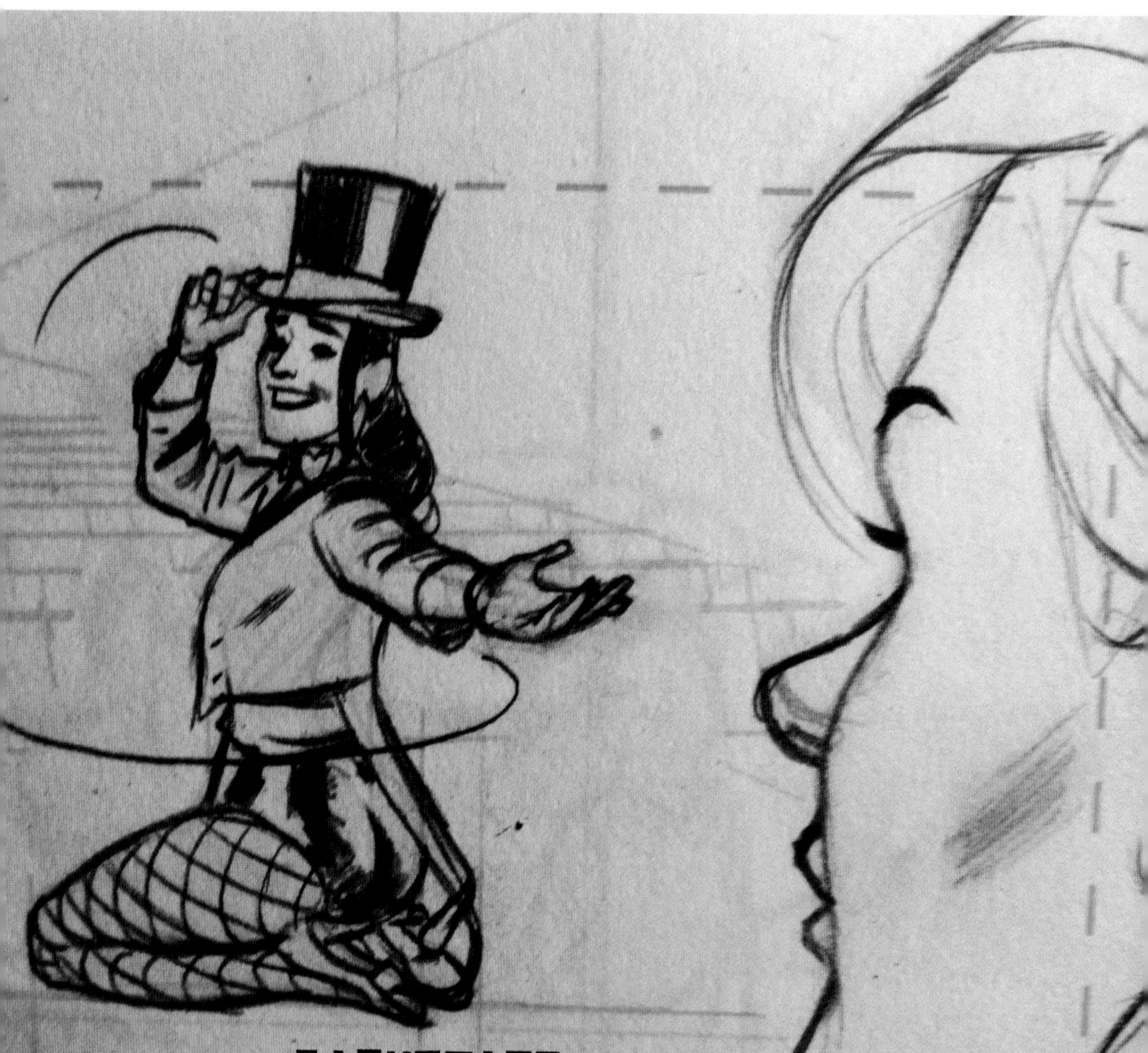

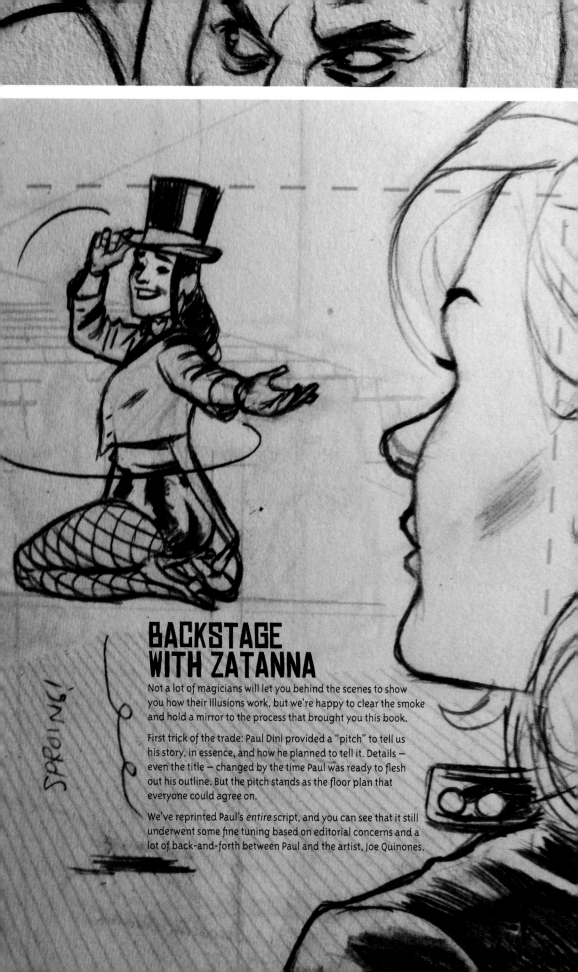

BACKSTAGE WITH ZATANNA

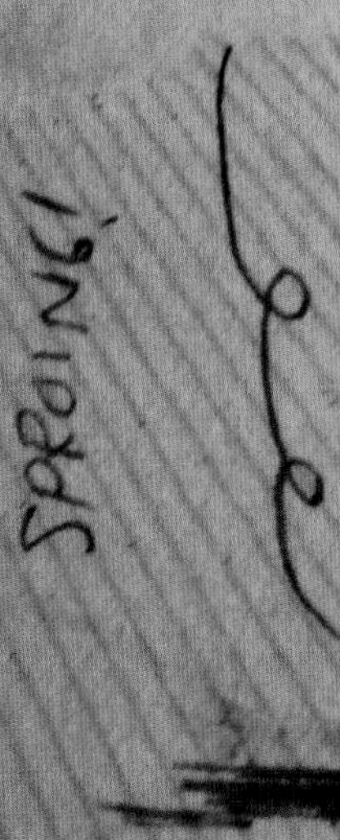

SPROING!

Not a lot of magicians will let you behind the scenes to show you how their illusions work, but we're happy to clear the smoke and hold a mirror to the process that brought you this book.

First trick of the trade: Paul Dini provided a "pitch" to tell us his story, in essence, and how he planned to tell it. Details – even the title – changed by the time Paul was ready to flesh out his outline. But the pitch stands as the floor plan that everyone could agree on.

We've reprinted Paul's *entire* script, and you can see that it still underwent some fine tuning based on editorial concerns and a lot of back-and-forth between Paul and the artist, Joe Quinones.

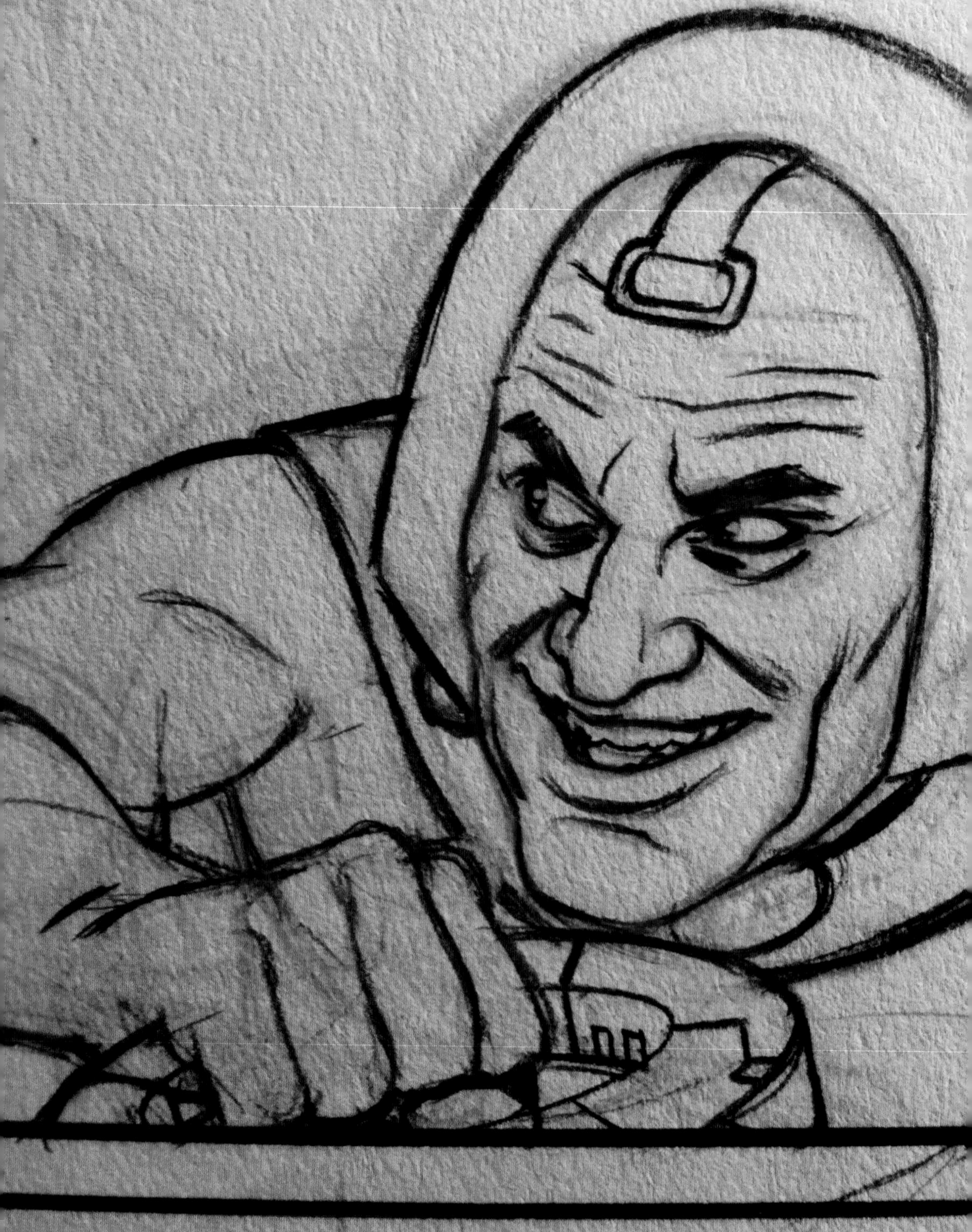

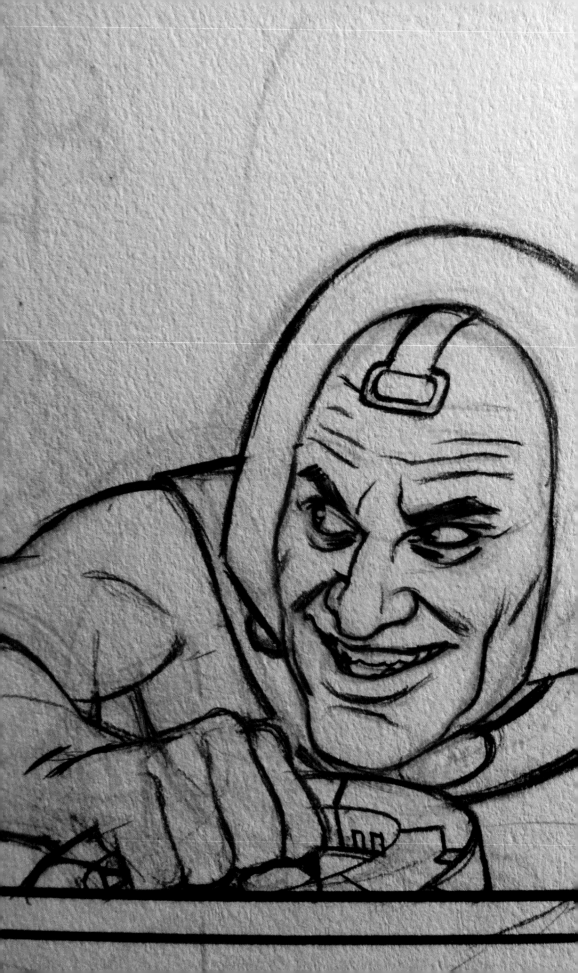

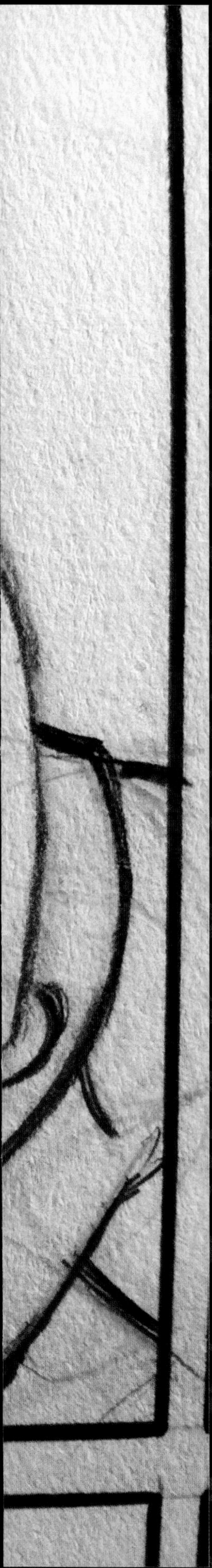

BLACK CANARY + ZATANNA
"JUMPER"
GRAPHIC NOVEL PROPOSAL BY PAUL DINI
11/11/05

Black Canary — Dinah Lance — mistress of martial arts. Zatanna Zatara — mistress of magic. Heroines, teammates, friends. Now, in this ninety-six-page graphic novel, two of the DC Universe's brightest stars join forces to combat a deadly new threat – a chilling supernatural foe that preys on their weaknesses and unleashes their awesome powers against each other.

One year ago...

Black Canary infiltrated a gang of ten female criminals set to pull a dangerous heist at a Las Vegas casino. Seems Dinah had been tipped off by one of the gang members in a plea for leniency. The turncoat suspected things were not what they seemed and she was right – the gang leader, Tina Boccali, had set up the other women to die in the robbery while she escaped with the money. Boccali was a definite loose cannon, beautiful in a tattooed biker-chick way, but ice cold. Skilled in hand-to-hand combat and with more than a passing interest in the occult, specifically black magic, she was one nasty customer. Just before the deal went down, the disguised Canary revealed herself to Boccali and fought her to a standstill. But rather than be taken by Canary or the law, she leapt to her death, vowing she would get revenge on Canary and her own former gang members. As Boccali was definitely, absolutely stone cold dead, her last words seemed an empty threat...

Until now.

One year to the day after Boccali's death, her former gang members start committing suicide. One at a time, each in a shockingly gruesome manner. Are they truly committing suicide or have they been targeted by Boccali's vengeful ghost?

Determined to learn the truth, Black Canary turns to her friend Zatanna to help investigate the deaths. The trail leads them on a cross-country journey as they try to locate the survivors before they take their lives. After rescuing one of them, Zatanna invokes a mystic rite and summons up the spectral superhero Deadman. He confirms what Zatanna has suspected: Tina Boccali has become a Jumper, a restless, evil ghost that jumps from person to person, possessing them and forcing them to kill themselves. This type of ghost is rare, but apparently Tina knew enough magic to "slip through the cracks" before she died, and has returned as sort of an evil variation on Deadman. Though he is able to help identify their adversary, Deadman cannot help Dinah and Zee in their battle. They will have to track the Jumper down themselves.

The ghost's trail takes the two heroines to Las Vegas, where the Jumper has taken possession of the casino owner she initially tried to rob. One thing about Boccali that never changed was her expensive tastes. Jumper also knows that the last member of her former gang is in Vegas, and she's out to kill her as well. However, Boccali is unaware that Zatanna is helping Black Canary, so Zee's gig as showroom headliner (with a less than enthusiastic Canary in disguise as one of Zatanna's assistants) gives them the perfect cover to infiltrate Jumper's lair.

This sets up the final battle where Dinah and Zee save the last woman just before Jumper can kill her. Though the final victim is safe, the two heroines have a murderous ghost to deal with, one who can possess them and force them to kill each other. Jumper leaps into Dinah and forces her to strike Zatanna in the throat, preventing her from casting a spell. The second Zee recovers, Jumper takes possession of her and directs her deadly magic blasts at Black Canary. Jumper takes great delight in forcing the heroines to torture each other, but thanks to their resourcefulness, fighting spirit, and belief in each other, the two allies eventually get the upper hand and banish the evil spirit forever.

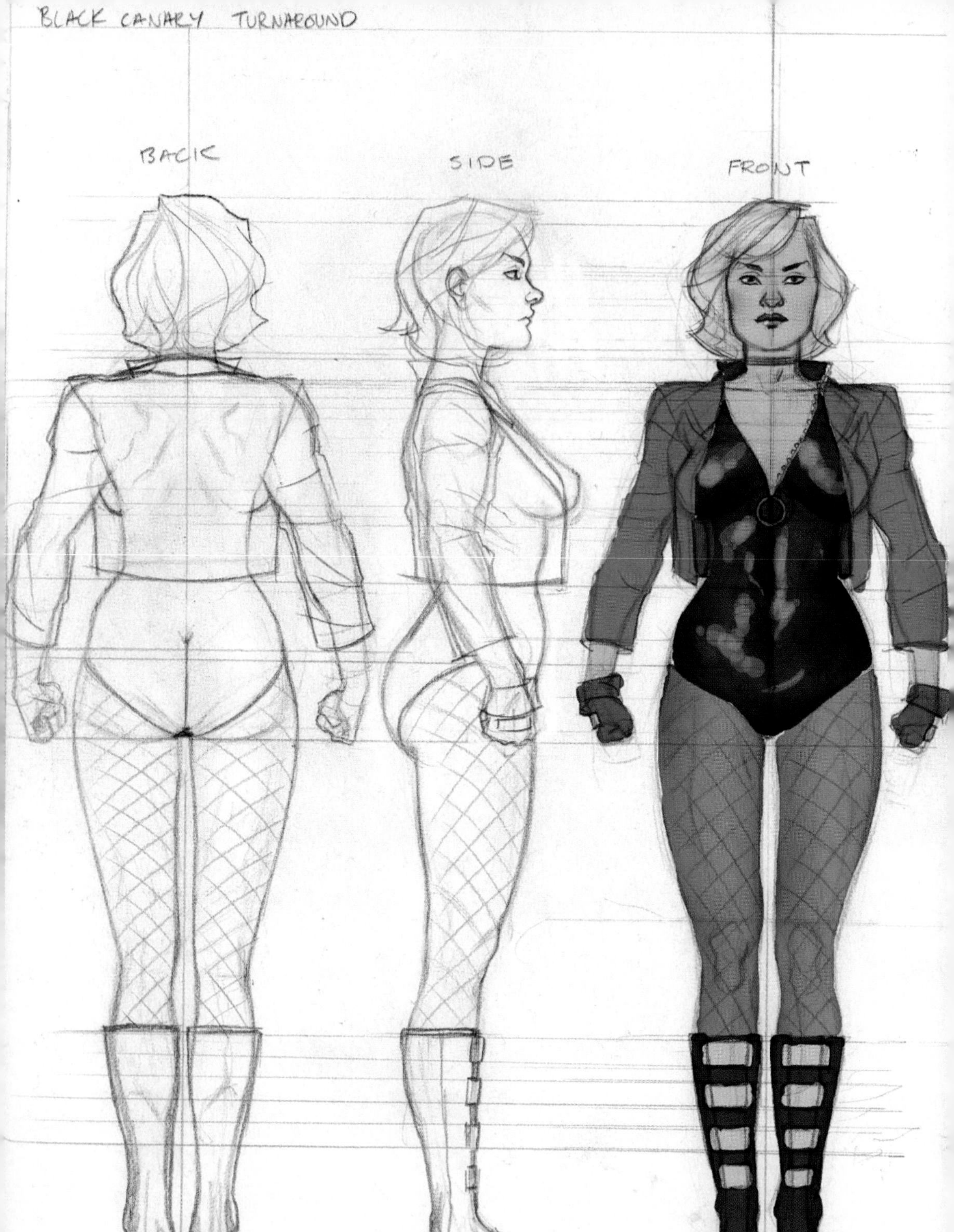
BLACK CANARY TURNAROUND
BACK
SIDE
FRONT
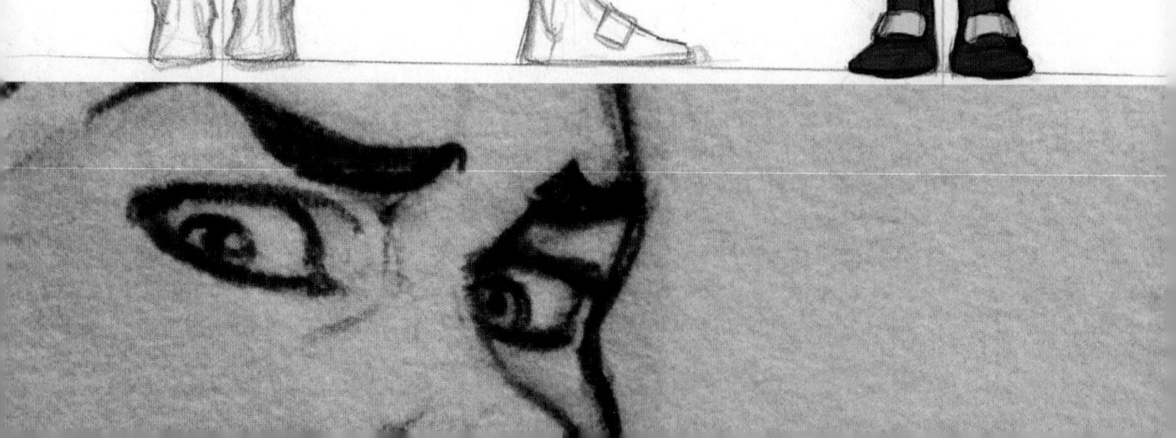

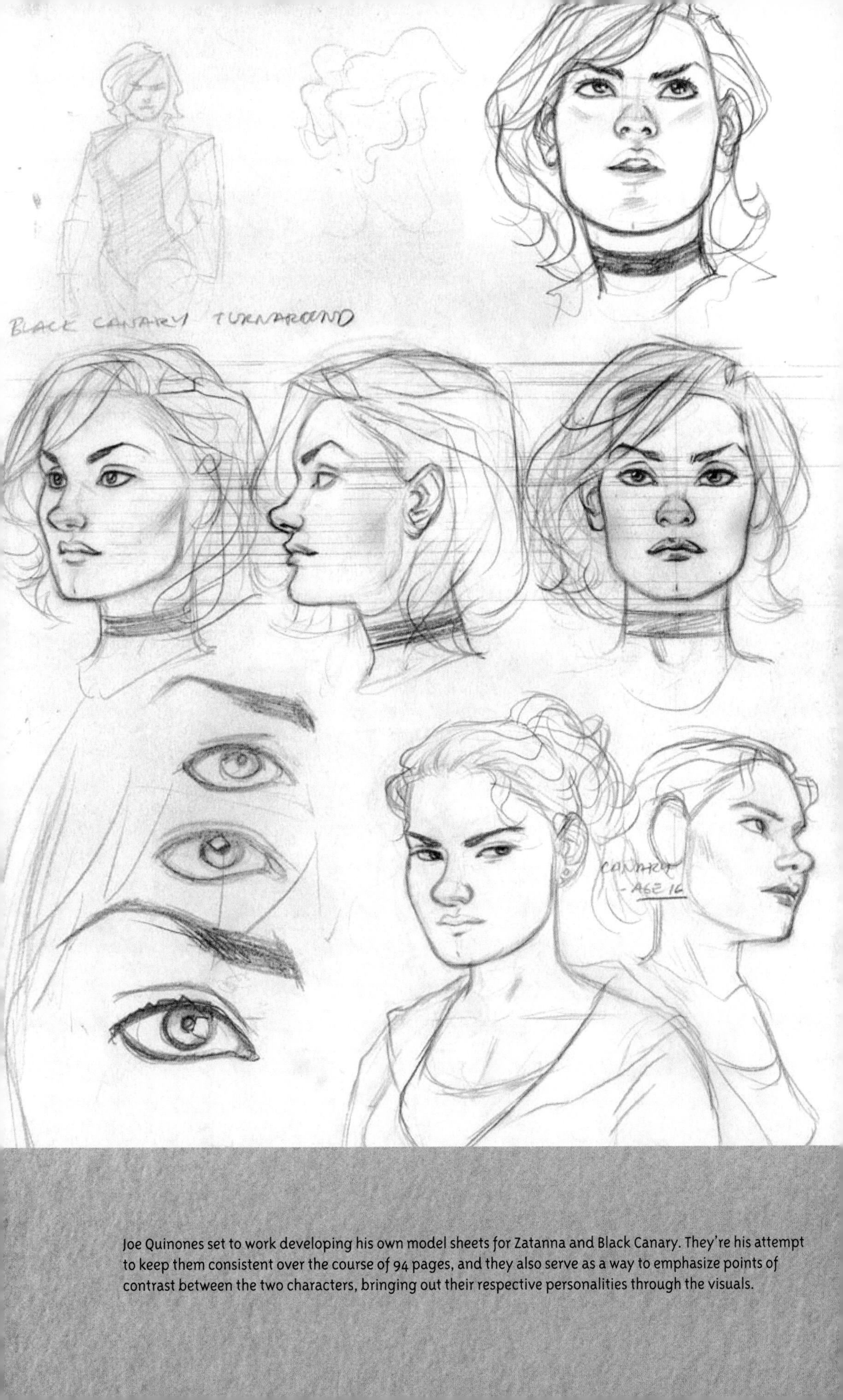
BLACK CANARY TURNAROUND
CANARY - AGE 16

Joe Quinones set to work developing his own model sheets for Zatanna and Black Canary. They're his attempt to keep them consistent over the course of 94 pages, and they also serve as a way to emphasize points of contrast between the two characters, bringing out their respective personalities through the visuals.

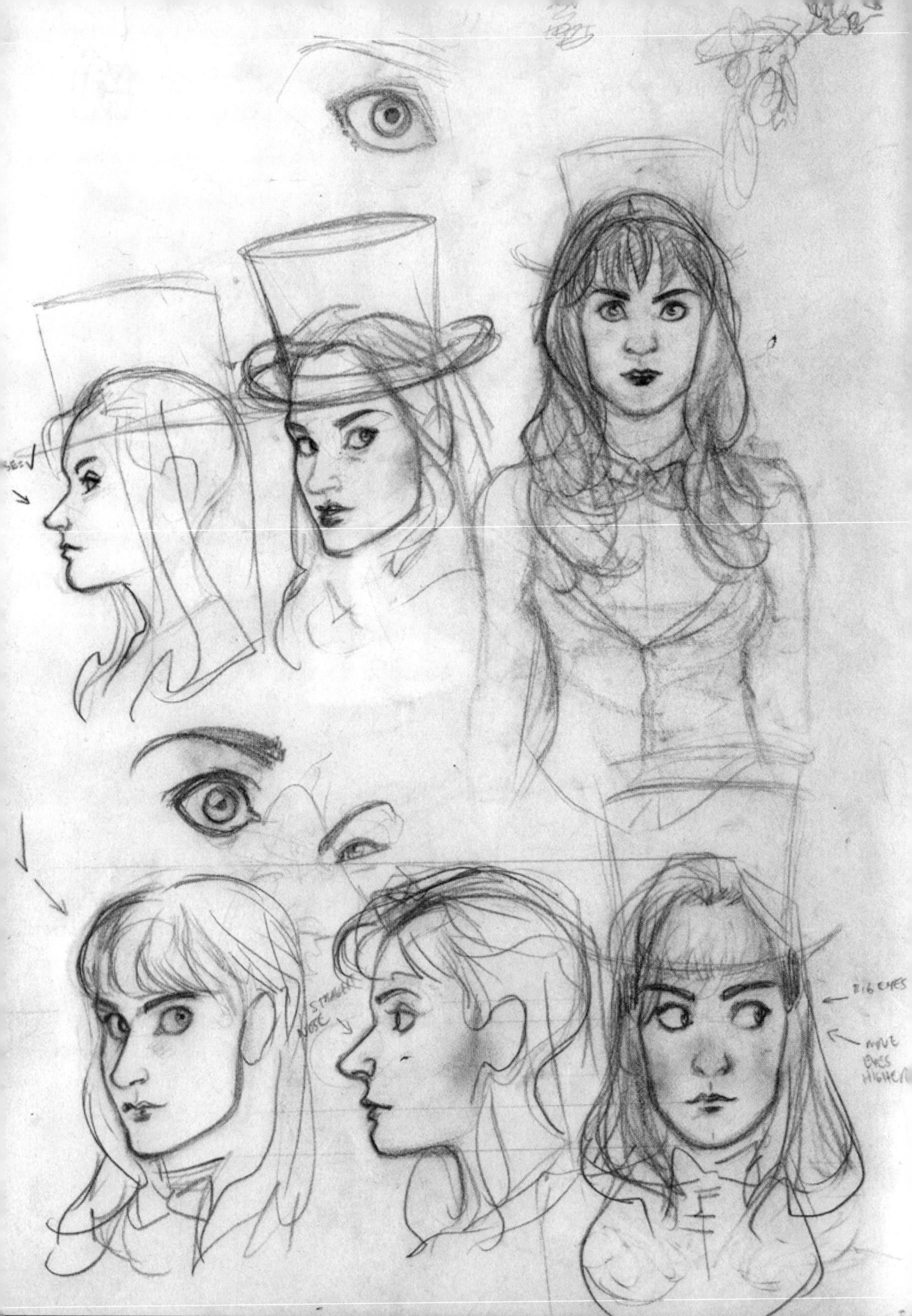

STRAIGHT NOSE
BIG EYES
MOVE EYES HIGHER

Can both Zatanna and Black Canary display a playful as well as a serious side? What would Zatanna look like as a twelve-year-old acolyte of magic? And how should a top hat fit anyway? These excerpts from Joe Quinones' sketchbook rise to the challenges of illustrating the script.

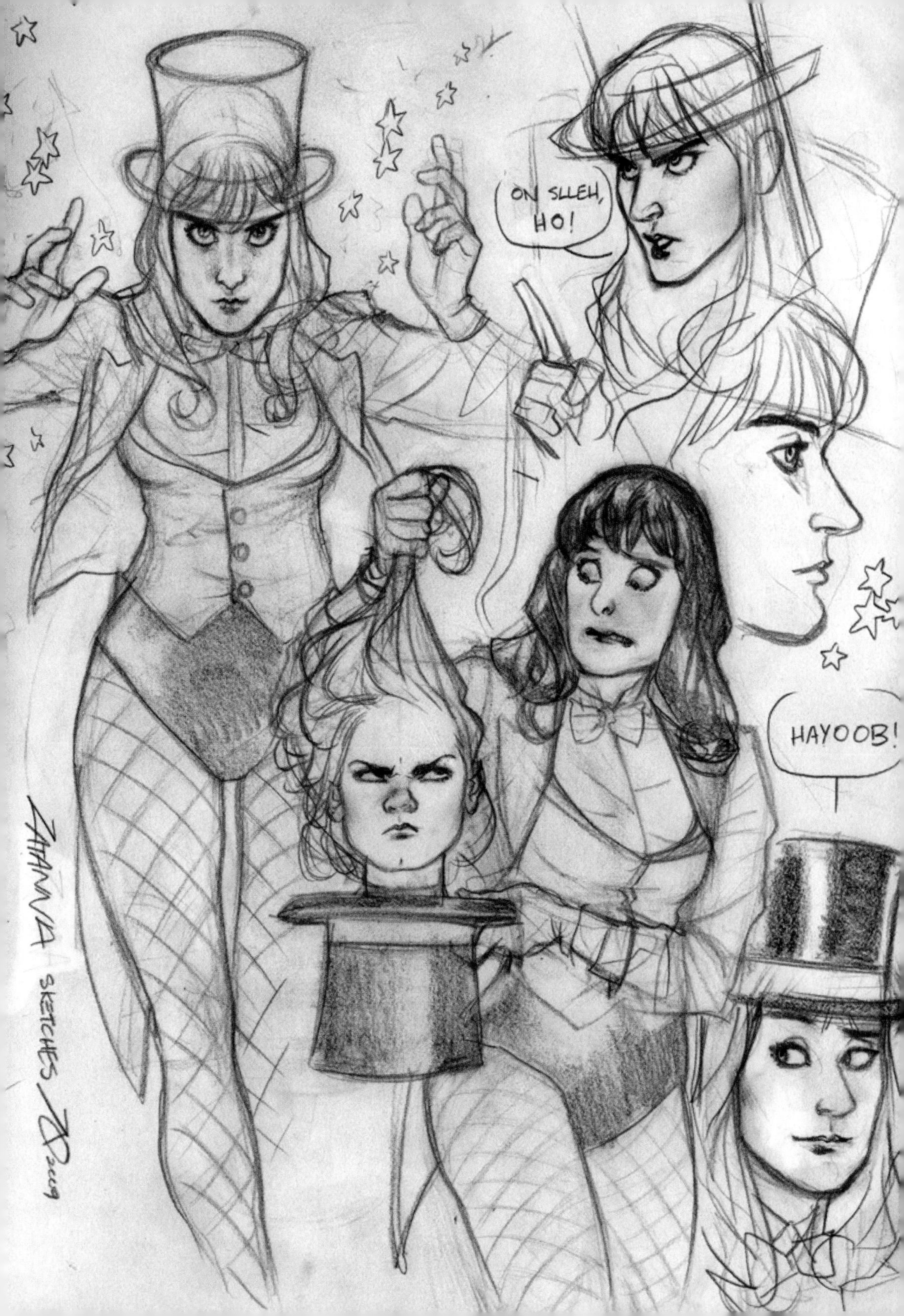
ON SLLEH, HO!
HAYOOB!
ZATANNA SKETCHES

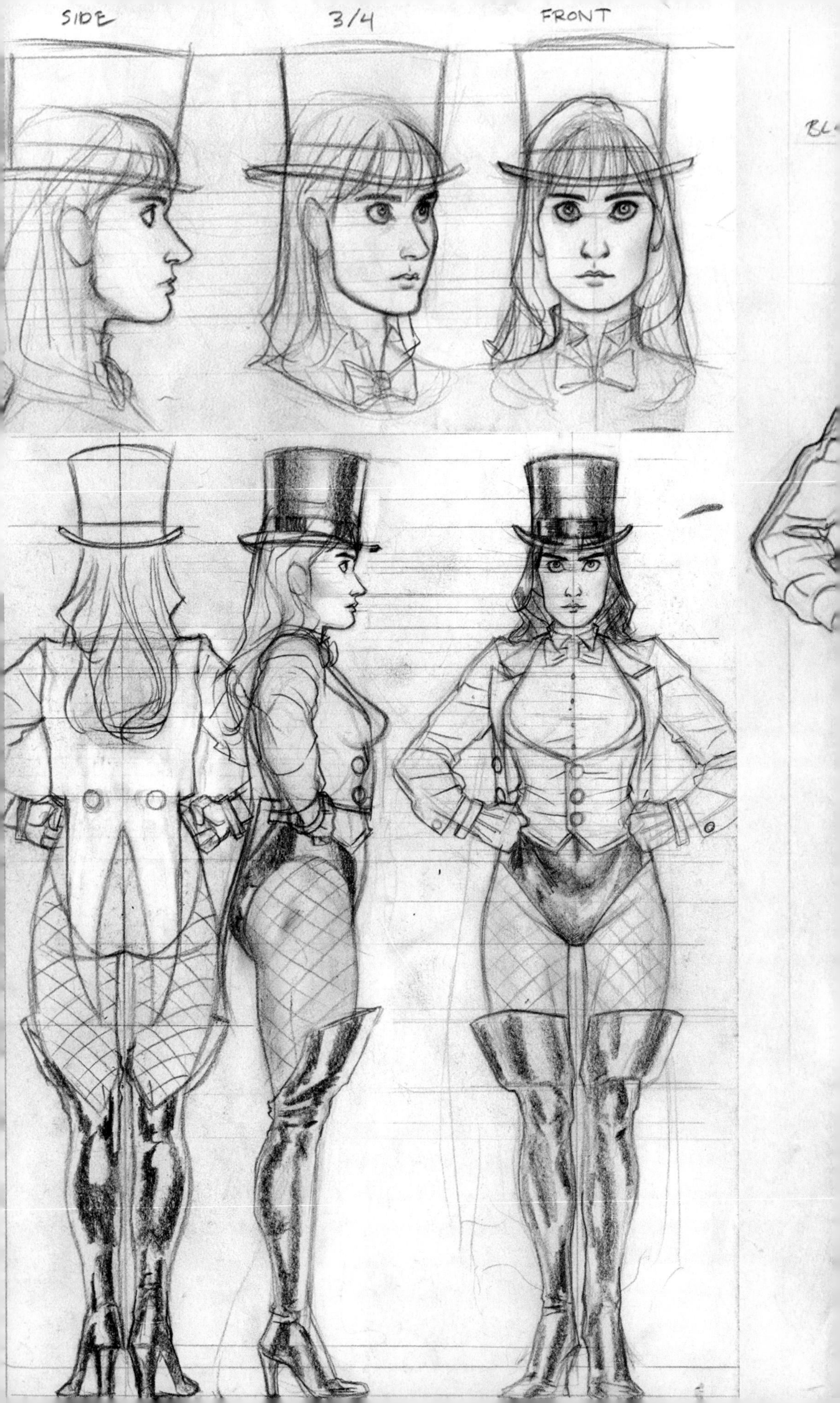

SIDE
3/4
FRONT
BL

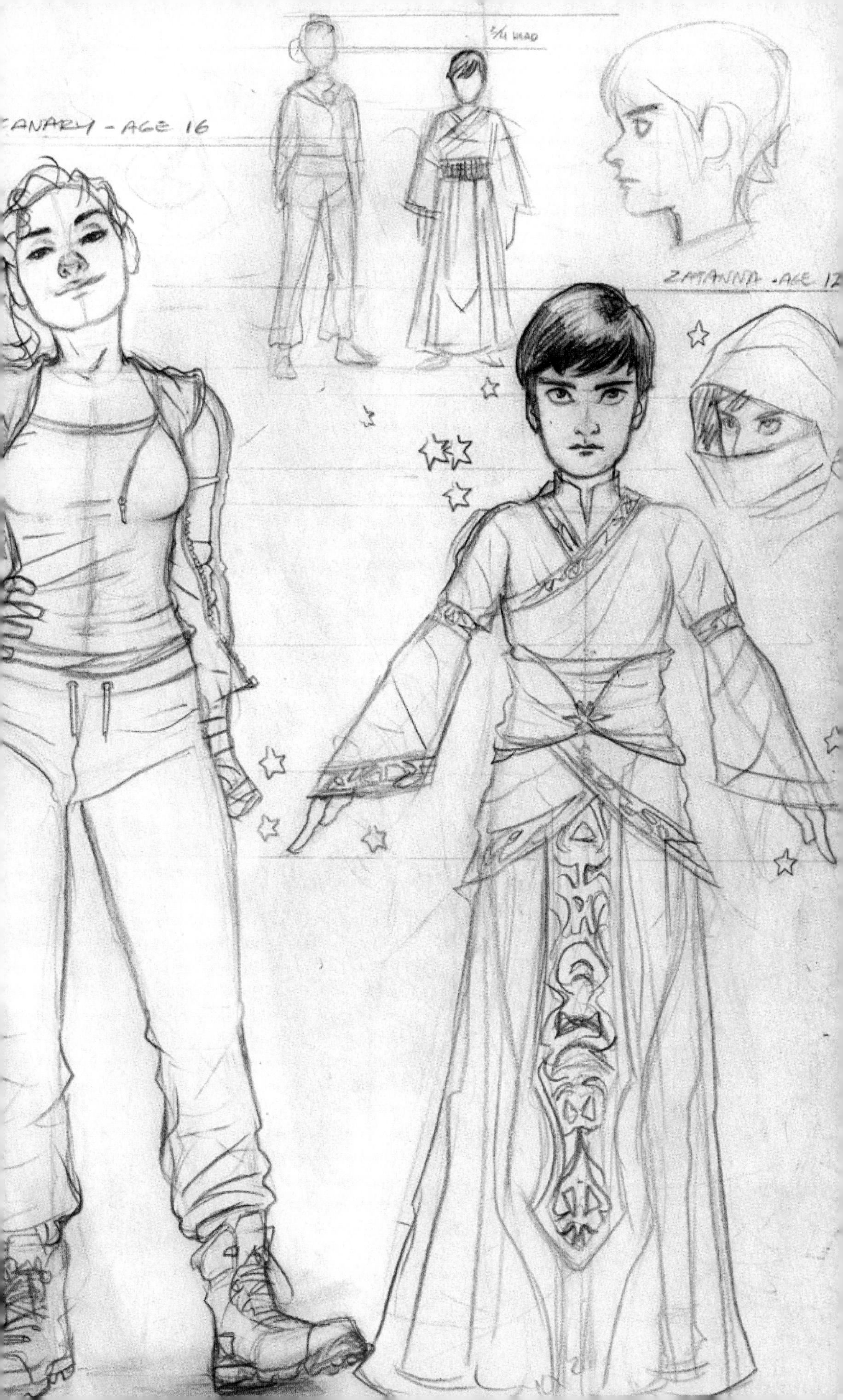

ANARY - AGE 16
3/4 HEAD
ZATANNA - AGE 17

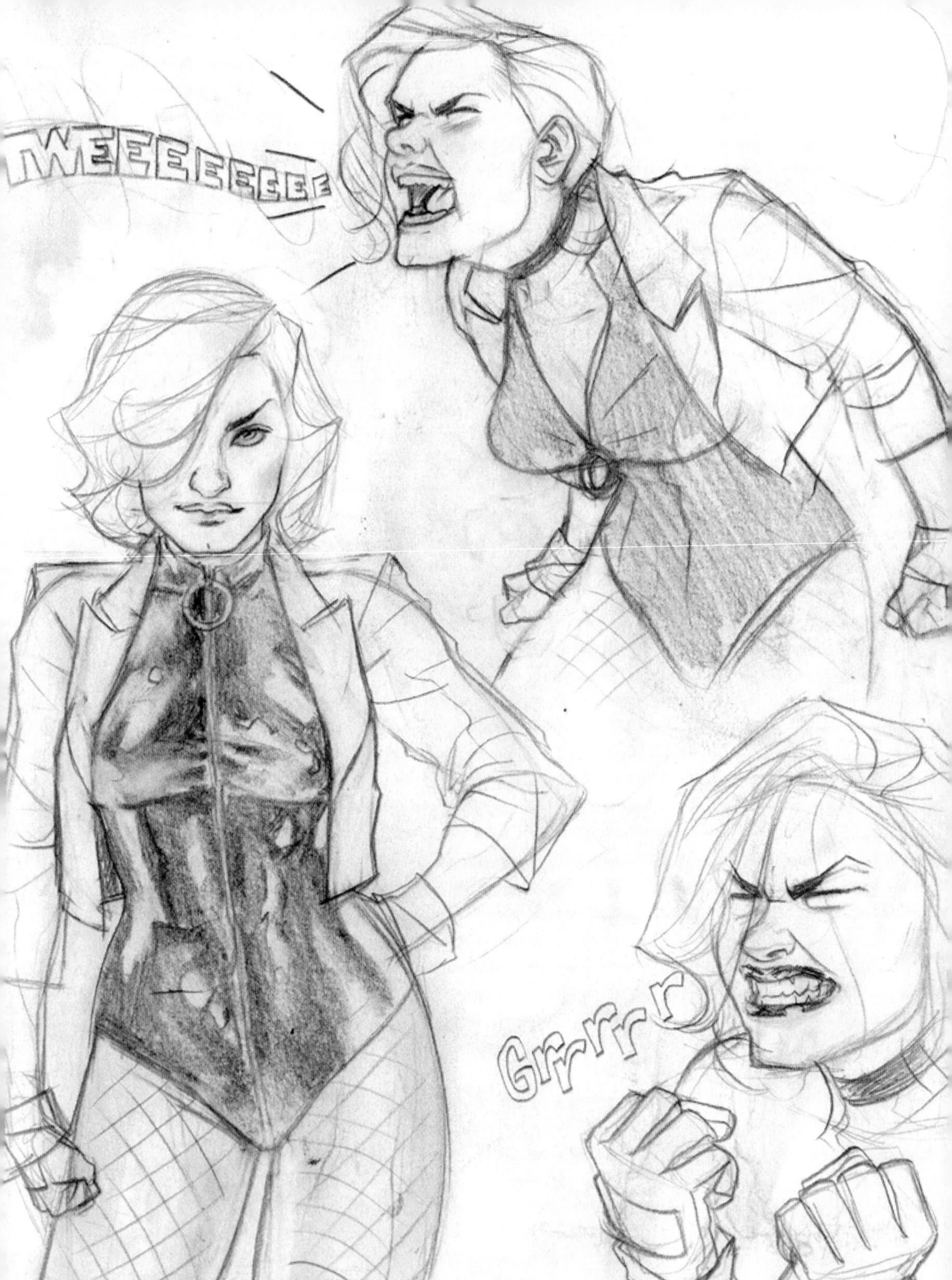
TWEEEEEEEE
Grrrrr

Clearly, Joe got the hang of it in short order. What follows is a near-final edition of Paul's script, punctuated by Joe's early layouts and final pencils -- as good a window into a graphic novel's creative process as you could hope for.

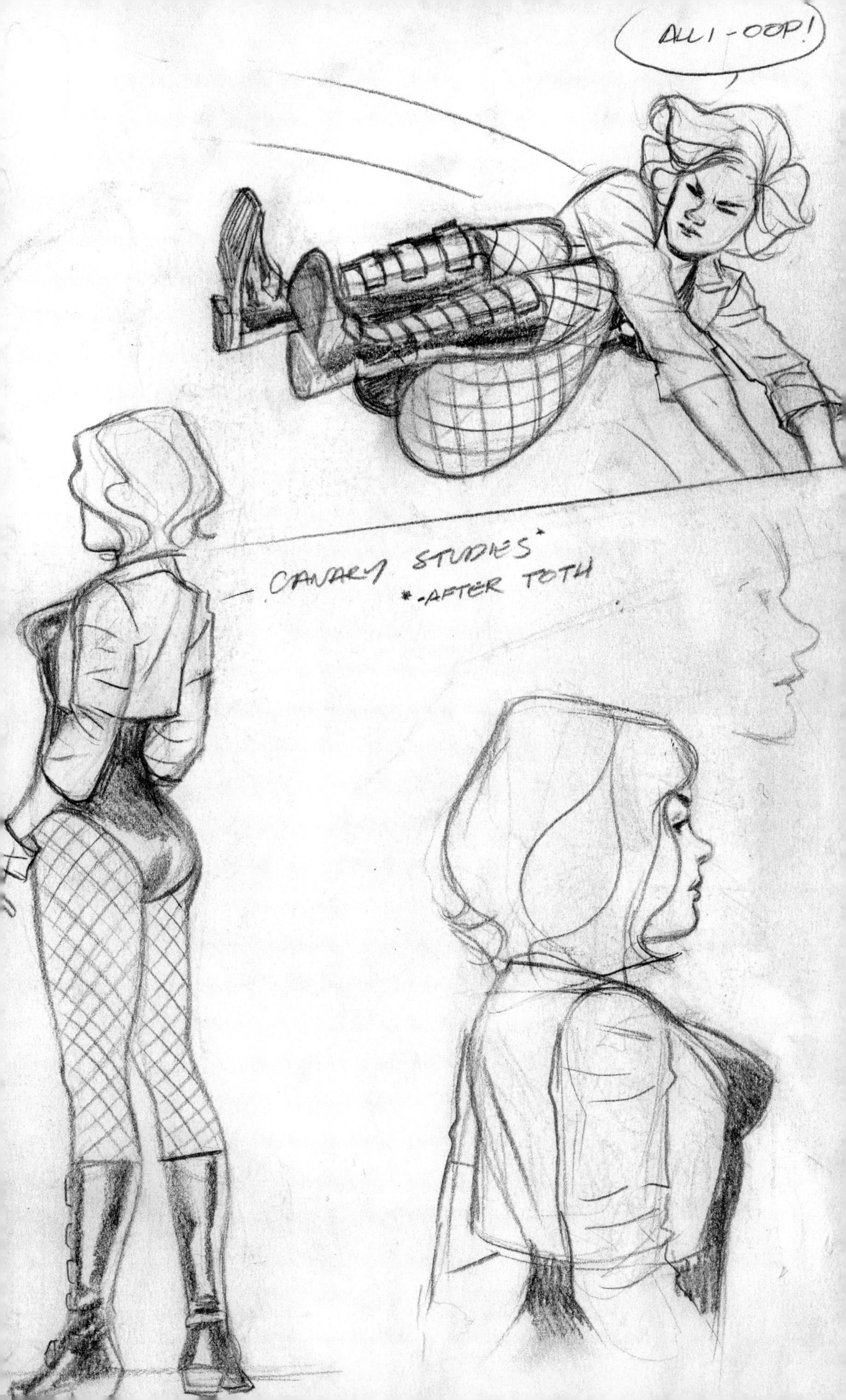
ALLI-OOP!
— CANARY STUDIES*
*-AFTER TOTH

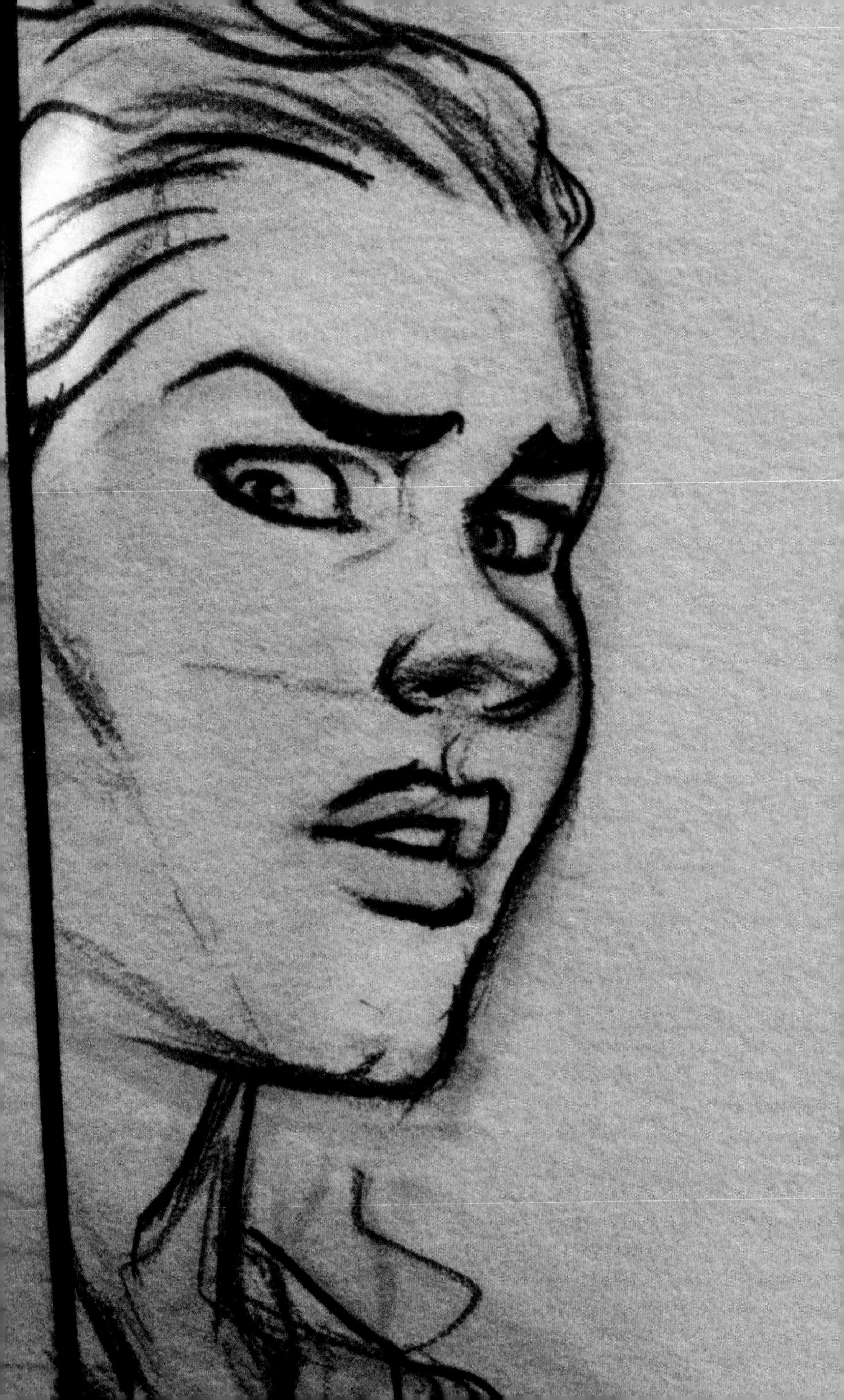

BLACK CANARY/ZATANNA
"BLOODSPELL"
WRITTEN BY PAUL DINI
REVISED
2/11/10

PAGE ONE

Panel One

The place — the Himalayas. It is cold and forbidding. Craggy, snow-capped peaks reaching up into the dark clouds.

ı CAPTION: The Himalayas - Fifteen years ago...

Panel Two

A procession of robed figures makes its way through a mountain pass. Carried in the procession's midst is an elaborate sedan chair.

Panel Three

The procession comes to a stop at the base of the mountain.

Panel Four

The robed figures part the curtains of the sedan chair. They bow reverently as a pretty young girl dressed in simple white robes, her black hair in a page-boy cut, steps out from the chair. Meet the enchanting female magician ZATANNA, at the tender age of twelve. Zatanna's attitude is that of a deeply nervous girl who is struggling to remain calm and focused.

Panel Five

Zatanna approaches a flat, clear area at the base. She glances to some nearby hooded and robed figures.

Panel Six

Under the hood of one of the robed figures we see the debonair features of Zatanna's father, ZATARA THE MAGICIAN (sans top hat, please). Though he looks serious, there is the slightest twinkle of pride and, yes, encouragement in Zatara's eyes as he nods ever-so-slightly back at his off-panel daughter.

PAGE TWO

Panel One

Zatanna stands in the center of the wide ring of cloaked figures. The girl centers herself, her arms extended in a meditation pose, her eyes closed, a look of gentle, though supreme, concentration on her face.

Panel Two

Close on Zatanna. Her lips part and she whispers a magic word:

ı ZATANNA: (Small lettering in balloon) Esir.

Panel Three

Zatanna's hair begins to gently fan out and her cloak floats around her as she slowly starts to rise into the air. It now becomes clear to us that this is Zee's rite of passage as a young sorceress, her magical Confirmation/Bat Mitzvah.

Panel Four

Downshot on Zatanna as she rises up, the cloaked mystics all looking up at her. She is not flying like Superman, but levitating in a straight up and down manner. Though she is concentrating deeply, the girl can't suppress the smile tugging at the corners of her mouth. Mystic rite or not, this is so cool!

Panel Five

Zatara kisses the hand of the cloaked mystic at his side. We see it is Zatanna's mother, the beautiful Homo Magi sorceress SINDELLA. She is also beaming with pride at her daughter's ascension. I know there are stories where Sindella and Zatanna did not meet until later, but continuity be damned, this is a family affair.

PAGE THREE

Panel One

A big long one that takes up the left side of the page and shows tiny Zatanna's rise up the side of the huge mountain.

Panel Two

Close on Zatanna, her eyes closed, the look of concentration on her face as the wind ruffles her hair.

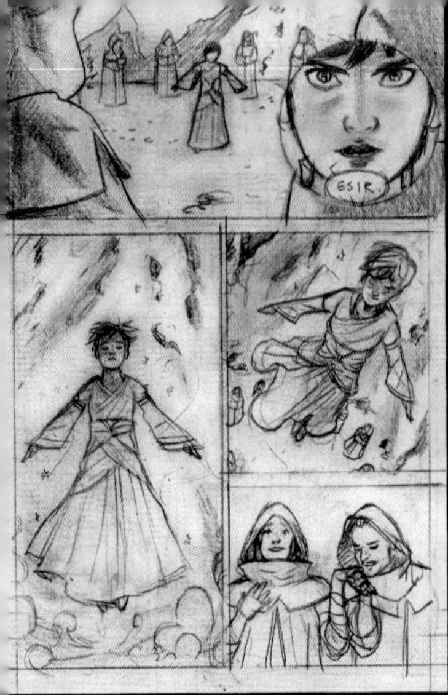
ESIR.
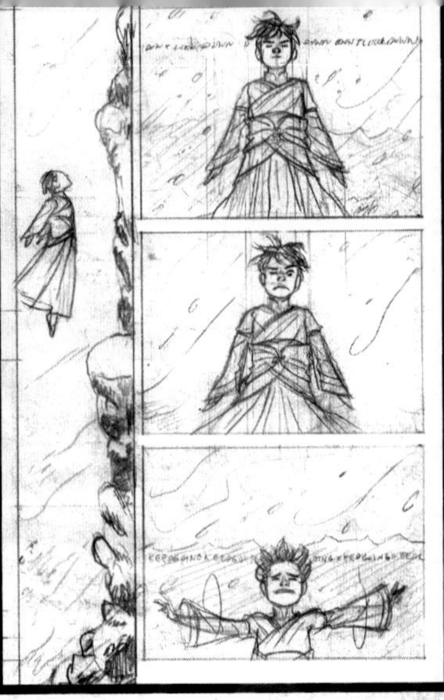
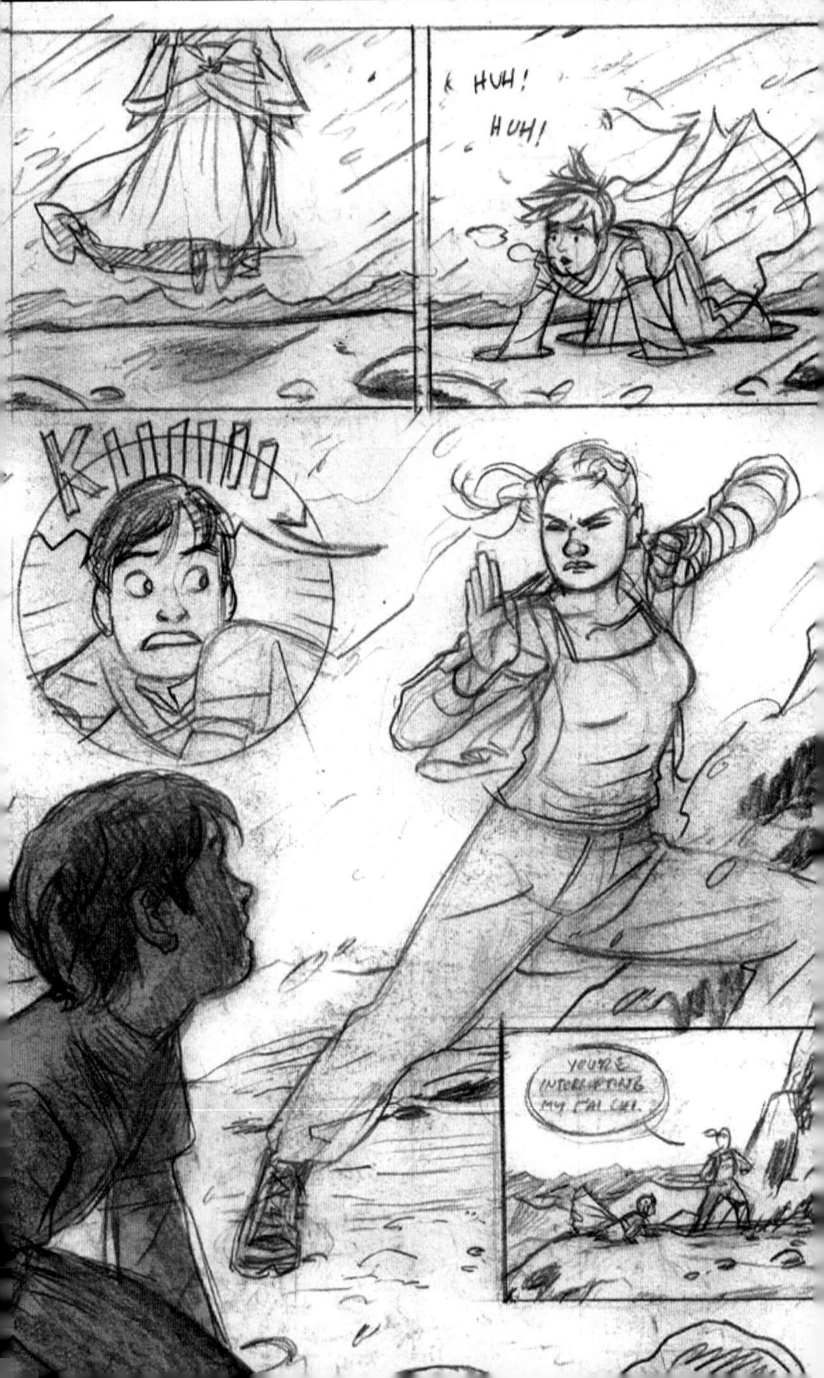
HUH!
HUH!
YOU'RE INTERRUPTING MY TAI CHI.

1 ZATANNA THOUGHT BALLOON: Don't look down, don't look down, don't look down...

Panel Three

Same angle. Zatanna glances down, perhaps peeking out of one opened eye.

Panel Four

Zatanna refocuses her energy fast. She bobs a little bit downward in the air – not a serious drop, but a slight flutter.

2 ZATANNA THOUGHT BALLOON: Keepgoingkeepgoingkeepgoing!

PAGE FOUR

Panel One

The top of the mountain is in sight. Zatanna rises up toward the small level area at the mountain's peak.

Panel Two

Zatanna lands on the snowy peak. Drops down on all fours is more like it. It's not the most graceful landing, but she made it. She breathes hard – it took a lot out of her and, damn, it's cold up there and the air is thin. Small puffs of air rise from her mouth.

ZATANNA (Breathing hard): Huh! Huh!

Panel Three

Closer on Zatanna, reacting with surprise to a loud martial arts cry to her right.

DINAH (OS): Kiiii!

Panel Four

Startled, Zatanna leaps away as a strange-looking girl leaps in and lands in front of her in a fighting pose. The girl is maybe four years older than Zatanna and clad in torn sweat clothes. Ridiculously ill-dressed for the freezing cold, but she doesn't seem to mind. Her stringy brown-blonde hair is tied sloppily behind her head. She seems to be a hippie who just happens to like practicing martial arts at 29,000 feet. Meet DINAH LANCE, the future BLACK CANARY, at age 16.

Panel Five

Dinah breaks her fearsome warrior's stance slightly to say to Zatanna:

1 DINAH: You're interrupting my t'ai chi.

PAGE FIVE

Panel One

Stuck for anything better to do, Zatanna apologizes.

1 ZATANNA: Sorry. How did you get up here?

Panel Two

Dinah points to where a small tent has been set in the snow. There are the remains of a campfire and a few other essentials scattered about. There is a small teapot on the fire.

2 DINAH: Climbed. You?

3 ZATANNA: Uh, magic.

Panel Three

Dinah's expression says she does not think much of Zatanna or her abilities.

4 DINAH: Hm. Must be nice. Wiggle your nose and all your wishes come true.

Panel Four

5 ZATANNA: Actually, I have to say my spells backwards.

6 DINAH: Really? How contrived.

Panel Five

Zatanna starts to explain her powers.

7 ZATANNA: It takes a lot of practice to get the inflection right. Not to mention concentration, visualization, willpower...

Panel Six

A snowball flies in and hits Zatanna in the face.

ZATANNA: Uh!

PAGE SIX

Panel One

Dinah smirks at the steaming Zatanna.

1 DINAH: Did I ask for an explanation?

Panel Two

Zatanna points at Dinah and casts a spell. Dinah starts to flip upside-down and frantically grabs at some rocks to try and stay right side up.

2 ZATANNA: Lrig pilf nwod-edispu!

3 DINAH: Whoa! Hey! Hey! I'm sorry, okay?

Panel Three

Zatanna removes her spell and Dinah falls hard on her butt.

4 ZATANNA: Nwod drah!

5 DINAH: Oof!

Panel Four

Dinah stands and brushes the snow off her rump. She flashes a peace-making smile at the still-wary Zatanna.

6 DINAH: Chill, Carrie! It was just a snowball.

Panel Five

The girls sit and have a bit of a chat. Dinah gives Zatanna a cup of tea from the pot on the small fire.

7 DINAH: So what brings you to this side of Everest?

8 ZATANNA: A mystic rite of passage I've been working toward all my life. Kind of a magical Bat Mitzvah, except there's no band or money.

Panel Six

In response to Zatanna's question, Dinah displays her chapped and torn fingers.

9 ZATANNA: How about you?

10 DINAH: Ah, I just wanted to see if I could do it. I worked my way over to Asia, and then dragged myself up here by what's left of my fingernails. Not everyone can take the easy way.

Panel Seven

Zatanna looks at this strange girl with concern.

11 ZATANNA: You might have been killed.

12 DINAH: So what? One less loudmouthed, pushy girl no one ever will miss. But I made it, so, yay for me.

PAGE SEVEN

Panel One

Zatanna still has questions, but Dinah (now wearing a jacket) is growing tired of the conversation and the company. She has pulled a backpack from her tent and is slipping it on.

1 ZATANNA: You mean your parents don't even know you're...

2 DINAH: Y'know, the air's thin up here and you're using up most of it. I'm not one for long goodbyes. The tent's yours if you want it.

Panel Two

There is a climbing rope tied to several pitons pounded into the rocks and snow. Dinah starts down the rope. She throws a couple of sarcastic remarks back to Zatanna.

3 DINAH: The Yetis are pretty noisy at night, but they won't attack unless you let the fire go out. Oh, and don't pet the snow leopards, they bite.

Panel Three

Dinah notices Zatanna's dubious look.

Panel Four

Dinah loosens up and extends her hand to Zatanna. Zatanna takes it.

4 DINAH: Just kidding about the Yetis. My name's Dinah.

5 ZATANNA: Zatanna.

Panel Five

Dinah has a "gee, that sucks" look on her face. Zatanna shrugs, somewhat embarrassed.

6 DINAH: Really? I'm sorry.

7 ZATANNA: Yeah.

Panel Six

Dinah starts to rappel down the mountain face. Zatanna watches her in wonder.

8 DINAH: If you get in trouble, I'm sure you can just yell "pleh" and make it better.

PAGE EIGHT

Panel One

Left alone, Zatanna is at a loss as to what to do next.

Panel Two

She goes into her concentration mode again, her robe and hair starting to gently rise.

Panel Three

Then she stops. A new determination is growing in her eyes.

Panel Four

Zatanna has moved over to the rope and is gingerly starting to edge her way down the mountain. It will be long and hard work, but she's determined to follow Dinah's example and do it the hard way.

Panel Five

A longer shot of Zatanna making her way down the mountain. Some snow starts to swirl up around her small image.

PAGE NINE - SPLASH

We're basically looking at a cross section of Las Vegas. Nighttime. The Strip lit up in all its gaudy glory. The top half of the page is the bustling strip right outside the new XANADU CASINO AND HOTEL. Like the Xanadu of the poem, it recalls Kubla Khan's stately pleasure-dome, but amped up for twenty-first century tastes. Tourists go about their normal lives, completely oblivious to what's happening in the tunnel below.

The bottom half of the page is said tunnel. The service tunnels that run beneath the Vegas strip. There, a female gang leader, TINA SPETTRO, is leading her five henchwomen in a loyalty ritual. Each woman has pricked her finger on the needle that Tina holds out. Well, each woman except one. The holdout is a tall woman with sandy brown hair.

1 CAPTION: Las Vegas -- One year ago...

2 JOY (Black Canary in disguise): I don't like this.

PAGE TEN

Panel One

Close on the group. Everyone but Joy is squeezing her finger to make a drop of blood appear at the recently pricked hole.

1 TINA: You scared of needles, Joy?

Panel Two

Closer on "Joy," flashing a sarcastic grin.

2 JOY: Ask the nurse I bit when I had to have a tetanus shot. I was pretty mean for a five-year-old.

Panel Three

Tina starts to get in Joy's face about the ritual.

3 TINA: I don't need a kid on this job, I need five loyal partners. Are you in or out?

Panel Four

Close on Joy. She stares at the needle. Is she hesitating or stalling?

Panel Five

Joy sighs and holds her finger out to Tina, who jabs her.

4 JOY: Shut up and stab me.

Panel Six

The girls touch their bleeding fingers together. (Bad Latin translation of "By our blood, our bodies are one." Can fix later.)

5 TINA: Per nostrum sanguis, nostrum corporis est unus.

Panel Seven

Close on Tina.

6 TINA: It's go time.

PAGE ELEVEN

Panel One

Inside the Xanadu Casino and Hotel, the opening ceremony is just starting. The hotel is Chinese/Mongol-themed, and like the summer capital of Kubla Khan's empire, it's square-shaped. The "Outer Square," being the guest rooms, surrounds the casino "Inner Square." The entire building is decorated with replicas of Asian art — tapestries, vases, statues, etc. It also contains REAL Asian art — but we'll get to that in a bit. Casino owner DALE HOLLISTER is center stage in the Casino and speaking at a podium to a crowd of well-dressed individuals. Dale is forty, looks thirty, and radiates charm and success.

1 DALE: "In Xanadu did Kubla Khan, a stately pleasure-dome decree."

Panel Two

On Dale, continuing his spiel.

2 DALE: Those words were written by Samuel Coleridge to describe the fantastic image of paradise he saw in a dream. Now comes MY dream made reality, the newest pleasure dome on the Las Vegas strip.

3 SECOND DALE BALLOON: Welcome, ladies and gentlemen.

Panel Three

Tina, now in a slinky black dress, walks away from the ceremony with a finger to her ear.

4 DALE (OFF): Welcome to Xanadu!

5 FX: CLAP! CLAP! CLAP! CLAP!

6 TINA (WHISPER): What's your position?

Panel Four

Tina's near a pillar, away from the crowds.

7 COMM: Directly under the piggy bank. We're ready when you are.

Panel Five

Closer on Tina as she goes over last-minute instructions.

8 TINA: On three, the bombs go off and you cut your way up into the vault.

9 COMM: Sixty million dollars, here we come!

Panel Six

Tina grabs the comm from her ear.

10 TINA: One... Two...

Panel Seven

And she tosses the comm on the ground.

11 TINA: Three.

PAGE TWELVE

Panel One

Tina walks away from the pillar... but no bombs are going off.

Panel Two

She puts on her best innocent "dumb rich girl" face and spills to a guard. She lays it on thick, complete with touching his arm.

1 TINA: Officer! Officer!

2 GUARD: I'm just a Casino guard, ma'am, not a cop.

3 TINA: I saw these five girls outside with a bunch of SCARY-looking equipment slip into the sewers! They were talking about, well... come here.

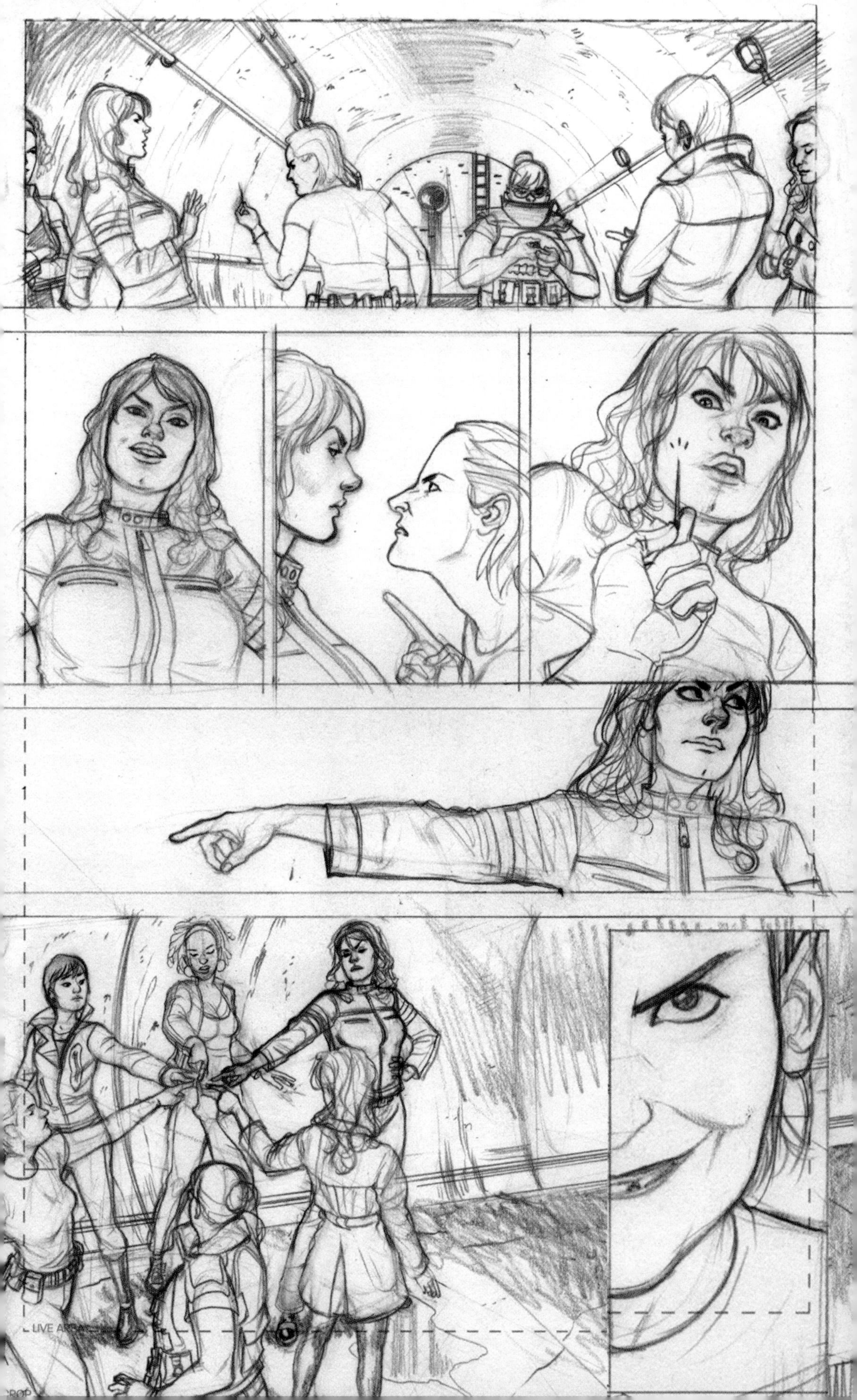

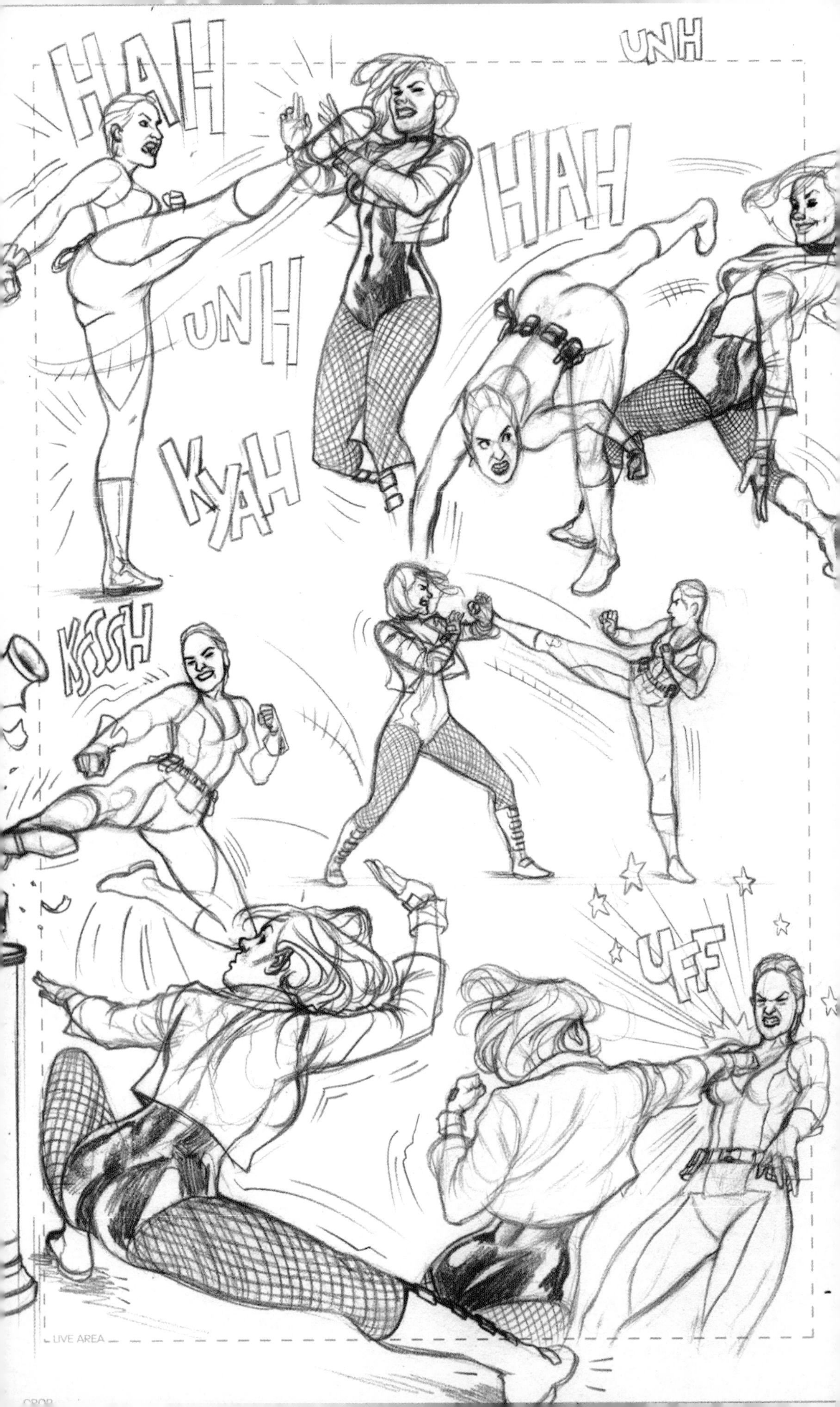
HAH
UNH
HAH
UNH
KYAH
KSSSH
UFF
LIVE AREA

Panel Three

She whispers in the guard's ear.

4 TINA: Breaking into the vault from below...

Panel Four

The guard's shocked. He grabs the walkie-talkie off his belt.

5 GUARD: Thank you for bringing this to my attention, ma'am.

6 TINA: No problem, officer.

Panel Five

The guard runs off while yelling into his walkie-talkie.

7 GUARD: We may have a SITUATION in the GAME room.

Panel Six

Tina slips inside the door the guard was stationed at as we see more guards in the background running — in the opposite direction of Tina.

8 TINA CAPTION: Smooth as a baby's behind.

PAGE THIRTEEN

Panel One

We're in the Xanadu Museum now. It's dark and no one else is around. Tina's dress has fallen to the floor to reveal a skintight sleeveless cat suit underneath. She also wears a utility belt with various thief tools.

Panel Two

She passes a black vase with a white dragon on it as well as a glass case full of ancient daggers.

1 TINA CAPTION: Three years, Dale. Three long, miserable years I played the part of one of your arm candy bimbos.

Panel Three

She passes a glass case with original tapestries as well as an ancient saddle and some paintings.

2 TINA CAPTION: And you treated me like all the rest, tossed out as soon as the novelty wore off.

Panel Four

Finally, she finds what she wants. We don't see what it is, but she's smiling.

3 TINA CAPTION: You don't GET to do that to Tina Spettro. It took me a long time to put this together, and the price I paid to make sure it went off easily, you don't want to know.

Panel Five

And the reveal. From behind, we watch as she's about to laser into a glass case full of very expensive-looking jewels.

4 TINA CAPTION: But this should compensate, for a starter.

5 JOY (Off): Not a bad plan.

PAGE FOURTEEN

Panel One

Tina whirls around to see Joy walking out of the shadows.

1 JOY: You rat us out to the guard so we'd get killed in a gunfight. Meantime that serves as your distraction while you make off with the real score.

2 TINA: Joy?

Panel Two

Joy gets closer, still a bit in the shadows.

3 JOY: Consider yourself triple-crossed. The girls got antsy about this caper and called some friends of mine. I took Joy's place to make sure you were caught with your hand in the cookie jar.

4 TINA: You a fed?

Panel Three

Joy comes out of the shadows. Her hair is now blonde and she's holding the sandy blonde wig in her hand. She's actually the Blonde Bombshell, BLACK CANARY, dressed in her trademark outfit.

5 DINAH: Worse. Justice League.

Panel Four

Joy/Dinah tosses the red wig at Tina's feet. Tina regards it coolly.

6 TINA: I'm impressed. Not as impressed as if they had sent Wonder Woman, of course, but Black Canary's no slouch.

7 DINAH: Smart girl. Now, are you smart enough to quit?

PAGE FIFTEEN

Panel One

Hardly. Tina high-kicks BC. BC blocks with her arms.

TINA: HAH!

Panel Two

Tina throws a volley of Tae Kwon Do kicks at BC, who counters each one with a kung fu/t'ai chi move.

1 DINAH: I guess... HAH... your UNH... loyalty oath... KYAH... was a bust...

Panel Three

BC ducks Tina's next kick in the wrong place, the kick destroys a priceless vase.

2 TINA: Time will tell.

Panel Four

BC finally gets in some offensive moves and shows what she's made of. She's in a low tiger stance and punches Tina HARD in the chest.

TINA: Uff!

3 DINAH: I don't plan on sticking around too long.

PAGE SIXTEEN

Panel One

Tina lands right next to the glass case housing the ancient knives.

Panel Two

She breaks the glass.

GLASS FX: CRASH!

Panel Three

She tosses the knives at BC.

Panel Four

BC ducks the knives, but they hit and ruin a priceless work of art.

1 DINAH: You can't win!

Panel Five

Close on Tina.

2 TINA: No --

PAGE SEVENTEEN

Panel One

Tina makes a run for it.

1 TINA: But I can run!

Panel Two

BC gives chase.

Panel Three

Tina opens an air vent on a wall. Inside is a jet pack.

2 DINAH: NO!

Panel Four

Tina's wearing the jet pack. She leans down to wave goodbye.

Panel Five

BC arrives just as the jets fire and shoot Tina up the shaft.

PAGE EIGHTEEN

Panel One

Shot down on Tina as she rockets up the shaft. She has a smile on her face. Behind her, we see a grappling hook catching up to her.

Panel Two

Same shot. Tina looks back confused as she hears the noise of the hook grabbing onto her rocket pack.

HOOK FX: CLANK!

Panel Three

BC lets off a CANARY CRY as she's dragged upwards by her rope.

CANARY CRY FX: EEEEEEEEEEEEEEE!!!!!!!!!!!!!!!!

Panel Four

The cry causes Tina to smack up against the wall of the shaft, but she just laughs.

1 TINA: Ha! Scream your lungs out. It's music to my ears.

Panel Five

Close on Tina's Hand — she presses a button.

PAGE NINETEEN

Panel One

The roof of the Xanadu. All is quiet. A lone airshaft sits disturbing no one.

Panel Two

The innocent airshaft is blown to bits, creating an escape route for Tina.

SHAFT FX: THOOM!

Panel Three

Tina shoots out of the smoldering shaft with BC still trailing by her grappling line. The jetpack and its riders streak up into the night sky.

Panel Four

Above the strip, Tina angles down while BC and her now burning rope keep going up.

Panel Five

Reaching its length, the fiery rope whips BC downward towards Tina.

ROPE FX: SNAP!

PAGE TWENTY

Panel One

BC grabs onto Tina.

TINA: Unh!

1 DINAH: Set us down or we'll both be killed!

Panel Two

Tina gets an evil gleam in her eye.

2 TINA: I'm not afraid to die. How about YOU!?

Panel Three

Tina dives hard towards the mock-volcano out front of the casino across the street.

Panel Four

BC pulls on the controls and angles them away just as the fire erupts from the mock-volcano.

Panel Five

They spin seemingly out of control a few feet off the ground as tourists jump out of their way.

PAGE TWENTY-ONE

Panel One

BC forces them back up in the air.

Panel Two

They rocket past a circus casino sign.

Panel Three

We're cheating with distance a little here, but now they're barely missing the cars and tracks of a prominent roller coaster.

Panel Four

Close on BC's face. It has "Oh no" written all over it.

Panel Five

And now we show why. They're headed DIRECTLY for the window of a revolving restaurant. There's no time to pull away.

PAGE TWENTY-TWO

These next four panels are a series of panoramic panels.

Panel One

BC lets out a CANARY CRY, shattering the window they're about to hit.

CRY FX: EEEEEEEEEEEEEEE!!!!!!!!

Panel Two

They knock over tables and patrons as they fly through the restaurant.

Panel Three

BC lets out another CANARY CRY to shatter the window on the opposite side.

CRY FX: EEEEEEEEEEEEEEEEEEE!!!!!!!!!!!

Panel Four

They safely shoot out the other side.

PAGE TWENTY-THREE

Panel One

BC looks up and sees the marquee of "Brutus' Palace" growing larger.

Panel Two

BC tries to grab the controls again but—

TINA: Won't do you any good, Canary.

Panel Three

A vicious kick and Canary is knocked away, half the controls to the jet pack ripped away in her hand.

DINAH: Ungh!

TINA: I'll be back to get even with you and every one of those two-faced skanks.

Panel Four

Canary in free fall, the Brutus Palace's pool far below her.

Panel Five

Tina spiraling out of control, getting closer to the sign. She's smiling – she wants this.

TINA (SMALL): Nostrum corporis est unus.

PAGE TWENTY-FOUR

Panel One

This is a large splash page of Tina flying right into the marquee. The release of jet gas causes a huge explosion. Tina is all but vaporized by it.

FX: WHOOOM!

PAGE TWENTY-FIVE

Panel One

Dinah bobs up out of the water, and looks up at the flaming wreckage of the sign.

DINAH: Ow. Scratch one crazy bitch.

Panel Two

BC, now dripping wet, climbs out of the pool, pretty much ignoring the stares of the tourists and late night bathers around her.

DINAH: I know, I should have showered first. My bad.

Panel Three

Canary has grabbed a towel and is drying off her hair in front of a bunch of people at the pool's bar. She points to the margarita held in the hand of some cute guy at the bar.

3 DINAH: Hey. Who's drinking that margarita?

4 GUY AT THE BAR: I...think that would be you.

Panel Four

Canary sips the drink as she walks away. She tosses her towel over her shoulder to the guy in the manner of Mean Joe Greene tossing his jersey to the kid at the end of the famous Coke commercial.

5 DINAH: Thanks.

PAGE TWENTY-SIX

Panel One

We are inside Dinah's apartment. Tasteful. Simple. She's never really there long enough to do much to the place except to sleep, work out and what she is doing right now. The CANARY CRY fires from off-panel and shatters a fancy crystal vase of roses on a normal-looking table in a dark room.

1 CAPTION: Today.

CRY FX: EEEEEEEEEEEEEEE!!!!!!!!!

Panel Two

Dinah and Oliver "Green Arrow" Queen collapse next to each other. We're in Black Canary's apartment. Ollie smiles.

2 DINAH: Sorry, Ollie. The vase was lovely.

3 OLLIE: So was that.

Panel Three

Ollie extends his arm toward Dinah. It looks like he is going to hug Dinah. She smiles adoringly, getting ready for her embrace.

4 OLLIE: Besides, what's a Waterford vase where passion is concerned?

5 DINAH: Aww...

Panel Four

But Ollie is really reaching for the TV remote. Dinah knows this trick and is getting pissed.

6 DINAH: Hey, hey!

Panel Five

Dinah punches Ollie in the shoulder as he flips through channels.

TV FX: Click. Click. Click. Click.

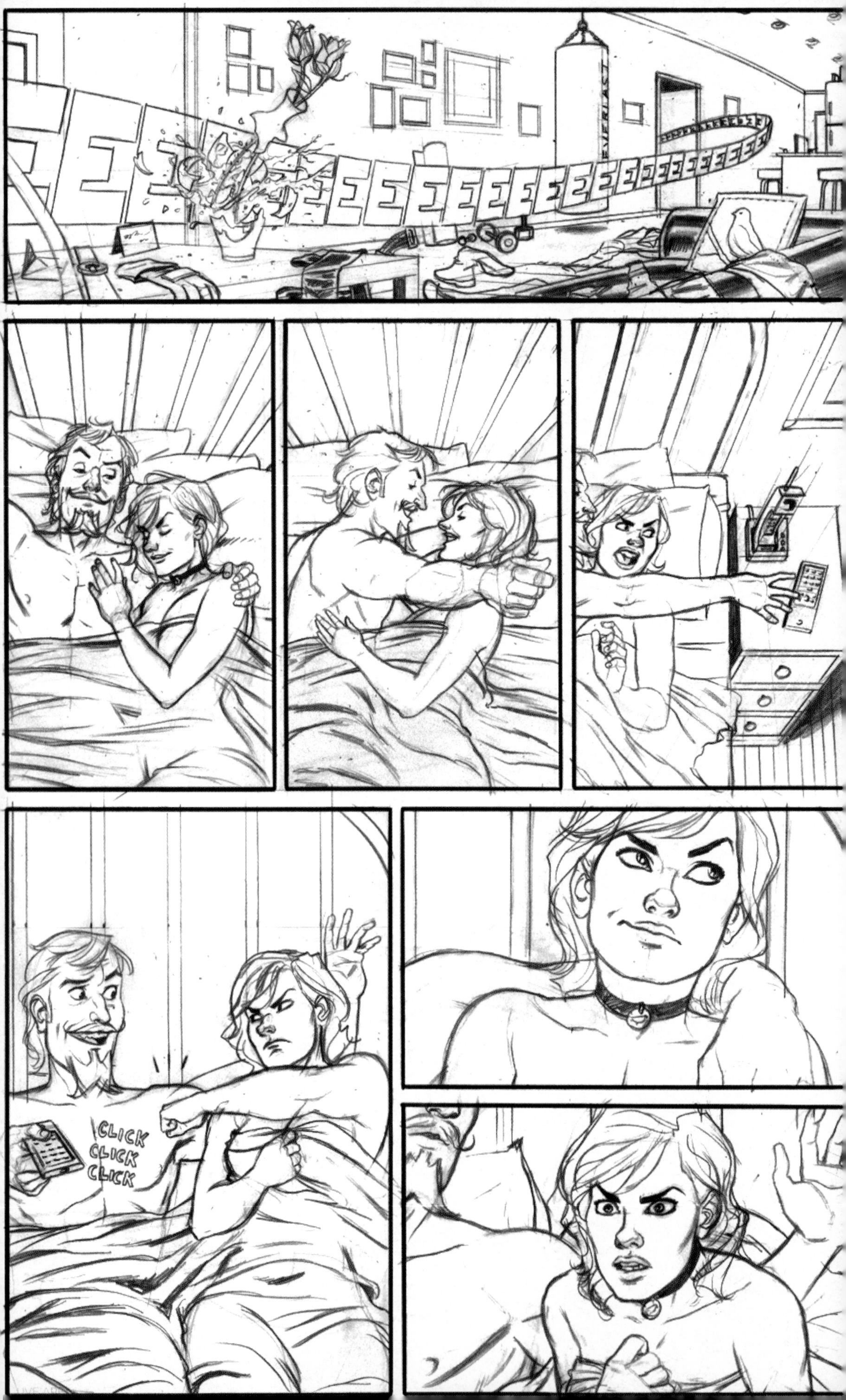
EEEEEEEEEEEEEEEEEEEEEEEEE
CLICK
CLICK
CLICK

7 DINAH: Bastard! Where are my cuddles?

8 OLLIE: Ow!

9 SECOND OLLIE BALLOON: This is work. If the world's about to end, TV will warn us.

Panel Six

Dinah rolls her eyes.

10 TV FX: Click. Click. Click. Click.

11 DINAH: I swear, next time I'm just gonna borrow your frequency-matching agitator arrow...

Panel Seven

Dinah suddenly points at the TV. Her face looks urgent.

12 DINAH: Wait. Wait. Go back!

13 OLLIE: What?

14 SECOND DINAH BALLOON: Go back!

PAGE TWENTY-SEVEN

Panel One

Ollie watches Dinah watch the television.

1 TV: —affic backed up around a popular restaurant following an accident this afternoon. A young woman crashed through a window of the rotating restaurant before plunging to the boulevard below. Police have not released the woman's name pending family notification, but have revealed that a suicide note WAS found.

Panel Two

Close on Dinah and Ollie.

2 DINAH: I think... I think I know her.

3 OLLIE: But they've got that mosaic thing over her body...

Panel Three

Dinah shoots Ollie a paranoid look.

4 DINAH: Trust me.

PHONE: RIIIINNNNGGGGG!

Panel Four

Dinah picks up the phone.

5 DINAH: Hello?

6 PHONE: Dinah? Is this Dinah?

Panel Five

7 DINAH: Betty Jo?

8 PHONE: You said... you told us to-to call this number if...

9 DINAH: Yeah, Bets. I did.

PAGE TWENTY-EIGHT

Panel One

Ollie looks concerned as Dinah is grabbing around for any clothes she can find.

1 PHONE: Meghan's dead, Dinah.

2 DINAH: I know, Bets. It's on the news.

3 SECOND PHONE BALLOON: The news doesn't know everything, Dinah. Meghan left a note apologizing... she apologized for betraying Tina...

Panel Two

Dinah's hopping on one foot to put on a shoe.

4 PHONE: I-I think I need to see yo --

5 DINAH: I'm on my way, Bets. I'm on my -- Bets?

Panel Three

Dinah stops what she's doing and gives the phone her attention.

6 DINAH: Bets!?

Panel Four

Close on the phone and one of Dinah's eyes.

7 PHONE: Sorry I bothered you, CANARY. The harbor ferry's about to leave and I plan to throw myself off it.

8 PHONE FX: Click.

Panel Five

Dinah tosses the phone to Ollie as she heads for the front door.

9 DINAH: Stay here.

PAGE TWENTY-NINE

Panel One

Dinah zooms along the streets on her motorcycle.

Panel Two

She weaves in and out of cars as she approaches the leaving ferry. The bridge is rising.

Panel Three

This panel takes up the bottom half of the page. Typical action movie moment. She's broken through the barrier and is jumping her bike across the large gap between the harbor and the moving ferry.

PAGE THIRTY

Panel One

Dinah's motorcycle skids across the deck

and is stopped by a hatchback. The owner stands dumbstruck with the door open. He must have been grabbing something from the car.

1 OWNER: MY CAR! You're PAYING for that!

Panel Two

Dinah stands and pays the man no attention.

2 DINAH: Send the bill to the J.L.A.

Panel Three

Dinah stops — she's looking at something. Perhaps in the foreground of the panel we can see an out-of-focus hand grabbing onto an out-of-focus rail.

3 DINAH: Betty Jo...

Panel Four

Downshot on Betty Jo. She's standing on the outside of the railing, leaning back against the rails. Her arms are wide and she's looking up with her eyes closed. We can see the beginnings of a VERY rough wake trail caused by the boat below. Behind her, Dinah approaches with her hand out.

4 DINAH: Climb back over the railing, Bets...

5 BETTY JO: One-way trip, Canary.

PAGE THIRTY-ONE

Panel One

Side shot of Dinah inching towards Bets. Bets is just standing outside the rails and looking away from Dinah with a smile on her face.

1 DINAH: If you fall, the wake from the boat will drag you under and you WILL drown.

Panel Two

Betty Jo turns around and smirks.

2 BETTY JO: OR... I'll get dragged through the propeller. I deserve worse for what I did to Tina.

3 DINAH: Stop joking around, Bets!

Panel Three

And suddenly Betty Jo looks scared.

4 BETTY JO: Dinah? Wh-where am --

Panel Four

And she loses her balance and falls. Dinah dives for her but...

5 DINAH: Bets!

BETTY JO: AHHHHH!!!!

PAGE THIRTY-TWO – SPLASH

She misses. And this is a very depressing down shot of Dinah looking over the railing, defeated. All we see is a splash in the wake.

PAGE THIRTY-THREE

Panel One

Back roads, nighttime. Dinah's back on her bike, but this time Ollie in his Green Arrow digs is riding on the back.

1 OLLIE: Sorry you had to pick me up.

2 DINAH: No problem, it was on the way. But, it may not be next time.

Panel Two

Dinah smirks. Ollie reddens.

3 DINAH: Hey, didn't you used to have an Arrowmobile or something?

4 OLLIE: ...

5 SECOND OLLIE BALLOON: No.

Panel Three

Dinah lightens a little to tease GA.

6 DINAH: Yeah, yeah you did. Whatever happened to it?

7 OLLIE: I don't wanna talk about it.

Panel Four

The cycle continues through the darkness.

8 DINAH: Bruce gave you a hard time about it, didn't he?

9 OLLIE: Hey, did you try to call the, uh... other girl from that undercover op?

Panel Five

Dinah gives up.

10 DINAH: Lauren.

11 SECOND DINAH BALLOON: She's not answering.

PAGE THIRTY-FOUR

Panel One

Establishing. Trailer park, nighttime. Dinah and Ollie pull up to a nearby trailer.

Panel Two

Green Arrow's getting off the bike. Dinah's knocking on the front door of the trailer. The light in the window is off.

1 DINAH: Lauren? Lauren, you there?

2 DOOR FX: Knock knock.

Panel Three

Ollie points to the window – the light is now on. Dinah rolls her eyes.

3 OLLIE: The lights are shorting out.

4 DINAH: Thank you, Batman.

Panel Four

The light is off. Ollie makes his way to the breaker on the side of the trailer. An extension cord trails off-panel.

5 OLLIE: Obvious though it may be, there's a reason for my observation.

Panel Five

Ollie unplugs the extension cord connected at the breaker. The window lights up behind him.

PAGE THIRTY-FIVE

Panel One

Ollie follows the cord around the back of the trailer. Behind it we see a small-sized above-ground pool. Several cords plug into a power strip. Their devices can not be seen as they're in the pool.

Panel Two

Dinah's right behind Green Arrow as he climbs the ladder to the pool.

1 OLLIE: Brace yourself, Pretty Bird.

Panel Three

On Dinah. She's gasping.

Panel Four

Down shot of the pool. Lauren floats fully clothed alongside a toaster, a hairdryer, and a small TV. What's really odd is that Lauren is dressed up nice like she was going out on a date – not at all like she was planning on committing suicide. She also sports several good luck charms around her neck, and a new tattoo of a mystical symbol that covers her right hand and extends to the tip of her index finger.

2 OLLIE: What do you suppose that symbol on her hand means?

3 DINAH: I haven't a clue...

Panel Five

Close on Dinah.

4 DINAH: But I know someone who might.

PAGE THIRTY-SIX

Panel One

Zatanna, in her typical magician outfit (black coat, 'nets, white vest, gloves, etc.) sits in the middle of a bunch of candles. Her top hat is brim up in her lap. The only light comes from the flickering flames. All around her are amoebic shadows. Zatanna's eyes are closed.

1 ZATANNA: I call upon the demons of the deep. Hear my prayer and respond.

Panel Two

Close on Zatanna's face. Her eyes are closed. Light flickers off of her ominously. What is she doing?

2 ZATANNA: Give us that which we desire. Give us that which will raise our spirits.

Panel Three

Her eyes open – the pupils are white.

3 ZATANNA: Evig su eht syeknom.

PAGE THIRTY-SEVEN

Panel One

And the reveal – This panel is the exact same layout, except now the lights are on and Zatanna's eyes are normal. We're actually in a small theater. Zee's smiling and raising her hands up in the air. The empty hat now has a small flood of adorable squirrel monkeys spilling out of it. The shadows were children. They are applauding. In the background, Dinah leans against a wall, smiling at the show. She's in her street clothes.

1 ZATANNA: Ta-da!

KIDS: YAAAAYYYY!

Panel Two

Zee, kids all around her, looks up and sees Dinah. She raises her index finger to say, "One minute."

Panel Three

Dinah nods.

2 DINAH CAPTION: Talk about having it all. Poise, power, successful career – and those kids just adore her.

Panel Four

On Dinah. She wears a nostalgic smile.

3 DINAH CAPTION: You've come a LONG way, kiddo...

PAGE THIRTY-EIGHT

Panel One

Establishing shot. Justice League Satellite.

1 CAPTION: Ten years ago.

Panel Two

We're aboard the old JL Satellite. Black Canary leans against a bulkhead and is watching a surprised and young-looking Zee teleport in front of her. Zee's about seventeen/eighteen here. It might be fun

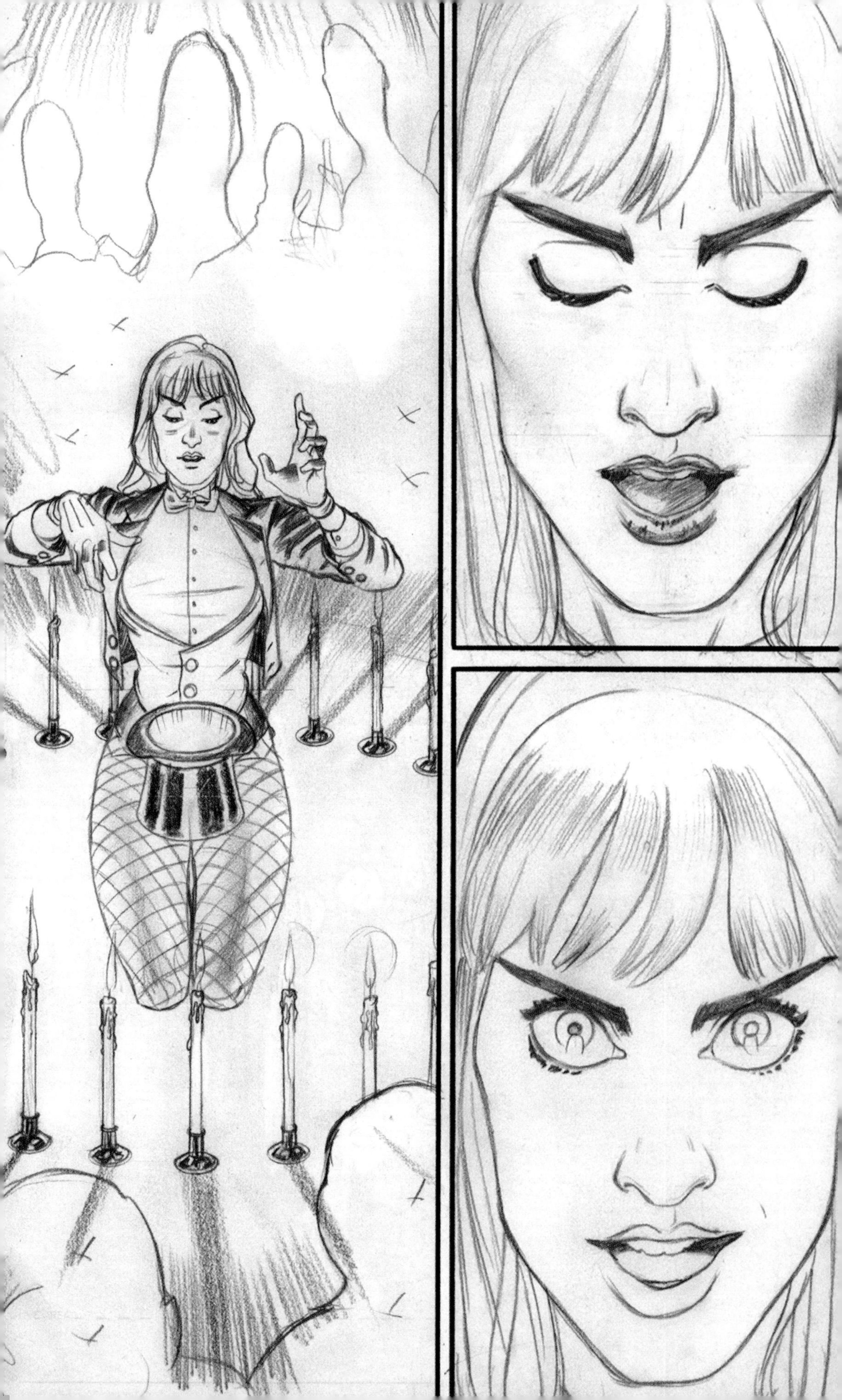

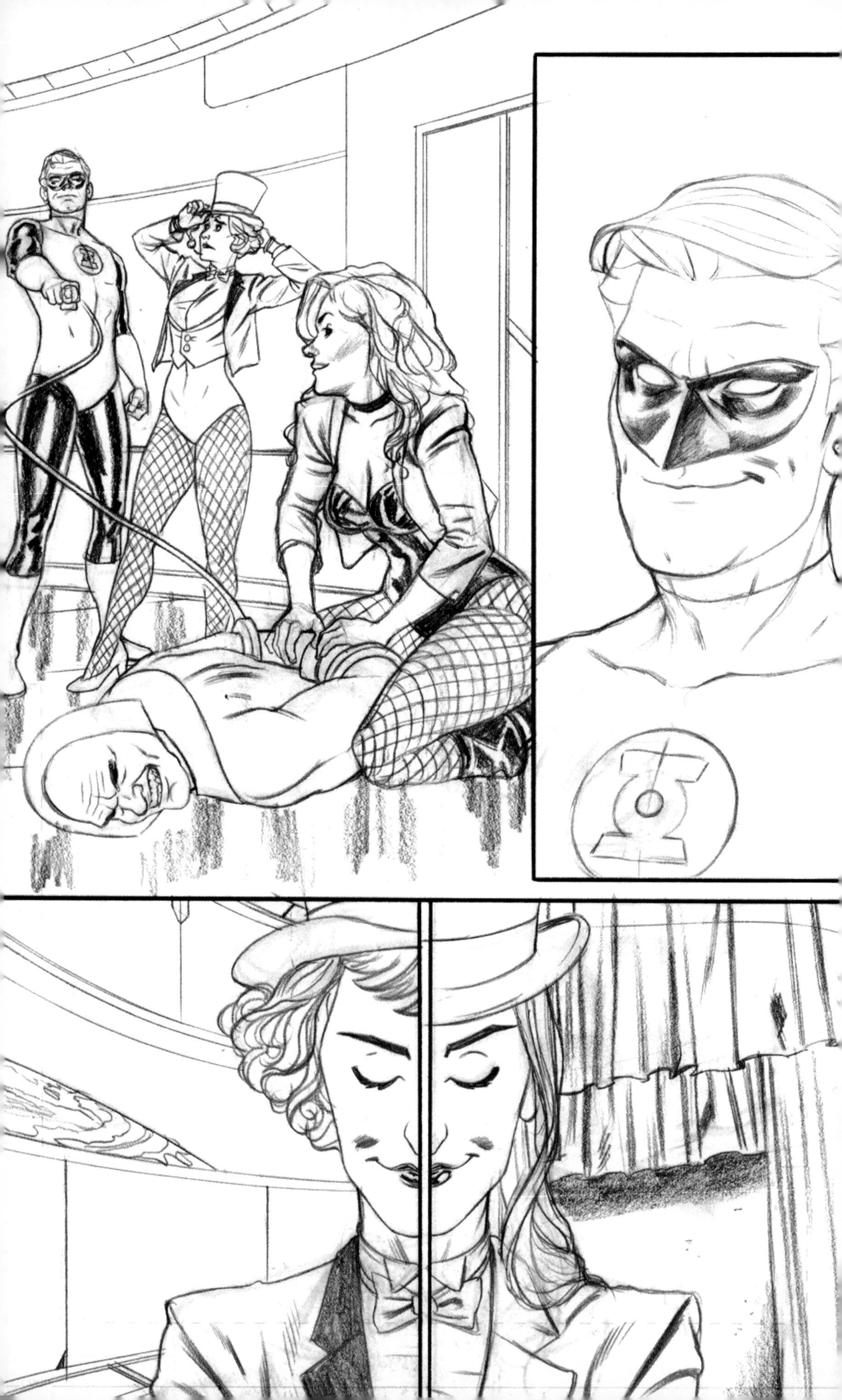

to go for an earlier look on her here, with the short hair and some variation of the blue tuxedo costume she first wore in that old issue of Hawkman from way back when.

2 DINAH: I'd think you of all people would be used to teleporting.

Panel Three

Zee straightens out her magician's outfit as she walks out of the teleport tube and smiles nervously at Dinah.

3 ZEE: That... That tickled a bit more than what I'm used to.

4 DINAH: Huh. Never heard it described QUITE that way before.

5 SECOND DINAH BALLOON: Glad you made the cut, Zee. The Hawks tell me good things.

Panel Four

BC waves Zee on. Zee nods as she nervously messes with her tie.

6 ZATANNA: I'm ACTUALLY on the REAL J.L.A. satellite! Nerves!

7 DINAH: Come on, I'll show you around.

Panel Five

They walk down a hall. Zee fidgets with her gloves uneasily. Her eyes follow Sue Dibny as she walks the other way.

8 DINAH: The layout may seem daunting, but you'll get used to it.

9 SECOND DINAH BALLOON: It just takes getting lost a few times.

PAGE THIRTY-NINE

Panel One

BC and Zee walk through the hall and run into Martian Manhunter.

1 DINAH: Here's someone I can introduce you to...

Panel Two

Zee's starstruck.

2 DINAH: Zatanna, this is --

3 ZEE: I know! I know! The Martian Manhunter!

Panel Three

Zee's smiling up at J'onn, who regards her coolly. Zatanna extends her hand.

4 ZEE: I totally GROK you!

Panel Four

J'onn looks at Dinah questioningly. Dinah just shrugs. She doesn't know what it means either. Zatanna forces a smile as she curls her formerly extended hand into itself. She feels like she swallowed a toad.

A thought balloon appears over Zatanna's head. In it, we see a Sergio Aragonés-style cartoony version of Zatanna being yanked off stage with an old-style vaudeville hook as an OS audience BOOS and throws tomatoes. Yes, while it IS technically Dinah having the flashback, the image is funny, so let's do it.

5 OFF-PANEL AUDIENCE IN THOUGHT BALLOON: Booo!

6 ZATANNA (Embarrassed): Heh...

Panel Five

And suddenly an alarm sounds. J'onn and the girls react to the alarm and comm voice.

ALARM: WOOP! WOOP! WOOP!

7 COMM: We have an escaped criminal. THE KEY has escaped during transport.

Panel Six

J'onn is already racing into action. Zee watches him leave with a heavy heart.

8 DINAH: You go, I'll stay with the kid.

9 ZEE: *SIGH* So much for first impressions.

PAGE FORTY

Panel One

Dinah pats Zee on the back.

1 DINAH: Don't sweat it, kiddo. You'll fit in just fine.

2 ZEE: I dunno. I'm not a boy scout or a hard-ass or even a scientist. I'm just...

Panel Two

Zee looks sort of sheepishly at Dinah.

3 ZEE: Me.

Panel Three

Dinah stops and looks seriously at Zee.

4 DINAH: You remember the first time we met?

5 ZEE: On the mountain? How could I forget? You were such a tool.

Panel Four

Dinah forces back a smile as Zatanna's white-gloved finger jabs her.

6 ZATANNA: And you lied. There WERE Yetis!

7 DINAH: Ha! Oh, yeah...

Panel Five

Dinah is all serious again.

8 DINAH: That aside, when I gave you a hard time, you sucked it up and CLIMBED

back down.

Panel Six

Close on Dinah.

9 DINAH: You proved to me right then you had the stuff. You'll fit in here just fine.

PAGE FORTY-ONE

Panel One

Pull back to reveal Ralph Dibny, the Elongated Man's head stretching around the corner towards Dinah. Actually, he's in between Dinah and Zee.

1 DINAH: Ralph? What is it?

2 RALPH: The Key... Don't let him free the prisoners!

Panel Two

A bright light shines off-panel and Ralph is knocked out cold.

KEY BLASTER FX: BZZZZZ!

Panel Three

Dinah has given Ralph a quick once-over. Zee looks worriedly at the unconscious Ralph.

3 ZEE: Is he okay?

4 DINAH: For the moment. We have to guard the prison.

Panel Four

5 ZEE: What prison?

6 DINAH: The one right behind us.

Panel Five

Zee looks behind her at the door marked "Prison."

7 ZEE: Oh.

PAGE FORTY-TWO

Panel One

And then the Key walks into view with a large smile, keys hanging wherever they can, and his key-shaped gun in his hand.

1 KEY: Ah, the Black Canary and...

Panel Two

He gives Zee a curious look.

2 KEY: ...And what are you supposed to be? A cocktail waitress?

Panel Three

Dinah pushes Zee behind her.

3 DINAH: You're NOT freeing the prisoners. I WILL stop you.

KEY: Forgive my proclivity towards stating the obvious, but...

Panel Four

The Key points to the unconscious Elongated Man on the floor.

3 KEY: You and what army?

PAGE FORTY-THREE

Panel One

Dinah lets out a CANARY CRY but the Key ducks.

CRY FX: EEEEEEEEEEEEEEEEEE!!!

KEY: Please, SUE put up a better fight.

Panel Two

The Key knocks Dinah down with a blow from his large key.

Panel Three

And points his gun at her.

2 KEY: Let me sing you to sleep.

Panel Four

Zee yells out her magic words and every key on the Key, including his Key Blaster, disappears. He looks very confused.

3 ZEE: S'yek syek hsinav!

KEY: Wha?

PAGE FORTY-FOUR

Panel One

Zee removes her hat and bows to Dinah.

ZEE: He's ALL yours!

Panel Two

But the vanished keys reappear — they fall out of Zee's hat and onto the floor. Zee's face matches her dialogue perfectly.

KEY FX: Ting! Ting! Ting! Ting! Ting!

ZEE (very small): yipes.

Panel Three

The Key leaps for his keys on the floor, but...

Panel Four

...smacks against the side of a circular green force field.

FX: WHUMP!

KEY: AH!!

PAGE FORTY-FIVE

Panel One

Dinah is kneeling on the Key's back and holding his hands together while GREEN LANTERN (Hal Jordan) cuffs him with a pair of glowing handcuffs made by his ring. Dinah smiles at Zee.

1 DINAH: Good job, Zatanna.

2 GREEN ARROW: Yeah.

Panel Two

Large panel — close on GL. Smiling encouragingly at Zee.

3 GREEN LANTERN: You did good, kid.

Panel Three

Close on Zatanna, grinning like a happy teenager, which is exactly what she is.

Panel Four

This happy image of Zatanna "fades" to show her ten years later, present day, a young woman at the height of her powers. It is after her show and she is signing autographs for an off-panel fan.

4 ZATANNA: So how do you spell "Orville," anyway?

PAGE FORTY-SIX

Panel One

We're back in the theatre. Zee's signing her last autograph for a kid, a little boy. Dinah's hanging around waiting.

1 LITTLE BOY: O-r-v...

2 ZEE: Never mind, I think I got it.

Panel Two

Zee tosses a wave to the last of her retreating fans as Dinah walks up.

3 ZATANNA: Glad you liked the show. Come again.

4 DINAH: You totally flashed on the cups and balls.

Panel Three

They hug like the old friends they are.

5 ZEE: The hell I did.

6 DINAH: On the other hand, you comped me, so what right do I have to complain?

Panel Four

They separate but keep up the high energy.

7 ZEE: How've you been? How's Ollie?

8 DINAH: He's terrific. Me, I'm not sure.

PAGE FORTY-SEVEN

Panel One

1 ZEE: What's wrong?

2 DINAH: Kinda hard to explain in here. You busy this afternoon?

Panel Two

Zee puts a hand to her forehead in imitation of a mentalist doing his act. Dinah raises a semi-amused eyebrow at that.

3 ZEE: My mystic powers tell me you are in sorry need of a girls' day out.

4 DINAH: Yeah, I just said that.

Panel Three

Zatanna puts a friendly arm around Dinah as they head toward the theatre dressing rooms.

5 ZEE: Then let me get changed and we shall adjourn to the Hall of Justice.

6 DINAH: What is that? Zee-speak for the local mall?

Panel Four

We are inside a mall, close on the sign of a lingerie store that reads: SEAMS AND DREAMS. There are half-body (waist down) female mannequins in the window that show off a variety of fishnet stockings. Zatanna and Dinah are exiting the store. Zatanna is not wearing her usual costume, though she still dresses somewhat bohemian — denim shorts (or skirt) over fishnets, boots, a leather jacket, maybe sunglasses or a ballcap with a Z on it. Zee and Dinah both carry bags of lingerie. Zatanna displays a wrapped packet of fishnets.

7 ZATANNA CAPTION: "Exactly."

8 ZATANNA: At the rate we go through these things, that place should give us a fifty percent discount.

9 DINAH: Amen to that.

Panel Five

Zee and Dinah continue on, approaching a big fountain in the middle of the mall. Three guys leaning against the side of the fountain leer at them lewdly and whistle.

10 GUY ONE: I'd love to get tangled in THOSE fishnets.

11 GUY TWO FX: WHISTLE!

PAGE FORTY-EIGHT

Panel One

Zee nods knowingly to Dinah.

1 ZEE: So you want to tangle with fishnets

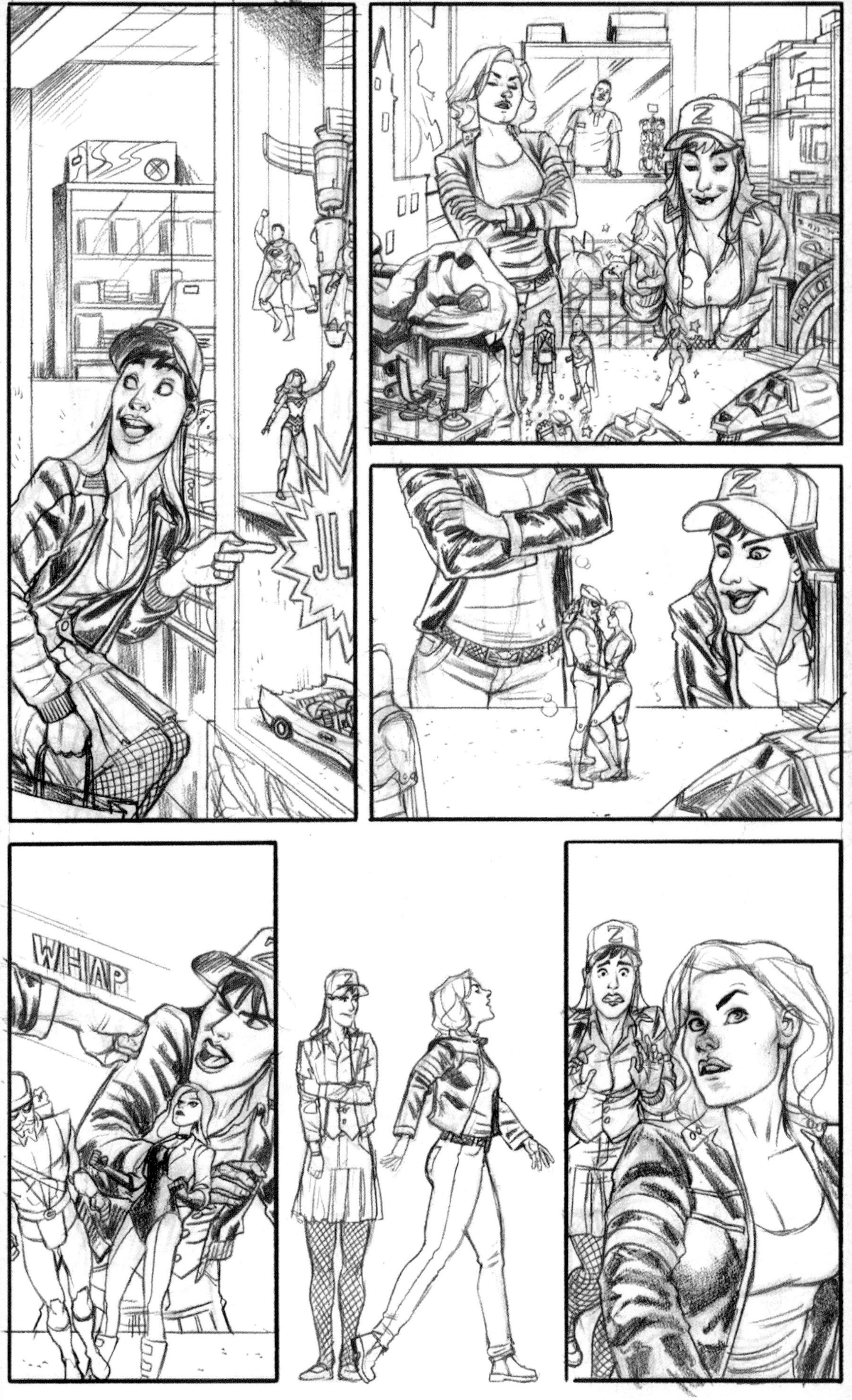
JL
HALL OF
WHAP

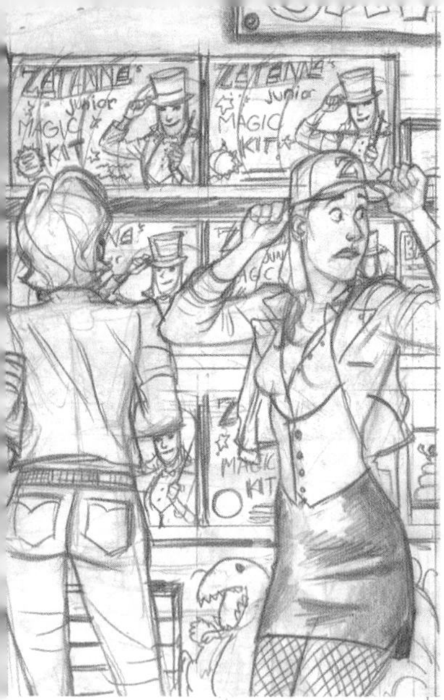
ZATANNA'S
Junior
MAGIC
KIT

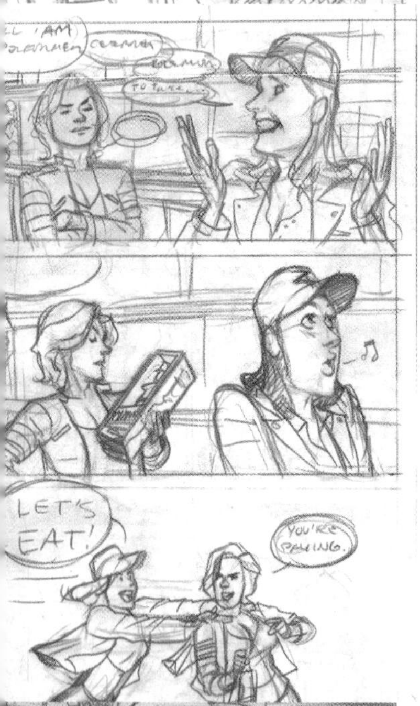
LET'S EAT!
YOU'RE PAYING.

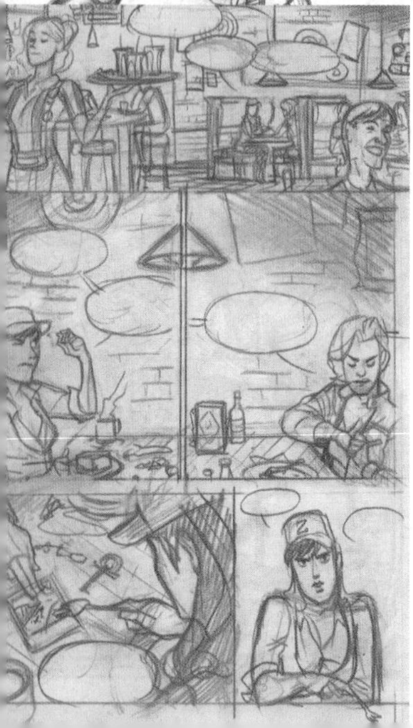

2 SECOND ZEE BALLOON (SMALL TEXT): Skrej emoceb hsifdlog.

Panel Two

Dinah shoots the mischievous Zatanna a disbelieving look.

3 DINAH: You didn't.

4 ZATANNA: I did. But only temporarily.

Panel Three

As the girls walk off, Dinah looks behind them and notices three big gold koi fish frantically flipping into the fountain where the jerks once stood.

5 ZEE: No one will miss them for an hour or so.

Panel Four

Zatanna and Dinah pass a big chain toy store.

6 ZATANNA: Oh, cool. You ever go into these places?

7 DINAH: God, no.

PAGE FORTY-NINE

Panel One

Zee points at the window. There is an assortment of Justice League character figures in the window. The figures include Wonder Woman, Superman, Flash, Martian Manhunter, Hawkgirl, Black Canary and Green Arrow.

1 ZEE: Really? I love toys.

2 ZEE (Second balloon, sing-songy): Look who's in the win-dow!

Panel Two

Inside the toy store. Zatanna and Dinah stand at a display of the dolls arranged against a small city backdrop. Zatanna flickers her fingers at the dolls. The Green Arrow doll and the Black Canary doll start to magically move as if guided by an unseen puppeteer.

3 DINAH: Oh, those. We okayed those to be sold for charity. The profits go to victims of super villains.

4 ZATANNA: Uh-huh.

5 GREEN ARROW FIGURE (Smaller balloon): Hey, Pretty Bird. I ain't seen you around the Barbie aisle before.

Panel Three

Dinah continues to explain as Zatanna has fun magically moving the toys around. The dolls continue to hit on each other.

6 DINAH: I guess you were on reserve when we made that deal.

7 ZATANNA: I'm not bitter.

8 SECOND ZATANNA BALLOON (Sings film music, musical notes in the balloon): Bount-chicka-bount-bount...

9 BLACK CANARY FIGURE: Hey, yourself, Robin Hood. Is that an arrow in your quiver or are you just happy to see me?

Panel Four

Dinah punches Zee in the arm. The dolls instantly turn back into lifeless toys.

10 SFX: Whap!

11 ZEE: Ow!

Panel Five

Dinah starts to walk down the aisle toward the exit. Zatanna follows.

12 DINAH: You're not missing out on anything, trust me.

Panel Six

As Dinah rounds a corner, her voice trails off as she sees something surprising off-panel.

13 DINAH: We don't see a dime from those...toys...

PAGE FIFTY - SPLASH

Dinah stops in her tracks as she notices an ENTIRE WALL of Zatanna brand "Junior Magic Kits." Each box has Zatanna's smiling face on it. Dinah's a bit taken aback. Zatanna hangs back a bit, embarrassed. She didn't really want Dinah to see this. She readjusts her sunglasses or cap so as to look anonymous.

1 DINAH: Huh.

PAGE FIFTY-ONE

Panel One

Zee tries to work up a credible explanation. Dinah raises an eyebrow.

1 ZEE: Well, I AM a performer. Celebrity. Role model...to the kids, y'know...

2 DINAH: Yeah.

Panel Two

Dinah holds up a Zatanna fashion toy in its Barbie-like box. Zatanna pretends to avoid the question, assuming a casual attitude, her hands in her back pockets, whistling, looking away, or otherwise trying to be evasive.

3 DINAH: And you donate the profits to...?

Panel Three

Zee avoids the question and pushes Dinah out the door.

4 ZEE: Let's eat!

5 DINAH: You're paying.

PAGE FIFTY-TWO

Panel One
At lunch, Dinah puts most of her cards on the table – well, the charms found on Lauren, anyway. Dinah's done with her food and has a cup of coffee. Zatanna is working on dessert – tiramisu.

1 DINAH: These were found on Lauren, the girl I told you about.

2 ZEE: Harmless. Trinkets to sell to Goth kids.

Panel Two

Zee shrugs as she examines one of the charms. She regards it the way a Tiffany jeweler would look at a paste diamond.

3 DINAH: Do any of them work?

4 ZEE: About as well as a four-leaf clover or rabbit's foot.

Panel Three

Dinah reaches into her jacket pocket and pulls out a photo. We don't see much of what's on it from this angle.

5 DINAH: Well, what about --

Panel Four

Dinah slides a photo of the tattoo on Lauren's hand across the table. Zatanna studies the photo and points to it with her fork.

6 DINAH: -- this?

7 ZEE: Now THAT actually has some mojo to it.

8 SECOND ZATANNA BALLOON: If the user is skilled enough, it can actually ward off some curses.

Panel Five

ZEE suddenly looks concerned.

9 ZEE: Dinah, what's this all about?

PAGE FIFTY-THREE

Panel One

Dinah doesn't like revealing this, but she's got no choice.

1 DINAH: The undercover job I told you about? The girl we were after, Tina, made us prick our fingers and touch them together. She said some kinda prayer...

Panel Two

Zee chokes on her tiramisu she's so shocked.

2 DINAH: "Per nostrum sanguis, nostrum corporis est unus"?

3 ZEE: *KAFF!*

Panel Three

Her composure regained, Zatanna throws her arms wide and says her magic words.

4 ZEE: EZEERF EMIT!

Panel Four

Dinah marvels as she looks around – everything is frozen. A waiter in mid-fall, dropping his tray.

5 DINAH: Whoa!

Panel Five

A customer getting a drink from the soda fountain, etc.... Dinah is impressed.

6 DINAH: Just like on "Bewitched"!

PAGE FIFTY-FOUR

Panel One

Zee looks at Dinah hard.

1 ZEE: Dinah, that was NO prayer!

Panel Two

Zee has gotten Dinah's attention back.

2 ZEE: She tricked you into a Bloodspell!

3 Dinah: A what? Can you break it?

Panel Three

Zee looks very serious and is shaking her head. Dinah protests.

4 ZEE: You took it freely of your own will...

5 DINAH: I WAS in disguise and under an assumed name. Does that count?

Panel Four

Zatanna stands, getting ready to cast a big spell.

6 ZEE: That DOES help, but you're still susceptible to its power.

7 SECOND ZEE BALLOON: I'd better call someone with a bit more experience...

Panel Five

Close on Zee

8 ZEE: I deen uoy.

PAGE FIFTY-FIVE

Panel One

A mystic wind stars to whip up in the restaurant. Dinah looks around, her alarm growing. She's used to physical action, and this hoodoo stuff creeps her out.

Panel Two

A silver light starts to grow in the center of the restaurant. Some unearthly messenger is crossing over into our world. We see the dim outline of a tall, thin man in the void.

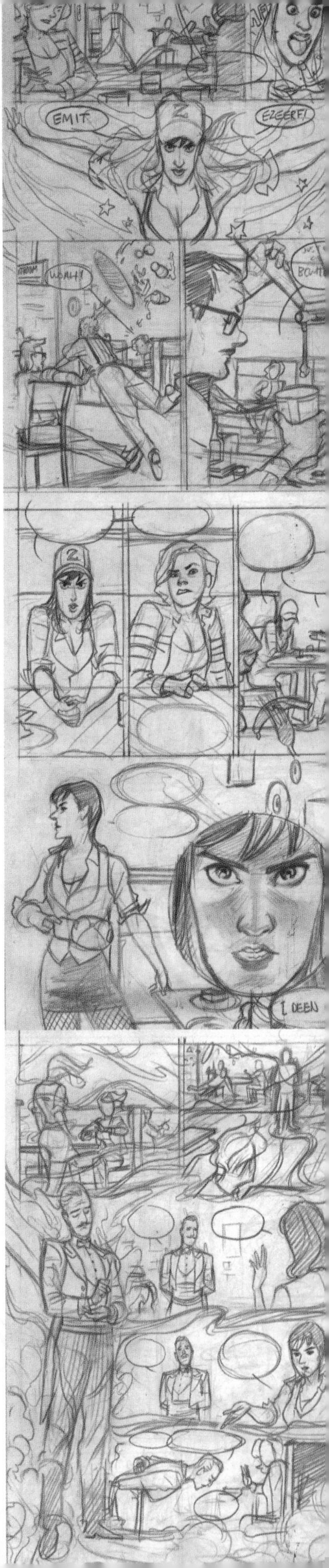
EMIT
EZEERF!
WOAH!
I DEEN

Panel Three

The silver light reveals the figure of Zatara the Magician. In spirit form, of course, but no less regal than we've known him in real life.

Panel Four

Zatara looks kindly at his daughter, Zatanna.

1 ZATARA: Hello, daughter.

2 ZATANNA: Hi, Daddy.

Panel Five

Zatanna directs her gently nagging father to Dinah.

3 ZATARA: I hope you finished your vegetables before ordering that tiramisu.

4 ZATANNA: Daddy, this is important. You remember Dinah.

Panel Six

The spectral wizard bows to Dinah. She gives him a wave back.

5 ZATARA: Of course. Nice to see you again, Black Canary.

6 DINAH: You too, sir.

PAGE FIFTY-SIX

Panel One

Zatara regards Dinah with sympathy as Zee explains the situation.

1 ZEE: Dinah's in trouble, Dad. She was tricked into a Bloodspell.

2 ZATARA: Oh, how unfortunate.

Panel Two

Zatara considers Zatanna's request.

3 ZEE: Fortunately, it was while she was in disguise and not with her real name. Can you help us?

4 ZATARA: The Bloodspell is an ancient and powerful method of self-preservation used by sorcerers.

Panel Three

5 ZATARA: At the time of their death, a powerful magician could use a blood bond to pass their soul into another human host body.

Panel Four

Dinah gets it now.

6 ZATARA: That soul can inhabit any and every person connected by the bond. A good sorcerer would leave the host in peace, though an evil wizard could force its host to harm or even kill themselves.

7 DINAH: Tina. While I was undercover,

her girls said she was into all that spooky-kooky candles and chicken blood stuff.

8 SECOND DINAH BALLOON: No offense.

Panel Five

Zatara tries to put a positive spin on it for Dinah.

9 ZATARA: None taken. If it's any consolation, the villain's hold on you is not as strong as the others. At least, not yet.

10 SECOND ZATARA BALLOON: Because you swore the oath in someone else's name, the curse has only a partial hold on you. But, still, you are FAR from being out of danger.

Panel Six

11 ZATARA: The more lives she claims, the greater her power grows. In time, she may claim you too.

12 DINAH: I think that's actually pretty high on her agenda.

Panel Seven

Zee also spells it out.

13 ZEE: Totally. She's killing the girls in front of you to break your resolve. If she wears down your defenses, you become vulnerable to anger and guilt.

14 ZATARA: And an easy target.

PAGE FIFTY-SEVEN

Panel One

Zatara thoughtfully considers alternatives.

1 ZATARA: The only way to get rid of this spirit is to magically banish her back to the afterlife.

2 DINAH: How do we do that?

Panel Two

It seems simple to Zatanna, who matter-of-factly says:

3 ZEE: We catch her.

4 DINAH (Not as hopeful): Oh sure. Why not?

Panel Three

The image of Zatara starts to waver.

5 ZATARA: My time is short. I think you can take it from here.

Panel Four

Zatara kisses his daughter on the cheek.

6 ZATANNA: Thanks, Daddy. Love you.

7 ZATARA: And I you, rabbit. Good luck.

Panel Five

Zatara gives Zee a loving touch on the nose.

8 ZATARA: For what it's worth, I was in the middle of baffling Houdini with a sleight-of-hand routine when you summoned me.

Panel Six

Zatara starts to vanish Cheshire Cat-style back into the silver light.

9 ZATARA: Imagine. The man can make an elephant disappear, but he can't master a simple thumb tip.

PAGE FIFTY-EIGHT

Panel One

Zatanna makes a wide magical gesture to the space around her.

1 ZEE: Ezeerfnu.

Panel Two

From here on out, everything in the background is moving again. That poor waiter drops his tray. Zee is putting a tip on the table.

2 ZEE: We'll have to act fast to save the last two girls... and you.

Panel Three

They hurriedly run out of the food court.

3 DINAH: Dottie and the real Joy are both still in Vegas.

4 ZEE: We need to get there FAST, but not in any way that would alert Tina's ghost to what we're up to.

Panel Four

They pass the fountain. Security guards are helping three very wet and confused men out of the water.

5 DINAH: No teleporting?

6 ZEE: Right.

Panel Five

They get to the exit and Dinah reaches for the handle. Zee smiles at Dinah.

7 ZEE: Up for a road trip?

PAGE FIFTY-NINE

Panel One

Panoramic shot of an arena on Apokolips. The living hellhole of a planet as seen from above. Huge fire pits, Parademons winging through the sky, giant statues of Darkseid, the whole works.

1 CANARY CAPTION: "Always."

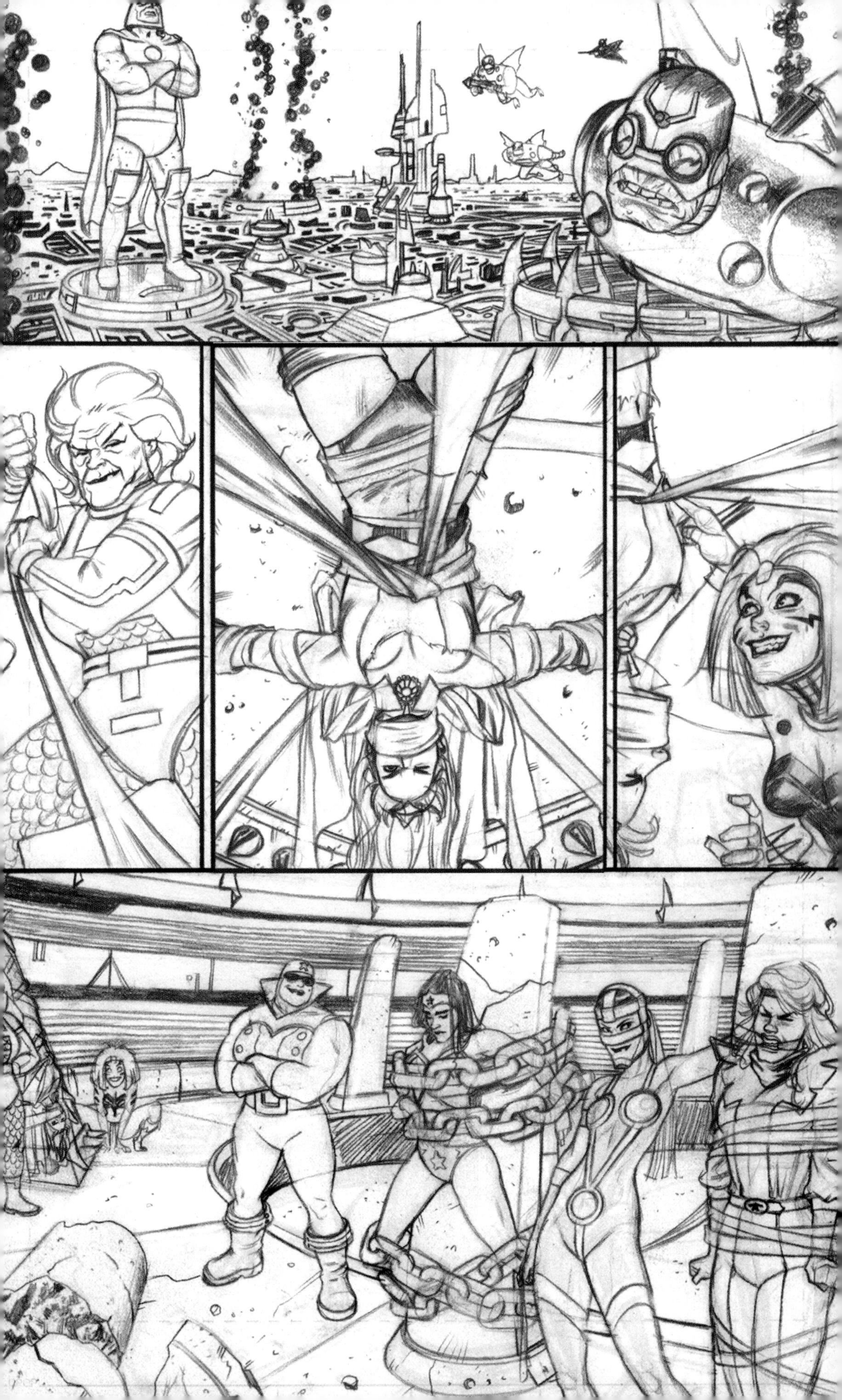

Panel Two

We are close on Darkseid's trusted hench-hag GRANNY GOODNESS. She is tying something up with what appears to be thick strands of red rubber.

2 GRANNY: My old protégé Scott Free, now THERE was an escape artist!

Panel Three

Zee is being tied by Granny to the front of some godawful huge machine, a Hellwagon. Nearby, Granny's own hench-girl, Female Fury MAD HARRIET, leaps in.

3 GRANNY: You have charms, lambkin, and skills to be sure.

4 GRANNY (To Harriet): Harriet, darling. Hold that knot.

Panel Four

Harriet places a clawed finger on the knot and leers at the gagged but defiant Zatanna as Granny pulls the knot tight.

5 MAD HARRIET: Hee, hee! Tighter, Granny!

6 GRANNY: But you're just not in the same class as Mr. Miracle, duckling.

Panel Five

Wider to reveal Granny has tied the unconscious rubber-like body of PLASTIC MAN around Zatanna like a rope. Nearby we see the Justice League has been fighting some big battle there and they've been beaten — badly. In heavy, huge chains is WONDER WOMAN, straining vainly to break free. Next to her, bound in LASHINA'S whips, is a gagged Black Canary. Lashina is enjoying Canary's struggling, as is the nearby muscle girl, STOMPA.

7 GRANNY: Trust your loving Granny Goodness. None of you are.

8 CAPTION: Apokolips.

9 SECOND CAPTION: Five years ago.

PAGE SIXTY

Panel One

Granny and the Female Furies are now seated in some crude arena, a place where the downtrodden slaves of Apokolips fight and die for the amusement of Darkseid and his followers. The captive Wonder Woman and Black Canary are close to Granny's seats. They are being forced to watch their teammates' demise. The Hellwagon rumbles into the arena. A wall of long spikes is at the other end of the arena.

1 GRANNY: Still, it will be amusing to watch you try to free yourself.

Panel Two

The Hellwagon races forward. Zatanna is headed STRAIGHT for the wall of spikes. Her eyes are wide in horror.

2 GRANNY (OFF): For the next three seconds or so.

Panel Three

Zee's even closer to the wall — how will she ever get out?

3 GRANNY (OFF): A toast, my lovely Furies.

Panel Four

Close on Granny and the Furies. Granny's about to take a swig from a mug. Her girls raise their mugs in a mocking salute to Zee's demise.

4 GRANNY: To a valiant, but woefully inferior...

Panel Five

Suddenly Granny and her girls find themselves hanging (by their arms, I suppose) over the very front of the Hellwagon where Zatanna was tied just a second before. Both she and Plas have vanished. Granny still has her raised mug and is looking in stunned, almost Wile E. Coyote-style shock at the wall of spikes less than a foot from them.

5 GRANNY: ...adversary?

PAGE SIXTY-ONE

Panel One

The Hellwagon hits the wall and EXPLODES!

1 FX: THOOM!

Panel Two

All but immolated, Granny and the Furies crawl out from the wreckage. They are Gods of a sort, after all, and while they are hurt, they are not completely destroyed.

2 LASHINA: Oww...

3 STOMPA: Oooh..

Panel Three

Granny stops at some feet and looks up.

4 GRANNY (Broken word balloon and lettering): Not fair...that was not...how?

5 ZATANNA (Off): Speaking words backwards or writing them, my magic still has power.

Panel Four

Up shot. Zee, a freed Wonder Woman, Black Canary and a shaky, but recovering Plastic Man look down at Granny and us. Zee is making a sign-language gesture with her fingers.

6 ZEE: And even bound and gagged, I was able to sign "switch places" backwards.

Panel Five

With her hands now doubled into fists, Zatanna, Wonder Woman, Plas, and Black Canary all advance on the groggy Furies.

7 ZATANNA: Now here's a hand signal I'm sure you'll all understand...

PAGE SIXTY-TWO

Panel One

We're inside what looks to be a HUGE lush loft. There is NO end in sight. Magic posters of Zee are on the wall, maybe a Hirschfeld-style caricature of her, as well. Zee stands in an expensive silk bathrobe practicing a ring-linking trick. Dinah soaks in a hot tub and laughs. A number of Zee's other big illusions and props are seen nearby.

1 DINAH: Sign language! Classic!

2 ZEE: Remember the time you went one-on-one with Grodd?

Panel Two

Dinah laughingly points at Zee. Behind Dinah, a large white tiger walks up to the hot tub.

3 DINAH: Yeah. After YOU turned him into a basketball!

Panel Three

Dinah notices the large cat and backs to the other side of the tub. The tiger laps water out of the hot tub. Zee looks over at the commotion.

4 DINAH: Um, Zee? Is there SUPPOSED to be a tiger in here?

Panel Four

Zee has let go of the rings she was practicing with. They stay floating in the air. She laughs as she walks to a nearby window. Dinah calms down a bit.

5 ZEE: Oh, that's just my friend Sasha. She's very tame AND obedient.

Panel Five

Dinah reluctantly pets Sasha. Sasha closes her eyes in contentment. The rings are still floating and Zee is looking out a nearby window.

SASHA FX: Purrrrrr...

PAGE SIXTY-THREE

Panel One

We're outside the window watching Zee watch us. Reflected in the window we see fluorescent lights of some kind.

1 ZEE: Dinah, we're almost there. You'd better suit up.

Panel Two

Pull out to reveal that they weren't actually in an apartment, but a tiny 16' trailer with a large Z painted on the side. The trailer is pulled behind a vintage convertible. Did I mention no one is driving the car? Okay, well, no one is driving the car. It's magically maneuvering itself through traffic on the busy Las Vegas strip. We can see Zee's face still in the window.

2 DINAH (OFF): I am NOT wearing this.

Panel Three

A bit closer on the trailer, but Zee's head is turning away.

3 ZEE: Yes, you ARE! Don't make me slap you.

PAGE SIXTY-FOUR

Panel One

Dinah is now out of the tub and in a robe and holding up a VERY skimpy magician's outfit. Sasha is rubbing her cheek along Dinah's hip like a house cat might do to your ankle. Zee walks up to Dinah.

1 DINAH: It's so skimpy!

2 SECOND DINAH BALLOON: I'll feel NAKED!

3 SECOND ZEE BALLOON: It's more than what you USUALLY wear.

4 SASHA FX: Purrr......

Panel Two

Dinah tosses the outfit onto the trailer's luxurious four-poster bed.

5 DINAH: That's my WORK outfit. I don't want to prance around in front of people in some showgirl costume.

6 ZEE: You have to have a disguise so Tina doesn't suspect we're working together.

Panel Three

7 DINAH: What would I say if someone recognizes me in that?

8 ZEE: Don't worry, they won't.

Panel Four

Zatanna points magically at Dinah, hitting her with a blast of magic power. Though mostly obscured by magical smoke and sparkles, we can just see that Dinah is starting to TRANSFORM.

9 ZATANNA: Emutsoc no dna revo-ekam!

10 DINAH: Hey!

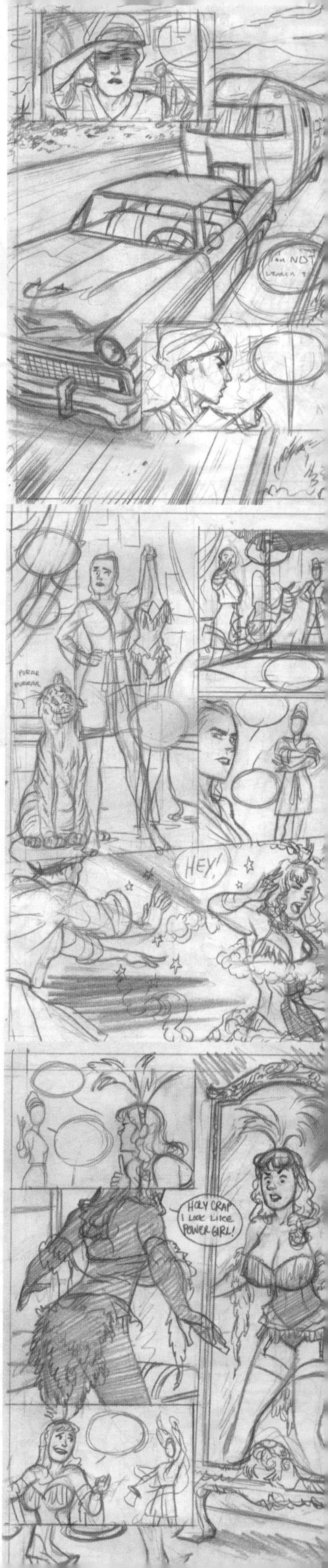
HEY!
HOLY CRAP I LOOK LIKE POWER GIRL!

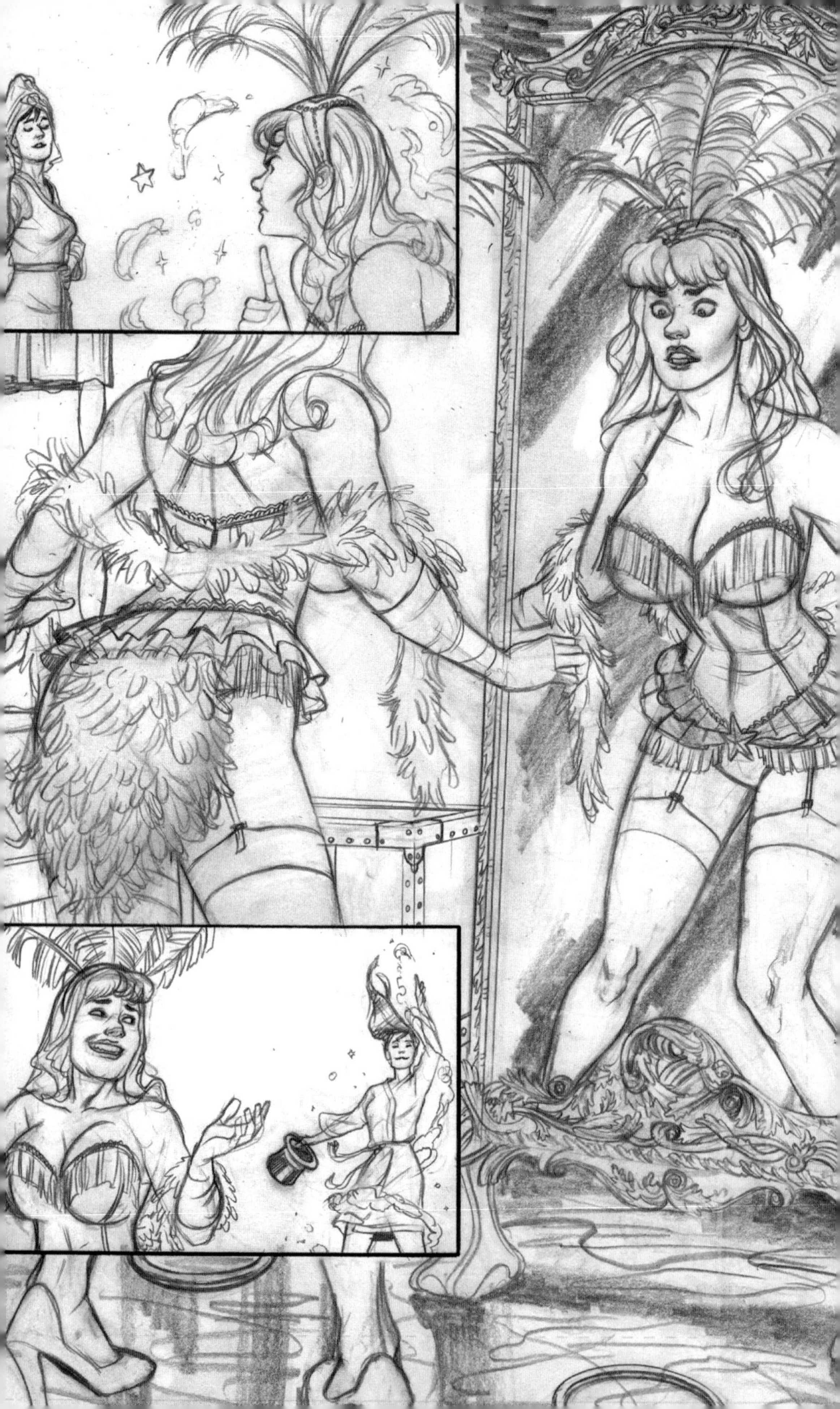

PAGE SIXTY-FIVE

Panel One

Not only is Dinah now wearing the costume (tight, skimpy, showgirly) but she also has red hair and looks like a completely different woman. She glares at Zee.

1 DINAH: THAT was not cool!

2 ZEE: Don't worry, it's not permanent. I'll lift the spell once I'm sure everyone's safe.

Panel Two

Dinah checks herself out in the mirror.

3 DINAH: Holy crap, I look like Power Girl!

Panel Three

Dinah shrugs at Zee, grinning a bit as she accepts the change.

4 DINAH: I'm not complaining, I'm just saying.

PAGE SIXTY-SIX

Panel One

We are now in the office of casino impresario Dale Hollister. Suddenly, Zee, (in full magician's outfit) the disguised Dinah, and Sasha all appear in front of Dale. He is surprised, to say the least.

1 ZEE: Hello, Dale!

Panel Two

Dale reaches out and shakes her hand furiously. Sasha does NOT seem happy.

2 DALE: Zatanna Zatara! Haven't seen you since you headlined my club in Tahoe! I've been trying to contact you ever since Xanadu opened.

Panel Three

Dale continues his pitch, but Zee stops him.

3 DALE: You'd make a GREAT headliner for --

4 ZEE: I'm afraid this isn't a business call, Dale. This is Black Canary.

Panel Four

Dale squints at Dinah.

5 DALE: Really? I never would have recognized her. (Small letters) Looks more like Power Girl...

Panel Five

Dinah throws a sour look to Zatanna, which the magician ignores.

6 DINAH: Hate you so much.

7 ZEE: She and a group of girls got tricked into a Bloodspell a year ago by Tina Spettro.

Panel Six

Dale glumly considers what Zee is saying. He accepts it.

8 ZATANNA: Tina is possessing and killing them off one by one.

9 DALE: Even dead, that witch is still a thorn in my side.

10 SASHA FX: Grrrrrr....

Panel Seven

Dale reaches out to shake Zee's hand.

11 DALE: Well, I can set you up in one of my showrooms. And I'll keep this whole thing a secret, of course.

12 SASHA FX: Grrrr...

PAGE SIXTY-SEVEN

Panel One

Sasha swipes a paw, cutting both Dale and Zee's hand.

1 SASHA: ROWR!

2 ZEE: SASHA!

Panel Two

Dale grabs Zee's bleeding hand (it was cut through the gloves she usually wears) with his own bleeding hand to pull her away. Sasha looks confused and suddenly calm.

3 ZEE: Sasha, what is WRONG with you?

Panel Three

Sasha hangs her head.

4 ZEE: I'm sorry, Dale. I don't know what got into her.

5 SECOND ZEE BALLOON: Laeh sdnuow.

Panel Four

He waves his healed hand at her. Zatanna's hand and glove are both healed as well.

6 DALE: It's okay. No harm done.

PAGE SIXTY-EIGHT

Panel One

That night, Zatanna is putting on her big illusion show for a sold-out crowd. She's holding a banner on a stick and standing next to Sasha.

Panel Two

She holds the stick out so the banner dangles in front of Sasha.

Panel Three

And pulls it away — Sasha is GONE!

Panel Four

Zee bows to a roaring crowd and holds her hat out.

CROWD FX: CLAP CLAP CLAP CLAP!

PAGE SIXTY-NINE

Panel One

And a 1/8th scale Sasha falls out of her hat.

Panel Two

Zee acts embarrassed and puts her hand to her lips. The crowd roars in laughter. In the background we see disguised Dinah peeking through the curtain.

1 ZEE: Oops.

2 SASHA: Mew.

CROWD FX: HA HA HA HA HA HA HA HA!

PAGE SEVENTY

Panel One

Backstage, Dinah's still peeking out through the curtain.

1 OFF: Excuse me, miss?

Panel Two

Dinah turns around. A stagehand hands her a note.

2 HAND: I was told to give this to you.

Panel Three

She looks at the note.

3 DINAH: Thanks.

Panel Four

We see the note in her hand. It says:

"Heard you were in town. My place: Oasis Sierra Apts #311 - Dottie."

PAGE SEVENTY-ONE

Panel One

Dottie's apartment. Low end. Messy. Dottie's opening the door to let Zee and Dinah in. In Dottie's hand is a drink. Dinah's still in disguise.

1 DINAH: Dottie, it's been forever.

2 DOTTIE: Dinah?

Panel Two

Dinah and Zee step into the apartment.

3 DINAH: I had some work done.

4 DOTTIE: Come in.

Panel Three

Dottie sits down in a lounge chair. She is a once-pretty girl in her late twenties now given in to misery. On the table next to her are a three-liter soda bottle and a bottle of rum. Dinah and Zee hover in front of a couch.

5 DOTTIE: Please, sit.

6 ZEE: Thanks.

7 DINAH: I'll just cut to the chase. Tina's back and taking us out one by one.

Panel Four.

Dottie's holding her drink close to her mouth.

8 DOTTIE: No surprise there. I heard about the others.

Panel Five

She takes a big swig.

9 DINAH: Dottie...

Panel Six

She scrunches her face up.

10 DOTTIE: Having the ghost of a vengeful witch after me, I need something to dull the insanity.

11 DINAH: Dottie, we're gonna figure this thing out.

PAGE SEVENTY-TWO

Panel One

1 DOTTIE: Why bother? Things haven't been that great since the robbery anyway.

2 DINAH: Dottie...

Panel Two

3 DOTTIE: Don't.

4 SECOND DOTTIE BALLOON: The reward money didn't last a week. My boyfriend ran off. The job market's bad enough, but with MY record...

Panel Three

Dottie is lost in her misery.

5 DOTTIE: Even my family doesn't want to talk to me anymore.

6 SECOND DOTTIE BALLOON: You know, there are times when I wish we'd just gone through with the job...

7 THIRD DOTTIE BALLOON: At least it was a chance at something better.

Panel Four

Dinah looks at Dottie with empathy.

8 DINAH: I had no idea...

9 SECOND DINAH BALLOON: Dottie, I gave you my number. It wasn't just for emergencies, I could have gotten you a job or... SOMETHING.

PAGE SEVENTY-THREE

Panel One

1 DOTTIE: I'm sorry. I'm grateful, really I am. I'm just tired. Tired of this, my life, everything.

Panel Two

Dottie turns to Zee. Zee smiles.

2 DOTTIE: You're some kind of magician, right? So change me into something better. A bird, maybe a cat. I like cats.

3 ZEE: Sorry, won't do that.

Panel Three

Dottie rolls her eyes.

4 DOTTIE: Great, a fake.

5 ZEE: It's not that.

Panel Four

Zatanna sits, tries to put the fantastic into layman terms.

6 Zee: It's just that... Well, let me put it this way...

PAGE SEVENTY-FOUR

Panel One

Close on Zee — she looks a bit creepy — creatively placed shadows.

1 ZEE: If I changed you into something else and left you that way for too long, you could never be brought back. You'd find yourself relying more on animal instinct and less on your human brain.

Panel Two

Dottie raises her drink as she stares at Zee with wide eyes. She hadn't expected this.

2 ZEE: You'd forget your favorite song, favorite color, the people closest to you, even that you had ever been born human.

Panel Three

Zatanna's explanation is a bit creepy and even Canary looks a little unnerved.

3 ZEE: It would be harder for you to think, almost as if you were slipping into an eternal haze of sights and scents, pain and pleasure.

Panel Four

Zee continues.

4 ZEE: After a day or so, no more than three, you would be changed completely, in body, mind and soul, and Dottie would be GONE.

Panel Five

Close on Zee – she's VERY serious.

5 ZEE: For ALL time.

PAGE SEVENTY-FIVE

Panel One

Zee's now smiling and a bit more cheery. Even the scene looks a tad brighter.

1 ZEE: However, I WILL cast a protection spell on you. That should guard you from all supernatural harm.

Panel Two

Zee starts to wave her hands for dramatic effect at Dottie.

2 ZEE: Tcetorp mor—

Panel Three

And suddenly her eyes look evil – her face enraged. She gestures wickedly at Dottie.

3 ZEE: Eittod nrut ot ssalg!

Panel Four

Instantly Dottie is transformed into a glass statue, a silent scream etched on her terrified face. Dinah looks horrified. Zee grins with evil pleasure.

4 DINAH: Zee! My God!

Panel Five

Dinah shakes Zee, who is holding her head and looking confused.

5 DINAH: What have you done?!?

6 ZEE: Wh-what?

PAGE SEVENTY-SIX

Panel One

Now Dinah looks enraged and evil. She turns towards Dottie. Zee realizes something's up.

Panel Two

Dinah tries to kick the glass Dottie, but Zee blocks the kick.

1 ZEE: Tsohg evael Hanid!

Panel Three

Dinah falls to the ground; in her place is the ghost of Tina.

2 ZEE: Tcetorp morf tsohg!

Panel Four

We now get our first look at Tina in her ghostly form. She looks like a transparent version of herself from the moment of her death: torn super villain-style unitard, frizzed hair and singed skin from hitting the electric sign, etc. She pounds against the mystic shield but can't get in. Dinah stands up in the shield, grabbing her head.

3 TINA: AHHHHH!

4 SHIELD FX: WHUMP! WHUMP!

Panel Five

5 TINA: No matter. Joy's next on the list anyway. And there's nothing either of you girls can do about it.

Panel Six

Tina turns to Dinah.

6 TINA: And after that...

7 SECOND TINA BALLOON: It's your turn.

PAGE SEVENTY-SEVEN

Panel One

Tina's vanished.

1 DINAH: Is -- is she gone?

2 ZEE: I think so...

Panel Two

Zee closes her eyes.

3 ZEE: Yes, yes she is.

Panel Three

She drops the shield.

4 DINAH: You have to change Dottie back!

5 ZEE: No. I have a better idea.

Panel Four

Quick cut to the Fortress of Solitude. SUPERMAN regards the statue of Dottie (complete with lounge chair) and reads a note that says:

6 SUPERMAN (reading note): "Clark, please keep this safe. I'll explain later. Z."

7 SUPERMAN: Oh-kay...

PAGE SEVENTY-EIGHT

Panel One

Back at Dottie's apartment.

1 DINAH: What'd you do with her?

2 ZEE: Sent her someplace safe.

3 DINAH: But all that talk about forgetting who she is...

Panel Two

4 ZEE: I'll return her to normal after the danger has passed. She's safer this way, trust me.

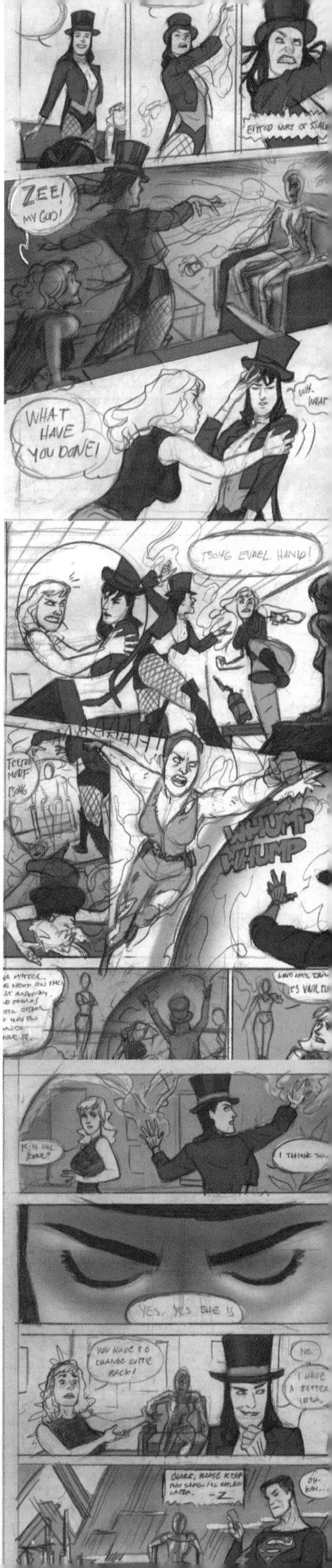
ZEE! MY GOD!
WHAT HAVE YOU DONE!
TSOHG EVAEL HANID!
WHUMP WHUMP
I THINK SO.
YES, YES SHE IS
YOU HAVE TO CHANGE DOTTIE BACK!
NO. I HAVE A BETTER IDEA.
OH-KAY...

Panel Three

5 ZEE: But we WILL have to work quickly or I won't be able to turn her back.

6 DINAH: And if Tina kills us?

Panel Four

7 ZEE: Then there will be no one left to save Dottie anyway. But don't worry, Tina won't win.

8 SECOND ZEE BALLOON: I WILL make her pay for using me against Dottie.

Panel Five

Zee adds with determination:

9 ZEE: Also, I know where she went.

PAGE SEVENTY-NINE

Panel One

Back at Xanadu performing hall, all of Zatanna's props are on stage. Including an impaling device. Joy is strapped to it and Dale Hollister stands next to it.

Panel Two

Zee and Dinah, now back in her Black Canary duds, appear on stage. Dinah sees Joy.

1 DINAH: Joy!

2 ZEE: It's over, DALE.

Panel Three

"Dale" laughs.

3 ZEE: Or should I say, Tina?

4 DALE: Ha ha ha ha.

Panel Four

"Dale" shrugs.

5 DALE: You caught me.

6 SECOND DALE BALLOON: I tricked Dale into the Bloodspell a few years ago when we were an item.

Panel Five

Dinah makes an "EW!" face.

7 DINAH: An ITEM?

8 DALE: Watch it!

PAGE EIGHTY

Panel One

1 DALE: When he made it big in Casinos, the bastard DUMPED me! The museum robbery was just my way of getting revenge.

2 ZEE: Aww, how SAD...

3 SECOND ZEE: Hsinab tso—

Panel Two

But something stops Zee. She stumbles and Dale collapses to the floor.

4 DINAH: ZEE!

Panel Three

"Zee" regains her composure.

5 ZEE: Zee's not here.

6 DINAH: Let her go, Spettro.

Panel Four

She walks towards Canary.

7 ZEE: When I died, I just jumped into his body. I've been running his empire this whole time.

8 DINAH: I said get out of my friend NOW.

PAGE EIGHTY-ONE

Panel One

"Zee" looks very creepy as she advances on Dinah.

1 ZEE: You know what I love about animals?

Panel Two

Zee looks over at Sasha in her cage next to cages of bunnies and doves. Sasha is growling.

2 ZEE: Even though it's risky, you can jump into their bodies without any kind of spell.

3 SASHA FX: GRRRRRRR....

Panel Three

Zee looks back at Canary.

4 SECOND ZEE BALLOON: And once I cut both Dale AND Zatanna...

Panel Four

On "Zee." She has a VERY evil smile.

5 ZEE: ...I got an ALL-access pass to one of the most powerful sorcerers on the PLANET.

Panel Five

"Zee" gestures to the prop drill. It starts to change, becoming sharper, deadlier-looking.

6 ZATANNA: Emoceb laer!

Panel Six

The drill starts to move toward the terrified Joy.

PAGE EIGHTY-TWO

Panel One

Dale, now recovered, is lunging at "Zee."

1 DALE: No, Tina! You can't!

2 ZEE: Ah, Dale! Like a true man of fortune, you bet everything on one chance...

Panel Two

"Zee" is pointing at Dale who is mid-transformation, shrinking, turning amphibious.

3 ZATANNA: And lost!

4 ZEE: Emoceb a daot!

Panel Three

Dale is now a toad completely. "Zee" raises her foot to squash it.

5 ZATANNA: Game over, sweetheart!

Panel Four

Dinah has reached over "Zee's" head and is pulling the rolled-up cloth INTO her mouth. The toad hops out of the way of the fighting women.

6 ZEE: MMMMM!!!!!

7 DINAH: I SAID... Get out of MY --

PAGE EIGHTY-THREE

Panel One

Gagged "Zee" rams the back of her head into Dinah's nose.

1 DINAH: Oof!

Panel Two

"Zee" kicks Dinah into a bunch of cages. Mostly rabbits and doves are in them, but also Sasha. A couple of the dove cages have fallen over and freed their occupants.

Panel Three

On "Zee." She reaches for the gag in her mouth.

Panel Four

On Dinah. She opens Sasha's door.

2 DINAH: Hey, girl. Be a good tigress and say hi to your mistress.

PAGE EIGHTY-FOUR

Panel One

Large shot of Sasha LEAPING out of her cage, claws extended, and ROARING like there's no tomorrow. Dinah steps out of the way.

SASHA FX: ROOOOOOOOOOOARRRRR!!!

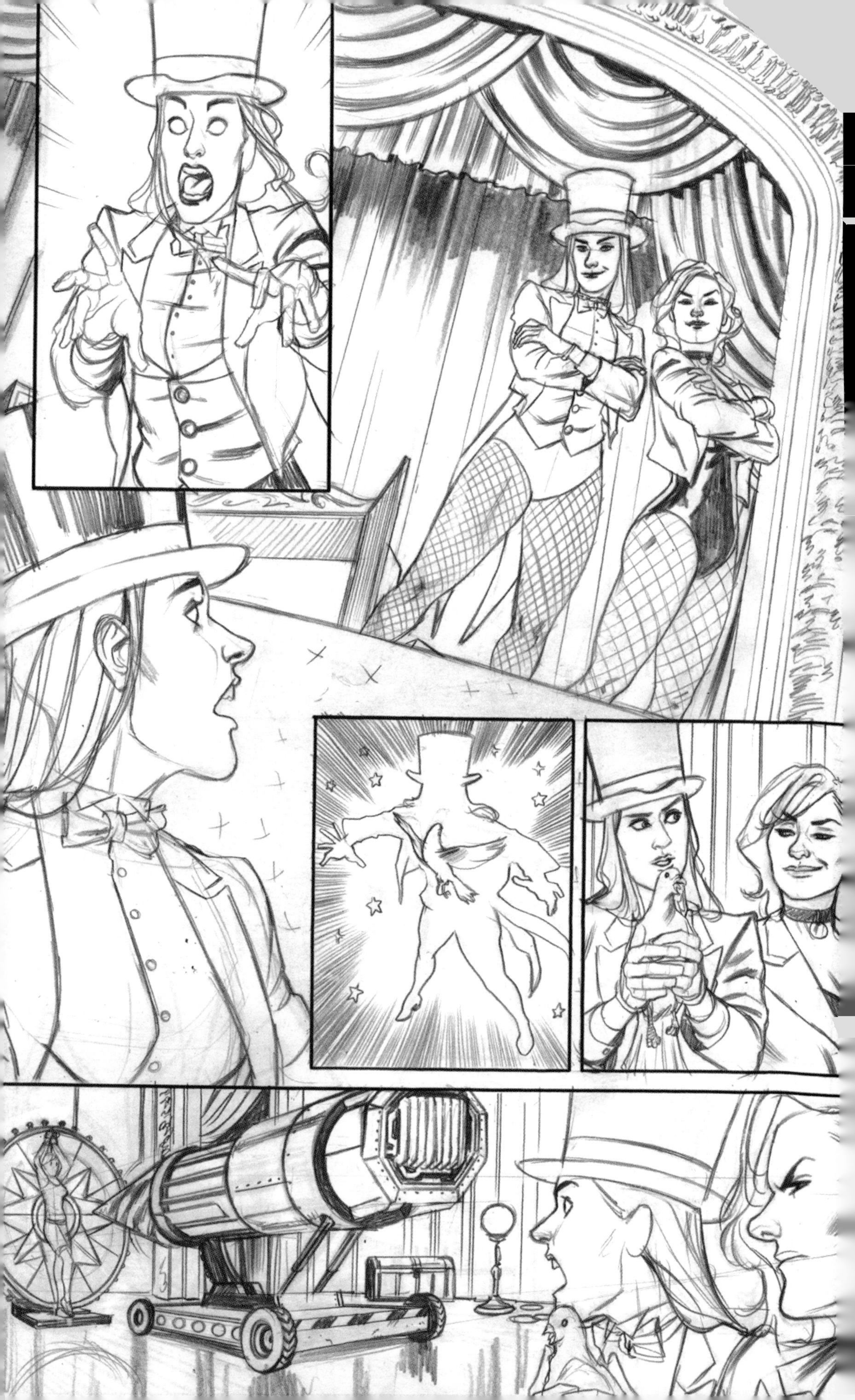

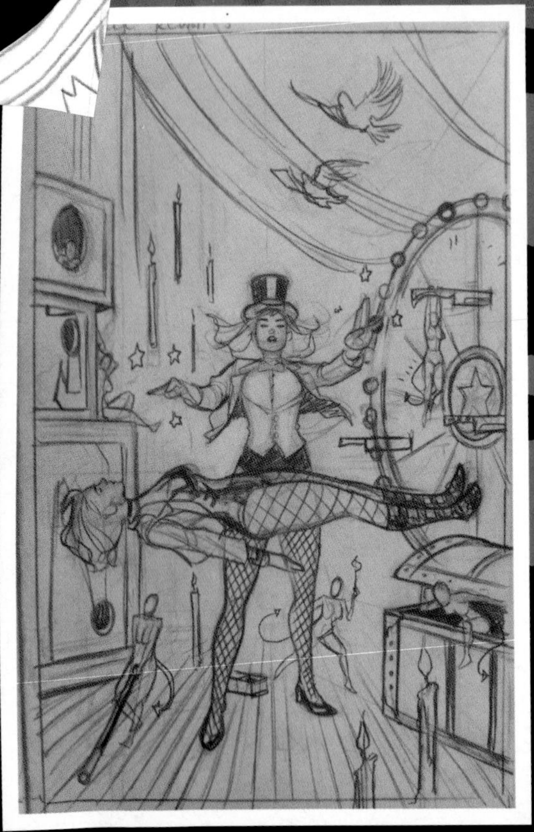

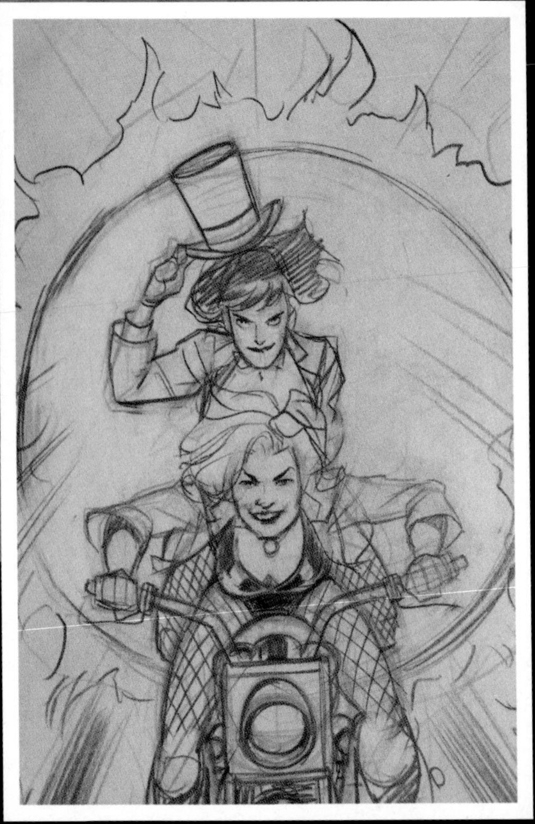

Cover sketches! The evolution of a good cover is seldom an easy one. The right elements and the right composition are vital, but it's equally important to convey some sense of the story's tone, of the experience the reader's in for. What attracts someone to a book is always subjective, but, hey, Joe must've done a good job or you wouldn't be reading this!

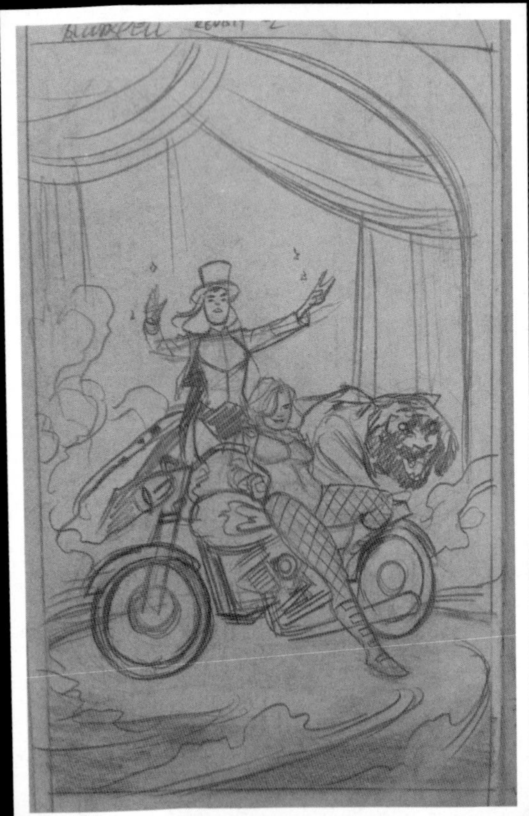

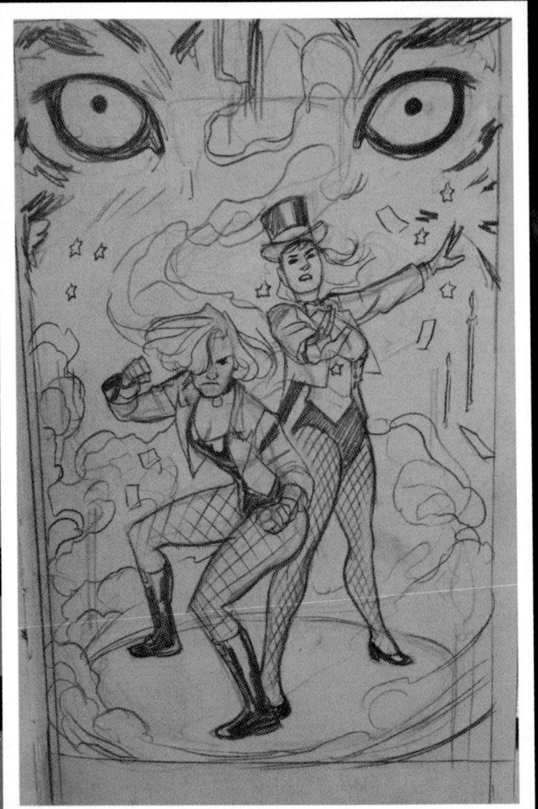